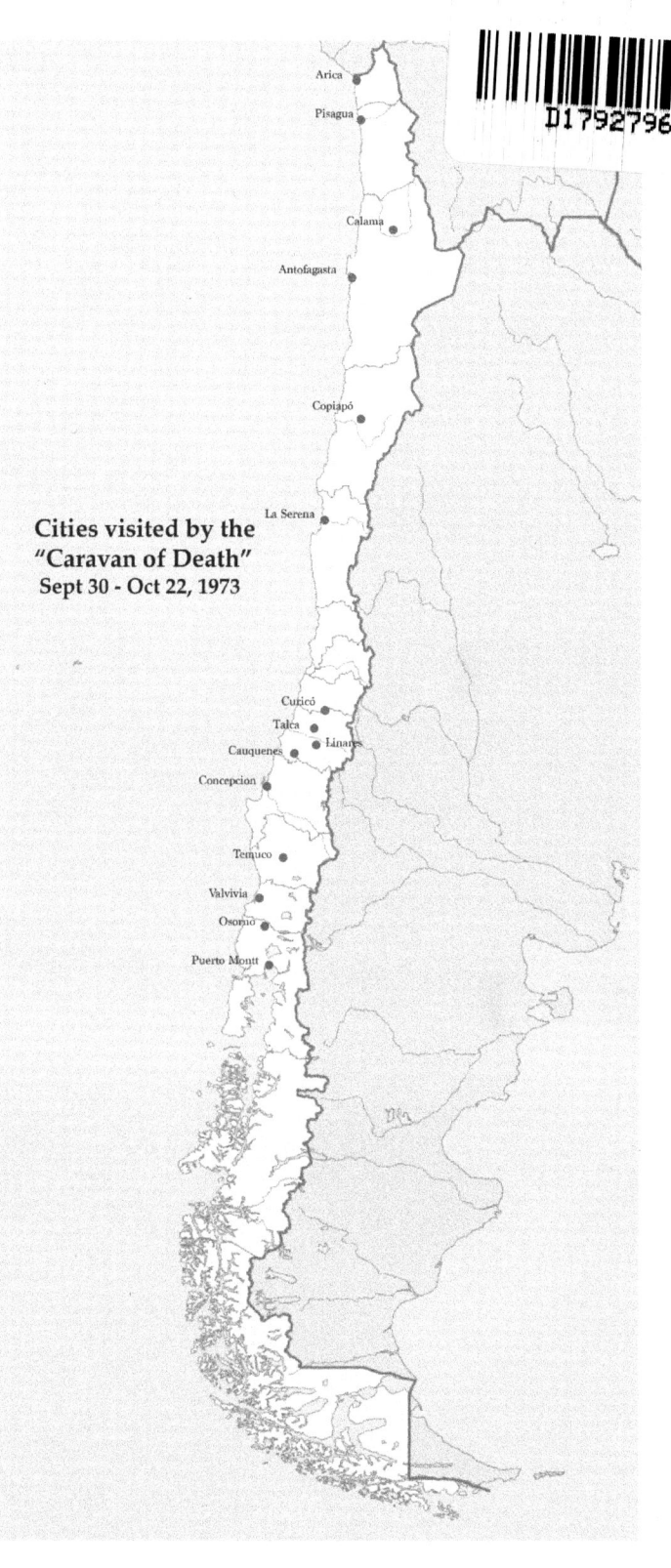

In Search of Spring

A SISTER'S QUEST TO UNEARTH THE TRUTH ABOUT HER BROTHER'S ASSASSINATION BY CHILE'S CARAVAN OF DEATH

Zita Cabello-Barrueto

The Berkeley Publishing Group
Berkeley, California

Copyright © 2014 Zita Cabello-Barrueto
The Berkeley Publishing Group
Berkeley, California
All rights reserved.

ISBN: 1500256757
ISBN-13: 9781500256753
Library of Congress Control Number: 2014911335
CreateSpace Independent Publishing Platform
North Charleston, South Carolina

*To my sons,
Felipe and Roberto*

*In loving memory of my brother, Wito
and
my parents, Elsa and Manuel*

Hope is a waking dream.
　　—Aristotle

ACKNOWLEDGMENTS

It is impossible to acknowledge by name all those who contributed to the story in this book. My infinite gratitude goes to the Center for Justice and Accountability, San Francisco, California; the law firm Wilson Sonsini Goodrich & Rosati, Palo Alto, California; and Robert Kerrigan of Kerrigan, Estess, Rankin & McLeod, LLP, Pensacola, Florida. Their generosity and support to see justice happen for my brother's murder gave me the story to tell.

I am indebted to those courageous Chilean souls who were willing to take a chance by entrusting me with their painful memories. I hope this book will help heal some of your wounds.

My warmest appreciation goes to the human rights lawyers in Chile who offered information, contacts, and assistance. I especially want to recognize Hugo Gutierrez, who generously gave his time and support at critical points along this journey.

My very special thanks go to Victor Canales for his daring and undeniable support. His energy, his confidence, and his welcome enthusiasm saved me many times from drowning. My many thanks to you, Victor!

This book was enriched through interactions with my students. My very personal appreciation goes to all of them for their fresh insights, suggestions, and kind words of encouragement.

I thank my daughter-in-law Erica, who made me understand that writing a book means letting others read it. Her encouragement and her question, "When are you going to show it to your sons, or do you expect them to buy it at Borders?" motivated me to search out my first two readers: my daughter-in-law Tiffany and my son Roberto, Erica's husband.

Tiffany, the first person to read the entire manuscript, copyedited it with patience and diligence. Her detailed readings and effective comments provided the inspiration and direction I needed, especially, "Zita, this is really, really, really good!" Thanks, Tiffany. I *really* believed you.

I thank my son Roberto for the enormous amount of time and commitment he devoted to this book. An incisive and critical reader, his probing insights, astute criticisms, and sense of humor invigorated the manuscript and provided me with detailed information that I greatly valued, perhaps more than he realized.

I could not have completed this book without the guidance of my editor, Kristen. I have been honored by her dedication, her clear understanding of the intentions of this book, and by her abundant generosity. Her constant editorial feedback sharpened and improved the book's initial draft in an unimaginable way. Until the last moment, in her usual calm and competent way, Kristen helped wrestle the manuscript into submission. Thanks, Kristen, I could not have made it without you!

I owe many thanks to my sister, Karin, who stood by me every step of this journey. I thank her for her faith and trust in my work. Karin, this is for you, too.

Finally, I want to thank the special members of my family. I owe it all to my sons, Felipe and Roberto, and daughters-in-law, Tiffany and Erica. It is difficult to imagine writing this book without their loyalty, emotional support, and understanding.

To my son Felipe, who accompanied me to Chile so many times and watched out for me, you gave me the biggest gift of my life: my first grandchild, Mazie.

Mazie, *mi bella niña*, you arrived into this life at precisely the perfect moment. Your smile and warm touch worked their magic in my spirit. I want you to know that I would never have been able to finish this book without you. My love.

And now we have Emilio and Amalia. Life could not get better! To my grandchildren, the greatest joy of my life, I dedicate this book to you. Many kisses.

PREFACE

My brother's name was Winston Dwight Cabello Bravo. Winston for Winston Churchill. Dwight for Dwight David Eisenhower. Born in Chile near the end of World War II, Winston was as rare a person as his name was uncommon in Chile.

As a child, I never understood why my father had chosen the name Winston Dwight for my older brother. Chile had not been involved in World War II, my father had never met Churchill or Eisenhower, and as native Spanish speakers, my family could barely pronounce the names. Today I understand my father's hopeful response to the horrors of war. My painfully sensitive father paid close attention to life and the world around him, and he suffered for what he saw. At the height of World War II, as my father read the daily news articles about atrocities committed in Nazi Germany, my mother's belly swelled with their unborn child. My father watched her anxiously and worried about bringing a child into that time of horrors, miseries, and frights.

On July 6, 1945, as World War II was drawing to a close, my brother Winston was born. Named after the Allied leaders my father most admired, in gratitude for their role in bringing peace to the world, Winston Dwight represented my father's hopes for the future. Twenty-eight years later, when Winston died at the hands of the *Caravana de la Muerte*, or Caravan of Death, those hopes died with him. My father never recovered from the loss.

For nearly forty years, I have tried to understand why my brother Winston was killed. Writing this book has been difficult. It is hard to know what to say and how to give meaning to my family's story in a way that is different from other accounts of human rights atrocities.

In 1973, General Augusto Pinochet led a coup in Chile to depose the democratically elected president, Salvador Allende. Since 1932, Chile had enjoyed decades of political stability. The country had been electing governments without political chaos, and numerous political parties were able to function freely. On September 4, 1970, thousands of Chileans joined in a coalition of seven political parties, known as the Popular Unity, to elect Dr. Salvador Allende president of Chile. President Allende was a physician and a member of Chile's Socialist Party, who headed the Popular Unity. The government of Salvador Allende was committed to overcoming problems of poverty, inequality, and the extensive neglect of women and children. It hoped to solve some of Chile's endemic problems: high unemployment rates, rampant inflation, and underutilization of national resources.

President Allende's program also included the nationalization of US interests in Chile's major copper mines, the advancement of workers' rights, and deepening of the Chilean land reform.

Immediately after the election, the United States expressed its disapproval and raised a number of economic sanctions against Chile. In declassified tapes, US National Security Adviser Henry Kissinger warns President Richard Nixon that the "model effect" of President Allende "can be insidious." Kissinger tells CIA Director Richard Helms, "We will not let Chile go down the drain," to which Helms replies, "I am with you."

Handwritten notes, taken by Helms, record the direction of Nixon and Kissinger to "make the economy scream" in Chile.

Three years later, the Chilean economy was screaming.

On September 11, 1973, General Augusto Pinochet broke Chile's long tradition of respect for democratic values and headed a bloody military coup against the democratically elected president, Salvador Allende. The Chilean armed forces claimed to be fighting for peace, freedom, and democracy; but for seventeen long years, they planned, organized, and carried out missions to kill, torture, and "disappear" people throughout the country. They broke their oath, on their honor as soldiers, to protect the lives of defenseless citizens.

A few weeks after the coup, Pinochet dispatched a Puma helicopter from Santiago carrying General Sergio Arellano Stark and his squad of Chilean army officers. The helicopter flew from the south to the north of Chile, stopping in small towns along the way. When the helicopter landed again in Santiago three weeks later, nearly one hundred political prisoners across the country had been savagely murdered. My brother was a casualty of this Caravan of Death.

On the twenty-fifth anniversary of Winston's death, Augusto Pinochet was arrested in London in connection with the Caravan of Death killings. When I learned that the "untouchable" Pinochet was being brought to justice in a foreign country for crimes committed in Chile, I thought that perhaps the officer directly responsible for Winston's death might also be located and brought to justice.

A team of US lawyers took my family's case pro bono. Over the course of two years, I traveled from the United States to Chile ten times searching for "unfindable" eyewitnesses to the Caravan of Death's atrocities. Former military officers, political prisoners, victims' families, and many others agreed to give voluntary testimonies for our case. In the end, I spoke with more than a hundred witnesses, including the gravedigger who buried my brother and twelve other victims; the civil servant forced to fingerprint the bodies; and the forensic pathologist who studied Winston's bones after Chile's mass exhumations. Each witness gave us a piece of the puzzle that told the greater story. As I worked with our lawyers, I continued teaching human rights courses at the University of California at Santa Cruz and San Francisco State University.

Our legal team faced challenges at every turn. Just as it seemed our lawsuit might fail, a tall lawyer in cowboy boots joined the case. Bob Kerrigan, a top US attorney, became an invaluable friend and ally.

After years of hard work, we filed in 1999 and won in 2003 a landmark civil lawsuit against Armando Fernandez Larios, the former Chilean army officer implicated in Winston's death. Our lawsuit marked the first time in US history that in a contested jury trial someone was found responsible for crimes against humanity. It was also the first time that any Pinochet operative had been tried in the United States for human rights abuses in Chile.

In 1990, Chile's Truth and Reconciliation Commission had ordered mass exhumations of Pinochet's casualties across the country. At the time, I did not want the victims in Copiapó to be exhumed. Shortly after Winston's death, I had learned that these thirteen political prisoners had not been shot during an escape attempt as reported by the military. They had been massacred. I had kept this secret from my family for fifteen years, wanting to spare them from knowing what really happened to Winston. I feared the exhumations would bring this painful truth to light.

On an emotional level, I am not sure it was worth it to me to learn how the Caravan of Death killed its victims. But our loved ones had their own way of telling the story. "There's something about your brother," a forensic pathologist said after examining Winston's remains. "He was speaking to us."

Chile's mass exhumations gave us a piece of the truth, but they did not offer justice. I wanted truth *and* justice, not just the remains of someone I loved. I did not want to accept my brother's body as payment from the government for keeping quiet. Winston was never theirs to take or give.

This book is an account of my personal experience. It is not a history of Chile, a study of the military coup, or an analysis of Allende's "socialist experiment." By sharing the testimonies gathered for our lawsuit, I hope to awaken a sensibility in readers that will help change behavior, so that together we can prevent such dark times from recurring. After every tragedy, the world cries, "Never again." We keep saying it, but the atrocities continue. I want to stop repeating "Never again."

I personally know families in Chile who do not want to hear what happened to their loved ones, and I understand that the truth presented in this book will bring pain to many. I do not know what to say to people who will learn here about their loved ones' encounters with cruel men like the defendant, Armando Fernandez Larios. This truly torments me. I hope the families will forgive me.

Like many who lost loved ones to Pinochet's brutal regime, my family felt alone after losing Winston. For decades we lived in silence and isolation. But through the process of working with our lawyers and searching for the truth, I discovered that there were people out there who could help us and who genuinely cared about truth and justice.

Filing our lawsuit gave my family a ray of hope. When our legal team finally won the case against Fernandez, the press was thrilled and our lawyers elated. I was happy, too, but to this day I wish we could hear of Fernandez accepting responsibility for his actions instead of always protecting himself and saying he was just following orders. Fernandez knows what happened that night in the Atacama Desert. We are left only to speculate.

We will probably never know why General Arellano and his men chose to kill these political prisoners. We are left with so many unanswered questions: Why was Arellano selected to lead this delegation? Why did the officers travel through Chile, killing prisoners? Was it to spread fear? Going from town to town, how did these officers feel about their activities? How did they choose their victims? Only Arellano and his men know the truth. A trial or a lawsuit reveals a great deal, but it is ultimately about winning, not presenting a complete historical record. I learned that in the process, as well.

Today as a human rights professor in the United States, I see many students who feel cynical about life and their power to shape the world. They feel there is nothing to get excited about. To my students I say: I hope this story will strengthen your sense of inner power. Whatever you go through in life, if you can treat any obstacle as a challenge, you will be more enriched than depressed. You can create a better future. You are more powerful than you know.

I often think of the people who are still holding onto some information about what happened in Chile. Wherever you are, I hope you will come forward now with the truth. Thousands of innocent victims remain disappeared. Thousands of families have no idea what happened to their loved ones; they cannot even find their remains. If you witnessed something, if you know someone who did, if you are holding even a small piece of information, please come forward and break the silence. Each piece of the truth, no matter how small or seemingly inconsequential, builds a greater historical truth. The information you are holding may be just what is needed to locate a disappeared person, restore the reputation of a falsely maligned victim, or even bring a human rights criminal to justice. By speaking the truth, you can restore dignity to victims and their families. You will also inspire others who may be afraid to come forward and are just waiting for someone else to speak first.

Silence may offer some comfort to families unable to bear the truth, but that same silence protects the very criminals who killed their loved ones. Human rights criminals must not be allowed to find sanctuary in silence just because they have committed crimes so terrible that no one wants to talk or hear about them.

Democracy has been restored to Chile, but seventeen years of a brutal dictatorship has left a deep scar. Even after thirty years, the fear in Chile is still very real. Some people are not even aware that they are afraid, but their responses and actions show just how deeply the fear is ingrained. For this reason, some witnesses chose not to officially testify for our lawsuit but offered their truth in conversation. From my careful notes, I have reproduced some of these conversations as faithfully as possible. The voluntary testimonies our legal team gathered are officially recorded and in the public record for all to see.

In pursuing legal action, I was able to tell the world about my brother Winston, who was kind, courageous, and true to the end. Ultimately, our efforts for justice will be measured by their usefulness as tools in protecting human rights around the world, as well as the impact our case has on future legal proceedings.

People often ask what this journey meant to me, how I felt after the trial, and whether I found it worthwhile. Through this transformative process, I found the truth I searched for, as well as love, companionship, and solidarity. I also found loneliness, abandonment, and profound grief. But in searching for truth and justice, I was at peace with myself. I did what I felt was right. I would do it all over again.

The day Winston died, my father stopped playing the guitar and never smiled again. For his remaining eighteen years, one question haunted his eyes: *Why did they kill my son?* Looking back, I feel that my siblings and I were very cowardly with our father—I most of all. My family had never talked much about feelings, and to do so after Winston's death would have meant exposing our utter devastation. I could not bring myself to do that, and I regret that I was never able to meet my father in his pain or offer even a single word of consolation. That is how the decades passed, with my siblings and me always avoiding talking about our lost brother. Until we started working on the lawsuit more than twenty-five years later, we never mentioned Winston's name, even among ourselves.

Today as the mother of two sons, I do not know how my parents survived such devastation. My greatest hope in writing this book is to spare other families from the kind of tragedy that we could not prevent for ourselves.

In 1948, a few days before Winston's third birthday, my father wrote him this letter:

To my son:

My son! At the birth of each day, and as I place another kiss upon your angelic face, I feel happier to have you by my side; and at the dawn of each new day, my spirit is gripped as I see you woven into the miserable humanity that men have forged as a product of their infinite pettiness.

The most beautiful flowers of my spiritual garden shall always shower their fruitful essences so that they may lavish you with, above all things, the most sublime warmth and thus contribute to making this life less burdensome for you, a life which holds but promises of unkindness.

And yet, I sense the finiteness of time, and the task that I have undertaken shall be silenced by the extinction of my materiality. And you, little son of mine, will go forward in the revelation of the ideals that shall contribute to spiritual peace.

Your sin—no, little son of mine! My sin consists of not having brought you to life in happier times. Nevertheless, you have arrived at the timeliest of moments. Your beautiful light eyes shall forever engrave upon your soul the picture that men hold before us and, as a product of that vision of horrors, miseries, and frights, within your spirit shall be born the ideal of renovation and elevation of feelings.

And so, little son, shall you in part pay your tribute to life; and so shall the essence of my spirit continue to sprinkle itself along all of those paths it chooses, paths that I shall never travel.

I saw this letter countless times as a child and could never understand why my father was apologizing to Winston for not bringing him into happier times. Today with children and grandchildren of my own, I understand my father better than ever.

It has taken me nearly forty years to be able to write this story, but limits do not exist for honoring my brother's short life. It is still very difficult to talk about Winston without recalling the circumstances surrounding his death. To remember my brother, to remember who he was, is so connected with the profound pain of losing him: the inexpressible pain that for so many years kept our family from even speaking his name.

My brother's name was Winston Dwight Cabello Bravo. Hopefully, I can tell this story with the dignity his life merits.

Zita Cabello-Barrueto
July 6, 2014

Generals Sergio Arellano Stark and Augusto Pinochet a few hours before the departure of the Caravan of Death in September 1973. (National Library of Chile/La Nacion Newspaper Archive)

PROLOGUE

Chile was a democracy, a highly civilized country where respect for human life was sacred.

Or so we thought.

On the morning of September 11, 1973, the commanders of the Chilean armed forces (General Augusto Pinochet), navy (Jose Toribio Merino), air force (Gustavo Leigh), and *carabineros* or police (Cesar Mendoza Duran) led a violent military coup in the heart of Chile. Armed soldiers flooded the streets of Chile's capital, Santiago, forcing civilians up against walls and facedown on the ground at gunpoint. Tanks and military trucks rumbled through the downtown area. Machine gun fire ripped the bright morning. Fighter jets screamed across the sky, bombing the elegant white presidential palace, *La Moneda*.

Through crashing fountains of ash and debris, smoke poured out of shattered windows, obscuring the Chilean flags flying in the palace square. Flames shot up through holes in the historic structure, devouring the rooftop, as fire began to engulf *La Moneda*.

With the presidential palace burning around him, Chile's democratically elected president, Salvador Allende, used the last free radio station to speak to any supporters who could still hear him. "My friends," he said. "Surely this will be the last opportunity for me to address you. The air force has bombed the antennas of Radio Portales and Radio Corporación…the only thing left for me is to say to workers, I am not going to resign! Placed in a historic transition, I will pay for the loyalty of the people with my life…History is ours, and people make history.

"Workers of my country, I want to thank you for the loyalty that you always had, the confidence that you deposited in a man who was only an interpreter of great yearnings for justice, who gave his word that he would respect the Constitution and the law and did just that…

"I address you, above all, the modest woman of our land, the *campesina* who believed in us, the mother who knew our concern for children…I address the youth, those who sang and gave us their joy and their spirit of struggle. I address the man of Chile, the worker, the farmer, the intellectual, those who will be persecuted…

"The people must defend themselves, but they must not sacrifice themselves. The people must not let themselves be destroyed or riddled with bullets, but they cannot be humiliated either.

"Workers of my country, I have faith in Chile and its destiny. Other men will overcome this dark and bitter moment when treason seeks to prevail. Go forward knowing that, sooner rather than later, the great avenues will open again and free men will walk through them to construct a better society.

"Long live Chile! Long live the people! Long live the workers!

"These are my last words, and I am certain that my sacrifice will not be in vain. I am certain that, at the very least, it will be a moral lesson that will punish felony, cowardice, and treason."

As the palace burned around him, President Allende placed an assault rifle under his chin. Refusing to legitimize the coup by resigning, he died of two self-inflicted gunshot wounds to the head. With him ended Chile's tradition of respect for democratic rule: one of the longest democratic cycles the modern world has seen.

The military junta appointed General Pinochet as supreme commander of the nation, giving him unprecedented powers throughout the country. Chile fell under military rule. For seventeen years, the Chilean armed forces killed, tortured, and disappeared more than three thousand people throughout the country.

Pinochet and his men invaded every part of civilian life. Day and night we were watched.

Soldiers patrolled the streets and came into our homes. A life was nothing to them.

They decided who lived and died.

PART ONE

Tell me how you die and I will tell you who you are.
—Octavio Paz

ONE

Winston, 20 years old

September 11, 1973, began like any other day. As light filled the morning sky, the people of Chile woke up, opened their windows, ate breakfast, and got ready for work and school. The cool breeze was alive with hints of spring, which was about to burst forth in the Southern Hemisphere. At our home in the copper mining town of Copiapó, I heard a bird sing in the tree outside our kitchen window as I asked my husband Pato to drive our one-year-old son Felipe to day care that morning. I kissed my husband and son good-bye and left the house around 8:00 a.m. to ride the bus to my teaching job at the Technical State University of Copiapó.

The bus was so crowded that I had to stand and hold onto a strap from the ceiling, swaying back and forth with the other passengers as we rattled through our sleepy desert town. About ten minutes into the ride, the driver switched on the radio at the front of the bus and suddenly a harsh voice filled the air.

At first, no one could make out what the voice was saying, but the jarring tone caught everyone's attention. We all fell silent. The garbled sounds of the military broadcast continued for a few minutes over the radio, and then we heard different, clearer voices in the *bandos* (proclamations) issuing orders to the Chilean people and announcing that a military takeover had begun. No one on the bus said anything or asked what was happening. We rode silently through town, trying to take in this shocking news.

I got off the bus at the Technical State University of Copiapó and walked quickly toward my office in the social sciences building, ready to teach my economics classes as usual. But when I arrived, everyone was streaming out the building. I followed the faculty and students to a large patio with a basketball court nearby and saw people running around in confusion. No one knew what to do. Finally someone figured out how to play the radio over the university's public address system. A harsh male voice shattered the silence.

"The junta of the military government calls on the populace to remain calm and exhorts all citizens to stay in their houses and workplaces and not to go into the streets, in order to avoid any lamentable misfortunes..." the voice reverberated across campus.

I stood in shocked silence, listening with the other faculty and students in the courtyard. The military edicts came in rapid succession.

"The armed forces and the *carabineros* [police] reiterate to the people of Chile the absolute unity of its command and troops and its unyielding decision to fight to the ultimate consequence to bring down the Marxist government," declared the voice. "To be reiterated once more is the fact that the fight is not against the people of Chile, but in defense of the people that love liberty..."

News of the coup in Santiago unfolded through a barrage of military broadcasts. Chile was in a state of siege. The armed forces had overthrown President Allende's constitutionally elected government. The presidential palace, *La Moneda*, was surrounded by tanks and armed soldiers.

President Allende was still alive. We knew that, anyway, because the military communiqués were warning him to unconditionally surrender.

"The Palace of *La Moneda* must be evacuated by eleven o'clock," the voice continued. "If not, it will be attacked by the Chilean Air Force. Workers must remain at their worksites, and it is strictly forbidden to abandon them. In the case that they should leave, they will be attacked by forces of land and air. Let the message of Edict 1 be reiterated, whereby it is warned that whatever act of sabotage will be punished in the most drastic form at the location of the infraction."

As I stood listening, my legs began to shake uncontrollably. Sharp pains shot through my calves. I looked around and saw my friend Inez Vincentti, a pretty young professor with freckles and dark curly hair. Our eyes met, and she smiled encouragingly. Across the courtyard, the university's twenty-one-year-old student body president, Raul Larravide, looked worried.

"The junta of the military government advises the populace of the following points," the voice proclaimed. "The Presidential Residence located on Tomas Moro had to be bombed due to the resistance of GAP personnel [Allende's bodyguards] to the armed forces and *carabineros*. It is advised that from this instant, the presence of groups of people in the streets is absolutely prohibited."

"Zita!"

I looked up and saw my older brother Winston, or Wito as we called him, waving at me from the driver's seat of his company's white Bronco. Slender and graceful with jet black curls, Wito flashed a boyish grin as I slid in next to him on the front bench seat, and then my husband, Pato, got back into the car beside me. As we drove through the quiet streets of Copiapó, I watched my brother and husband talking together. Friends for years, they were about the same age and height, but where

Wito had delicate, angular features—high cheekbones, thin shoulders, honey-colored eyes that slanted when he smiled—Pato's features were more rounded, and he had tight black curly hair, broad shoulders, and thick black-framed glasses. As we drove home for lunch, Wito and Pato chatted as if it were a normal day.

Suddenly the car radio blared: "The people whose names appear on the list that follows must voluntarily turn themselves in by 16:30. Failure to turn oneself in will signify that they are subject to the provisions of the junta of commanders in chief with the foreseeable consequences…"

We listened anxiously as the voice named one hundred of the most respected, prominent people in Chile: government ministers, senators, leaders of national political parties, all the people most closely associated with President Allende. But everything looked normal as we drove through our sleepy town surrounded by the Atacama Desert. Copiapó felt so isolated, so far away from the political upheaval in Santiago that we fell into a false sense of security. We were not activists or political people; who were we to matter to anyone? Driving home for lunch that day, we only wondered what the military would do to *other* people—not to us.

We walked into the kitchen, and my mother, who was visiting from Malloco, looked up and smiled. As I handed her one-year-old Felipe, whom we had picked up from day care on the way home, Pato switched on the portable radio.

The jarring voice filled the kitchen. "The government junta wishes to stay informed of the public opinion about national events. In accordance with the provisions of the decrees already issued upon finding the country in a state of emergency, it has been provided that a strict censorship of the press shall be exercised over mediums of publications.

"As a preliminary measure of precaution, during the day of September 12, 1973, publication of only the following newspapers is authorized: *El Mercurio* and *La Tercera de la Hora*," the voice droned. "Authorization for other publications will come gradually. The enterprises not indicated by this decree should consider themselves effectively closed."

Hearing that voice on my kitchen radio, in my own home, suddenly made the coup feel much more real. Now it was invading personal space, not just public space like the university.

"An office for press censorship has been designated, which will act from the Military Polytechnical Academy of the Army (San Ignacio N 242)," the voice said. "It will have under its control all authorized written publications; the system to be employed will be that of censorship of the printed edition. Therefore, the directors of the newspapers mentioned will have the responsibility to turn in daily, before their publication the respective samples to be able to proceed with their revision. It is advised that the publication of all other bodies of written press not properly authorized will be seized and destroyed."

My mother, setting out plates for lunch, seemed not to notice the announcement.

"The military government is determined to achieve a purification of the press," the voice continued, "so as not to have to accept henceforth insults to people or institutions, and to likewise end the impudent language, for which an immediate solution is needed in order to reestablish the national coexistence and ethical norms."

We began speculating on life changes that might be coming and wondered what would happen to Wito's and Pato's government jobs. A few years earlier the Allende administration had appointed my brother and my husband, both economists, as local managers of agricultural and copper mining regions.

As my family was sitting down to lunch, Wito said casually, "Mr. Tarifeño stopped by the office today to ask me if the tires of the vehicle were in good condition. He offered to take me to Argentina through the mountains." *Isn't that a silly proposition?* my brother's grin seemed to say.

Are the tires okay? I thought.

No one at the table said anything. We did not know how to respond to the idea that the military government might target Wito. To this day I struggle with the question: Why didn't I encourage my brother to take Mr. Tarifeño's offer? The only answer I can offer: it didn't cross my mind that his life was in danger. We Chileans were so proud of our long tradition of respect for human life that we failed to see the approaching evil.

Over lunch we listened to more military communiqués on the radio, and when the junta announced that there would be a curfew from 6:00 p.m. to 6:00 a.m., Wito and Pato drove back to the office of regional planning to quickly finish some work so they could comply with the edict. I stayed home with my mother and son, watching the junta's announcements on television. At 5:00 p.m., Wito dropped Pato off at our house and then drove straight home to check on his wife, Veronica, and one-year-old daughter, Susan.

Why didn't I ask Wito to take Mr. Tarifeño's offer that day? Would my brother have responded as I think he would have: "Why? I haven't done anything. Why should I run?"

Mr. Tarifeño, a lifelong gold miner, knew the rugged mountains that separated Chile from Argentina. Apparently he also knew what life would be like under military rule. While my family hesitated, Mr. Tarifeño's instincts could have saved my brother.

Some people managed to save themselves by going into hiding after the coup. Others went into hiding, only to be discovered and arrested by the military. My family never imagined that there was any need to go into hiding, because we were not people who had any reason to be considered a threat to the new regime. Had we been political people, perhaps we would have had a more realistic sense of the dangers facing the broader population.

I sometimes think of a night shortly before the coup, when Wito, Pato, and I were sitting at my kitchen table talking about the possibility of a military takeover in Chile. A coup attempt had already failed in June, and the Allende administration was facing serious problems, including an acute economic crisis. That night, Wito talked about atrocities recently committed by the military in Brazil and about the thousands of people who had been incarcerated and tortured in that country for years.

"That will happen here, too, if we have a military coup," I said anxiously.

"No," Wito replied. "In this country if there is a coup, the military will incarcerate many people across the nation in the first few months. It's too expensive for a country like ours to keep people in jail, so a large number of them will be killed. A practical solution. This is not a rich country. Chile is not in any condition to waste money keeping people incarcerated for too long."

Wito, Pato, and I talked until well past 2:00 a.m., speculating on the future of our country. Intellectually we thought we were prepared for life under military rule. But when it actually happened, my brother Wito—who believed in the fundamental goodness of people—was as unprepared for the brutality as I.

TWO

"In light of the obstinate attitudes of certain subversive elements attempting to resist the patriotic decision adopted by the armed forces and command recognized by all the country," the voice on the radio announced the next day, "the junta of the government declares the following:

"1. To be granted a period until 15:00 hours today, Wednesday, the twelfth of September, that will allow those persons or groups of persons opposing armed resistance to the new government of the Chileans to cease their attitude and turn in their arms to the representatives of the armed forces and *carabineros*.

"2. All persons who insist on the suicidal and irresponsible attitude previously mentioned will be subjected to a definitive attack by members of the armed forces and *carabineros*. Those taken prisoner will be shot in the act.

"3. The junta of the government reiterates once more that attacks on the armed forces and *carabineros*, carried out by irresponsible individuals who compromise the lives of innocent people in surrounding villages, factories, and other populated centers, will only elevate hatefully the price of national liberation."

The morning after the coup, the most powerful man in Copiapó—Commander Oscar Haag—summoned all local public officials to a meeting at his office. Many of Wito's coworkers at the office of regional planning urged him not to go, but as head of the department, my brother felt he should attend.

After the meeting, as everyone was leaving to go back to work, Commander Haag pulled Wito aside and said he had received an anonymous tip that the office of regional planning's company vehicle had been seen in "suspicious places" on the day of the coup. Wito had not been the only person to drive the company's white Bronco that day, but Haag arrested him on the spot and sent him to the public jail for immediate detention. Without warning, Wito became the first political prisoner in Copiapó.

Back at the office of regional planning, Wito's coworkers watched anxiously as the other public officials began to come back from the meeting at Haag's office. When Wito did not return, they feared that Haag had detained him. My husband, Pato, went down to the public jail and learned that Wito had been arrested *only* because of the anonymous tip about the company vehicle, and he told me about it when I got home from work that night. Trying to convince myself that nothing would happen, I asked Pato, who was normally very rational and good at explaining things, if he thought there was any chance that Wito might be killed. Pato lowered his eyes and would not look at me. Clearly he had no answer, and that terrified me.

"The armed forces, *carabineros*, and *investigaciones* wish to give special thanks to the patriotic attitude of the Chilean citizenry," intoned the voice on the radio, "which, in keeping with the historic democratic tradition and in defense of the high interests of the country, has permitted with its timely information the control and destruction of important extremist centers and the completion of the profile of extremists and subversive foreign residents, and to clean our country of undesirable elements that have no part in our land and common origin."

That night at the public jail, the guards put Wito in with the common criminals. There was no established procedure for dealing with political prisoners, and since Wito was the first and only one in Copiapó, the jail administrators had no idea how to handle the situation. In the holding cell, one of the criminals offered to show Wito how to escape if he wanted to. "This is not going to be good for the political prisoners," the man said.

The next day my family went to visit Wito at the jail. My brother came out to see us, smiling as always, and asked if we knew what was going on, since no one had told him anything. It was all so confusing and upsetting, but if it was hard for me, it was even worse for my mother. She could not understand why her son was being detained. During our visit, I felt desperate to get information but did not ask questions or say anything that I thought might further upset my mother. My family talked about things we could do that might be helpful, but again, to avoid distressing my mother, no one expressed any major concern.

On our way home from the jail, my mother began to cry.

"Nothing's going to happen," I said, trying to calm her and managing to give myself a false sense of security, as well.

On September 14, 1973, the military junta dissolved the National Congress and declared that the congressmen's positions were vacant. In Copiapó, as was happening across the country, the military began to arrest more political prisoners: good, ordinary people like Alfonso Gamboa, a journalist and local radio station director; my friend Inez Vincentti's husband, Leonello, a bookish physics professor; and Raul Larravide, the twenty-one-year-old student body president at the Technical State University of Copiapó. Trying to make sense of the senseless, my mind attempted to find comfort in this new development. *There are more people now*, I thought. *It's not just one. These are good people. Everything should be okay.*

Soon the military transferred Wito and the other political prisoners to the garrison, a more threatening environment, surrounded by armed soldiers under Commander Haag's direct supervision. Before the coup, Copiapó's military and civilian populations had remained mostly separate. We knew the military existed in our town, but they had their own society—the barracks, the military hospital, their own clubs—and we did not really think about them. Suddenly, after the coup, soldiers were everywhere.

A week and a half dragged by. We could learn nothing about what to expect for Wito. My parents were frantic. Our lives began to settle into a new "normal" routine. We did our best to make sure that Wito had food, clean clothes, and books to read, and on visiting days we went to see him. But the only communications were those the Pinochet regime wanted us to hear, and those came with regularity over the radios, televisions, and public address systems.

The last time that my mother and I went together to visit Wito at the garrison, we were shocked to see that they had shaved his lovely black curls. Wito's almond eyes were smiling as he kissed us and said, "Look, they shaved my hair." When my mother saw him she began to cry. "They did that to my son," she wailed.

Many times after Wito's arrest, Pato wanted to go to Commander Haag's office and ask what was happening with my brother. Terrified of what might happen, I asked him not to go. One day while I was at work, Pato went to Haag's office to inquire about Wito. Haag's assistant arrested Pato on the spot without charges and sent him to the public jail for immediate detention.

Our friend Mauricio came to the university to tell me that Pato had just been arrested. I felt so anxious to get to my husband that I did not even want to wait for the bus, so Mauricio and I started walking from the university to the jail. My mind raced to try to make things seem normal, but my legs were shaking and hurting so badly that I nearly fell and twisted my ankle many times during our long walk to the jail.

Finally we reached the jail. We were not allowed to see Pato. Suddenly and without provocation, my husband and brother, like thousands of other innocent Chileans, were labeled "enemies of the state."

My family struggled to cope with the absence of Wito and Pato. My son, Felipe, and Wito's daughter, Susan, were only about one year old at the time. The children could not understand where their fathers were and cried for them to come home.

A few days later, my mother flew home to Malloco. Knowing I would not be able to take good care of Felipe while trying to help Wito and Pato, I asked her to take my son with her.

Weeks passed. There was no one we could ask for information about Wito and Pato. We heard about more people being detained. Then we started hearing about people being tortured. Many started losing their jobs. Outside the jail, wives and children clustered near the gate because their husbands and fathers were inside.

With Pato imprisoned indefinitely, my friends Adriana and Natacha came to stay at my house. Adriana, a university professor, had been fired after the coup when Pinochet declared philosophy a "subversive subject." Natacha's husband, Ronnie Ramirez, an economist working for a copper company in the town of El Salvador, had recently been arrested and transferred to the Copiapó public jail. Natacha had sent their children to stay with her parents in Santiago and followed Ronnie to Copiapó. She had no place to stay, so she stayed with me.

Every Sunday, and sometimes during the week, the military allowed visiting days for the political prisoners. On Sunday, October 14, I set out early to visit Pato for our allotted fifteen minutes. As I walked through Copiapó's quiet streets, I recalled a recent visiting day when my whole family had gone to see Wito at the garrison. The guards had escorted my brother to the patio, and when Wito's daughter, Susan, had spied her father, she had run toward him delightedly shrieking, "*Papi, Papi, Papi!*" Grinning playfully, Wito had bent toward his little curly haired girl, spreading his arms wide to scoop her up for hugs and kisses.

Smiling at the memory, I arrived at the public jail and stood outside the front gate with the other visitors. Soon the heavy gate swung open. As we walked through the jail entrance, I saw a guard on duty who was widely feared for his mental instability. A small, dark man with missing front teeth, he stared intensely as I walked by, then ordered me to stop. I stood motionless as he slowly walked toward me, a menacing smile on his face. The other visitors continued on toward the patio where the political prisoners were waiting.

The guard led me across the empty jail yard to a small room off the main corridor. Without a word he began roughly patting my sides and pockets. He grabbed my purse and dumped the contents onto a table. Mockingly he went through my personal things.

Then he ordered me to follow him to the patio. But before we reached it, he told me to stop and wait in the corridor while he fetched my husband. Trembling with fright and humiliation, I stood where he left me, and soon I saw him return with Pato. I felt desperate to put my arms around my husband, but before he could reach me, the guard told him to stop. Smiling broadly, the guard forced Pato and me to stand ten feet apart, facing each other. Then he began to laugh.

I looked at the guard, then into Pato's brown eyes, and then I burst into tears. For fifteen minutes, I did nothing but cry. I could not manage a single word to Pato. The guard stood at my side the entire time, laughing.

When our time was up, I dragged myself out of the jail, still crying, and slowly walked ten blocks to the garrison to see Wito. The military had erected some small, light-colored tents on the front patio for visiting day, and soldiers in olive green stood around, supervising. These soldiers seemed to have no emotional connection to the people or situation in front of them. They were not welcoming or friendly, nor were they extremely harsh; they just seemed to be doing their best to follow orders in a situation that was new to them, too.

Wito, escorted by a guard, soon appeared on the garrison patio. Smiling, he strolled over to kiss me hello but saw instantly that I had been crying. Without mentioning it directly, my brother began trying to cheer me up.

As Wito and I walked toward the military tents, I was relieved to see that the officers I feared most—Diaz, Marambio, and Ojeda—were not on duty that day. Widely feared for their hateful manner, these three young officers seemed to take pleasure in inflicting pain and humiliation on the visitors and prisoners. Of the three, Captain Patricio Diaz was considered the cruelest.

Wito and I sat on an empty bench inside one of the tents, and he related his recent conversation with the military prosecutor, Major

Carlos Brito. "Everything is going to be fine," Wito said with a sunny smile. "Pato and I will be released this coming weekend. If you see Pato before Tuesday, tell him that he will be brought here to speak with Brito sometime on Tuesday afternoon. Maybe we will be sent to some small town into internal exile. Major Brito will tell us on Tuesday."

Wito radiated optimism, but as he spoke I just sat motionless on the bench.

"Come on, Zita," Wito said. He got up, squatted in front of me, and placed his hands on my knees. His warm touch made me feel safer.

"Don't worry, Zita," my brother said gently. "We are going to be just fine."

THREE

Three days later, my friend Mauricio's wife, Gloria, called me at work. "Did Adriana arrive yet?" she asked.

"No."

"Okay, Zita, don't believe anything that she's going to tell you."

Soon my friend Adriana came into my office at the University and asked to speak privately. We walked to a coffee shop around the corner.

"A few minutes after you left home, Veronica came to the house," Adriana said. "She heard rumors that Winston was killed during the night."

My hands started shaking so violently that I dropped my coffee cup on the table.

"Do you want to go home now?" Adriana asked.

Wito's wife, Veronica, and my friend, Natasha, were waiting for me in the living room. No one spoke for a long time.

"It can't be," I said, finally. "It just can't."

We spent the day with Veronica, searching for news, and walked several times to the garrison hoping to speak with anyone who could tell us that Wito was fine. But armed soldiers now surrounded the garrison entrance. There was no way for us to get inside. Around 6:00 p.m. we remembered our lawyer—the same man my friend Inez Vincentti had hired after the military arrested her husband, Leonello. That night I went to our lawyer's house, and when he opened the door, I explained that I'd just heard that Wito and some other prisoners had been killed.

That was not possible, the lawyer said, inviting me in. I sat on his living room sofa, crying uncontrollably. The lawyer told me to wait a few minutes while he went to find out what had happened, and when he returned he said not to worry, that he had just seen Pato and Wito, and that Wito was doing exercises. They're well, they're fine, absolutely nothing had happened, the lawyer said, adding that he had spoken with Commander Haag and I did not need to worry, but that I should buy a newspaper the next morning because details of the prisoners' upcoming release would be published. I wanted this to be true, so I chose to believe him. The lawyer said to meet him at his office the next morning and to bring Inez Vincentti with me. "Don't forget to buy the newspaper," he repeated, as I left his house.

The next morning, Veronica, Inez, and I arrived early at the lawyer's office in downtown Copiapó. We realized that we had forgotten to buy a newspaper, so Veronica went out to get one while Inez and I waited in the reception area. The door to the street was open, and when I glanced up again I saw the lawyer standing in the doorway.

"Hi," I said. The lawyer stared at us, surprised to see us chatting so calmly.

"You didn't buy the newspaper?" he asked.

Just then, Veronica walked into the lawyer's office holding a newspaper out to me. I knew from her face that something dreadful had happened. My hands trembled as I took the paper and read:

INMATES' ESCAPE ATTEMPT

> **Two days ago, a massive escape plan was uncovered in the Copiapó Jail of inmates detained by the Military Justice. The plan was denounced by one of the detainees implicated in this case.**
>
> **Due to the lack of security and overpopulation at the Copiapó Jail, the military prosecutor's office yesterday proceeded to transfer a group of the most dangerous prisoners of the Military Justice to the jail of the city of La Serena.**
>
> **The transfer began at 01:00 a.m. yesterday, Wednesday, by military personnel in a truck from the garrison.**

According to the report by the Chief of the Commission and after proper investigation, it was verified that the vehicle had an electrical malfunction near the summit of *Cuesta Cardones*, which forced the driver to pull over on the shoulder of the highway.

Seeing that the driver and his assistant were busy trying to fix the electrical problem, the prisoners suddenly took advantage of their guard's distraction, jumped out of the truck, and fled toward the *pampa*. Despite the fact that the guards shouted "Stop!" several times and even fired warning shots into the air to frighten the prisoners, they did not stop.

In light of this situation, the guards proceeded to fire at the prisoners, wounding thirteen of them, who died immediately at the scene.

The affected ones are: Fernando Carvajal Gonzalez, Manuel Cortazar Hernandez, Winston Cabello Bravo, Agapito Carvajal Gonzalez, Alfonso Gamboa Farias, Raul del C. Guardia Olivares, Raul Leopoldo Larravide Lopez, Ricardo Mansilla Hess, Adolfo Pallera Norambuena, Pedro Perez Flores, Jaime Ivan Sierra Castillo, Atilio Ugarte Gutierrez and Leonello Vincentti Cartagena. Their remains were buried at the local cemetery.

COMMANDER OF THE ZONE UNDER STATE OF SIEGE
ATACAMA PROVINCE
October 17, 1973

Wito's name was third on the list.

Inez was watching me closely, waiting for news of her husband. I grabbed the lawyer and started shaking him. "You lied to me!" I cried. "You lied to me! Why didn't you tell me?"

When Inez heard that Leonello had been killed, she started crying and nearly collapsed. Everything I had wanted to deny to myself had now happened. I was furious with myself for believing the lawyer.

"I'm sorry, I'm sorry, I'm sorry," the lawyer kept saying. Later we learned that this lawyer was a military informant who had been reporting our conversations. When he had told me the night before that everything was fine, he had already known that Wito was dead.

Reeling from shock, we caught a cab home. As the taxi pulled into my driveway, Susan's tiny face appeared in a front window of my house, looking for her father's car. I saw her mouth forming the words *"Papi, Papi, Papi."*

I stumbled out of the cab and through my front door, past Adriana, Natacha, Gloria, and Mauricio, who had gathered at my house after hearing the news. I crawled into bed and prayed never to wake up, but even as I was slipping out of consciousness, part of my mind was fighting to stay awake.

"Where is Pato?" I screamed suddenly, sitting up in bed. "Is he also dead?"

My friends just looked at me with eyes full of pain.

"I have to save Pato!" I heaved myself out of bed and ran frantically out of the house and through the streets of Copiapó, knocking on doors and asking everyone I saw if they'd heard any news of my husband. No one could tell me if Pato was alive or dead.

FOUR

That night after curfew, the lawyer came unexpectedly to my house and asked to speak privately. The fact that a civilian was freely walking around after curfew should have made us suspicious of him, but we were so traumatized that we did not care. Natacha, who was staying with me, had hired this same lawyer in hopes that he could help her husband, Ronnie.

"Don't tell Natacha yet, but today there was a court-martial," the lawyer told me. "Ronnie got a death sentence. They plan to carry out the execution tomorrow. I have a meeting in the early morning with Commander Haag and the other members of the court-martial to see if there is any chance they would change their minds. I'll be back tomorrow to let Natacha know the final decision."

I shared this with Adriana, and we decided to wait and tell Natacha in the morning. What would happen to her if she went out after curfew? But Natacha was gone when I awoke, and she spent the day going back and forth between the jail and the garrison, trying to see her husband. I did pretty much the same, trying to find news about Pato. At the end of the day, Natacha and I had not been able to learn anything about our husbands, but we were horrified to hear that three of Ronnie's coworkers at the El Salvador mining company, including the general manager, had just been killed after a court-martial. At curfew, we went home and ate dinner in silence.

Around 8:00 p.m., a sharp knock came at my door. Fearing the worst, we opened it, and the lawyer rushed in with a bottle of champagne. "Let's celebrate!" he cried. "Ronnie got life in prison!"

We drank gratefully that night to Ronnie's life sentence. I never saw that lawyer again.

A few nights later, after curfew, a lower-ranking soldier named Adolfo Gonzalez appeared at my home. Adolfo worked at the garrison as an assistant to the military prosecutor, Major Carlos Brito. I had befriended Adolfo during my many visits to Pato and Wito.

On the night Wito was killed, Adolfo had come to Veronica's house to give her the news. Adolfo had been drunk, and Veronica had not believed him. Now he was standing on my porch with some news for me. "I came to tell you what happened to your brother," he said.

"Please, tell me about Pato first." I had not been able to learn anything about my husband and did not even know if he was still alive.

"Patricio is fine," said Adolfo, following me into the kitchen. "You can visit him this coming Sunday at the garrison."

Trembling with relief, I sank into a chair at the kitchen table. I offered Adolfo a drink, but he refused.

"Zita, the night your brother was killed, a general came from Santiago with a group of military officers," Adolfo said. "It was that general who gave the order to execute the prisoners."

"What's the name of the general?"

"I don't know. You have to believe me, Zita. If I could have saved Winston, I would have done it. I couldn't," said Adolfo, starting to cry. "Your brother's death was a terrible crime. You need to forgive me, Zita."

My voice failed. I could only nod.

"Upon their arrival, they all met with Commander Oscar Haag to review all prisoners' folders, and in a few hours they selected the prisoners they wanted to kill," he continued.

"Just like that?"

"Yes, just like that. They removed all thirteen victims from the garrison a few minutes after midnight. They put them in a truck and drove them to *Cuesta Cardones*. I don't know the name of the people who came from Santiago. But they took them out of the garrison with the help of a few local officers who joined the party."

"Party?"

"That's what they called it," said Adolfo, describing how three local officers—Captain Patricio Diaz, Second Lieutenant Waldo Ojeda, and Second Lieutenant Marcelo Marambio—had also participated. "They all started drinking *pisco*. By the time they left, they were all drunk and in a celebratory mood. They even invited me to join them in the celebration, but I refused. A young lieutenant insisted that Winston's name should not be removed from the list. I tried, Zita, but I couldn't take your brother's name off the list. You have to believe me."

I just nodded. Years later, I learned that Armando Fernandez had been the lieutenant who insisted Wito's name remain on the list.

"Twenty minutes after the truck left with the prisoners, I heard shots," Adolfo said. "Then I drank a whole bottle of *pisco*, and I went to Winston's house. That night I might have said things that were not true. But I'm sober now. Everything I'm telling you tonight is the truth."

"After you left Winston's house, where did you go? We looked for you everywhere. We didn't believe what you told Veronica, yet we wanted to speak with you."

"I was guarding the bodies all day long," said Adolfo. He added that the military had buried the victims somewhere in the Copiapó cemetery around 11:00 p.m. on October 17.

"Do you know where they buried them?"

"No."

I started to cry. "Tell me, what can I do for Pato?"

"You can do nothing, Zita."

"Why is he detained?"

"People who wanted to destroy our freedom destroy our way of life," Adolfo began.

"Are you telling me that the evil you are committing is necessary for the good of the country?" I demanded, interrupting him. "Can you tell me what my brother did to deserve to be killed? Can you tell me what my husband did?"

Adolfo looked at the floor. As I waited for his answer, it struck me how out of place this young uniformed soldier looked in my kitchen. "I can't explain why Winston was killed," he said, finally. "I just can't. I can't explain either why Patricio is detained."

"So he could be killed?"

Suddenly, Adolfo stood and raised his right hand. "Zita, I promise you. Nobody will ever touch Patricio. If another general comes from Santiago, I will hide him. I will take him out of the garrison, I will do anything, but he won't be killed. I promise this to you."

I responded as Wito would have wanted me to: with faith in humanity. I stood up and embraced Adolfo.

Then he walked out of my house and into the night.

FIVE

Immediately after the killings, everything changed in Copiapó. If the objective of killing innocent people was to spread fear among the civilian population, the military accomplished that. Now we knew there was no limit to what they could do. From that moment on they flaunted their power everywhere. It was a different town. They could kill with impunity. They took over everything.

The military canceled all visits to political prisoners. I had not been able to see Pato since October 14, the last day I had seen Wito. Finally, the military announced a visiting day at the garrison: on Sunday, November 4, at 3:00 p.m., I would be able to see Pato for ten minutes.

Under the chilling surveillance of armed officers in combat fatigues and dark glasses, I walked slowly along the inside of the garrison fence, searching for Pato. Officers stared down from watchtowers and patrolled the yard, where prisoners and visitors clustered together trying not to attract attention. As people visited they spoke quietly, glancing nervously around to see where the officers were, what they were doing, who they were watching. Despite the crowds, the garrison yard was eerily quiet.

Finally I saw Pato waiting for me at a distance. I walked toward my husband, timidly opening my arms to embrace him.

"Get back!" shouted a harsh voice. "Five feet away from each other!"

I froze. Captain Patricio Diaz was walking slowly toward me across the yard, carrying a rifle. Diaz had always frightened me, but now that I knew he had participated in Wito's murder, I was terrified.

I waited, trembling, not daring to look directly at Captain Diaz. He stopped in front of me and stared down through dark glasses for what felt like an eternity. My legs began to shake. Then he shoved me away from Pato and walked away across the yard, pushing everyone out of his path. He did not look back.

My heart was pounding. I looked up and saw two other officers approaching. Marambio and Ojeda—the other local officers who had participated in Wito's murder—were heading toward us. Pato and I stood motionless, afraid to speak or even look at each other.

Marambio and Ojeda moved on.

When the officers were far enough away that we felt we could speak, Pato hurriedly told me what had happened on October 16, the day of his transfer to the garrison.

"The military prosecutor, Major Carlos Brito, ordered the transfer because he wanted to meet us both, Winston and me, to discuss our release," said Pato. "Since your brother had spoken with Brito earlier that day, Winston brought me up to speed while we both waited outside his office. Brito told your brother that he had decided to release us because there were no charges against us. Winston told me that we were going home on Sunday, October 21, or would be sent into 'internal exile' to live in a small town close to Copiapó. On Tuesday the sixteenth, Brito was going to discuss those details with us. But we never had the chance to do it.

"Around 4:00 p.m., we were still waiting outside his office when unsettling activities began to occur. At one point, two guards came to us and without warning ordered all prisoners to get inside the barracks. Since I was imprisoned in the jail, I expected somebody to take me back there. Instead they instructed me to go inside the barracks where the prisoners at the garrison slept. Winston thought that was a strange order, so he offered me a place to sleep in his bunk bed. He briefly explained to me how the prisoners had organized their time and space. We ate inside, which Winston said was 'totally unusual.' Sometime between 6:00 and 7:00 p.m., we heard the noise of a helicopter landing in the patio. Ominous noise. A few moments later total silence, deadly silence, fell over the entire place.

"Winston had a pretty bad cold that night, so I offered him a scarf of mine to keep him warm. We were all in bed by 9:00 p.m. It was probably about 11:00 p.m. when a group of soldiers burst into our sleeping quarters. One of them was Patricio Diaz. And there were two others Winston did not recognize. We assumed they had come with the helicopter we heard earlier.

"The two unknown soldiers, both dressed in combat uniforms and carrying machine guns, looked at each other. One of them, the youngest one, said, 'So it is here where the little doves sleep.' We felt the sarcasm in his voice. Then he said, 'Look Marcelo, they even have cake, these sons of bitches,' pointing to some leftover birthday cake. They left after that. There was something quite disturbing about their visit. They looked very different from the local soldiers.

"Once they left, we all got quiet. We forced ourselves to fall asleep. At midnight, a loud noise woke us up. The door banged open, and the same three officers who'd come earlier walked inside the room. They looked really drunk. One of the unknown officers stood at the very end of my bed. I could see the lower half of his face and the rest of his body down. He was smiling a dreadful smile, holding a machine gun in his hands, and a few more weapons were hanging from his body. I even saw a grenade on him. He kept smiling when Patricio Diaz began reading names. The first name was your brother's. When Wito heard his name, he said, 'Here.'

"'Get up, son of a bitch!' the officer screamed at him.

"Winston quickly put his pants on over his pajamas, plus the green sweater your mom knitted for him, and his shoes. He didn't have time to tie them because they screamed at him, 'Hurry up, motherfucker!' I reminded him to take the scarf. He did. He never came back."

Pato spoke urgently as if he wanted me to hear every detail of that night, as if there would be no other opportunity to tell me. I wanted to tell him to stop, that I could not bear any more, but I could not make a sound.

"At 7:00 in the morning, a friendly guard took me aside and told me Wito had been killed," Pato said, choking back tears. "And the others as well."

Our ten minutes were up.

I walked slowly home from the garrison, not knowing when I would see Pato again. I had never felt so alone.

SIX

My visit with Pato left me in desperate need of hope. Natacha and Adriana wanted to hear everything when I got home, but I did not feel like talking or eating. I could not express all the pain in my heart.

"You don't have to talk if you don't want to, Zita, but you do need to eat something," Natacha said, cooking a simple dinner. The three of us ate in silence, and then sat on the living room sofa talking quietly in the dark. Adolfo had warned us that patrolling soldiers grew suspicious if they saw lights on after curfew. As I was sharing what Pato had told me, a sudden, sharp knock came at the door. We froze.

"I know you are there," called Adolfo. "It's me."

I ran to the door. Afraid to ask questions and dreading the news he might have, I offered to make tea for everyone. A few minutes later, Natacha, Adriana, Adolfo, and I were seated around the kitchen table, holding the steaming cups in our hands.

"Commander Oscar Haag received an order today from Santiago to transfer all political prisoners held in the garrison and in the jail to Chacabuco," said Adolfo, avoiding my eyes. "That includes Patricio."

I stared in horror. Chacabuco, an old, abandoned mining town in the desert, was now a notorious concentration camp. Scorching in the day and freezing at night, this deadly place was surrounded by barbed wire, watchtowers, and landmines, with patrolling tanks pointing their cannons in toward the prisoners. Every night the guards chose prisoners for terrifying mock executions, or worse, took them away forever.

"All the prisoners, around fifty total, will be transferred this Saturday, November 10, to Chacabuco," Adolfo said.

I felt suddenly sure the military would kill my husband. "I can't let that happen to Pato."

"Zita, there is nothing you can do."

"I'll go to speak with Commander Haag," I said. "He can't send Pato to Chacabuco. He just can't."

"It's too late to do anything," Adolfo said. "The entire list of prisoners was already prepared and sent to Chacabuco and Santiago. This was done under Commander Haag's orders a few hours ago."

"Why can't I speak with Commander Haag to ask him to remove Pato from the list?"

Adolfo reminded me that Commander Haag had personally detained Wito the day after the coup, and that Haag's assistant had arrested Pato when he had only asked for information. "You have to remember, he is the most powerful man in the region," Adolfo said. "He is the governor and the highest military authority in the region."

"I know that," I said, desperately. "Don't you think that's exactly why he is the only one who can help Pato?"

"What makes you think he will even listen to you?"

"He killed my brother."

"Zita," said Adolfo, panicking, "don't ever say that again. You need to remember that what happened to your brother can happen again. You need to be safe. Haag is a powerful man, a lot of power in one man's hands. But you are right. He bears responsibility in your brother's death."

My mind was racing as Adolfo spoke. What could I possibly say to persuade Commander Haag?

"You have to pack things for Patricio," Adolfo continued, looking steadily at me across the kitchen table. "All the prisoners at the garrison will be transferred tomorrow to the jail. You will probably be able to see Patricio on Wednesday and Saturday before they leave for Chacabuco. Nobody knows about this transfer yet. They will be notified on Wednesday."

Adolfo left my house around 10:30 p.m., and I went to bed soon after with just one thought in mind: I could not let Commander Haag send Pato to Chacabuco.

All night I lay awake, trying to figure out how to prevent the transfer. At the first light of dawn I got out of bed, feeling I could not wait another moment to get over to Haag's office. Although I knew nothing of Commander Haag's schedule, I thought I would be safer going to the governor's office than the garrison.

I was heading out the door when I caught sight of myself in the mirror. It was not a good image. Although I was twenty-six years old, the thin, anxious girl with long brown hair and a miniskirt who was peering back at me looked barely seventeen. If I was going to meet Commander Haag, I had to look professional. I raced back to my bedroom and tried on five different outfits, but nothing helped. Finally I pulled on pants and a sweater and rushed out of the house.

At 7:50 a.m., I walked into the reception area of Commander Haag's office. Fifteen men were already seated there, and I stood awkwardly by the door, unsure what to do, until a kind older man finally told me I needed to sign the waiting list.

A tall, blond officer soon appeared. Frowning, he glanced around the reception room, picked up the waiting list, and walked out. A few minutes later, he returned.

"Zita Cabello."

Everyone stared at me. *I had nothing to do with this*, I wanted to say as I walked past the seated men.

The young officer led me down a silent hallway and offered me a chair inside his office. "How can I help you?" Haag's assistant asked, sitting down at his desk.

"I want to speak with Commander Oscar Haag," I blurted, suddenly afraid to identify myself.

"Why do you want to see him?"

Realizing that Haag's assistant probably already knew who I was, I calmed down a little. "I'm Winston Cabello's sister—he was killed on October 17—and also the wife of Patricio Barrueto, who is a prisoner at the garrison. My husband is scheduled to be sent to Chacabuco this coming Saturday. I want to ask Commander Haag to change his destination and send him into internal exile instead, maybe to a remote island of his choice where our little son, Felipe, and I can join him."

Haag's assistant studied me with piercing blue eyes. He did not move a muscle. "Come back tomorrow," he said finally. "I'll speak with him."

Early the next morning I returned to Haag's office. Within five minutes, I was talking with Haag's assistant.

"I spoke with my commander," he said. "He asked me to tell you not to worry. Your husband will go to Chacabuco, where he will have a place to sleep and food to eat."

"Please," I said timidly. "I really want to speak with him."

"Why do you still want to speak with him? He is going to tell you exactly what I already told you."

"I still want to speak with him."

"He can't change your husband's destination," Haag's assistant said. "Chacabuco is a safe place. You shouldn't worry."

"Please, let me speak with Commander Haag," I pleaded. "I'm not asking for my husband's release. He can send him to a remote island if he wants. He won't escape from there. Our little boy and I could go with him."

"I'm sorry. I can't help you."

"Can you ask him again, please?"

The young officer did not know what to do. He waited for me to leave. I did not move. "Okay," he said finally. "My commander will be here tomorrow morning. He has a meeting at 9:00 a.m. I will ask him again. Come back tomorrow."

The next morning, my friend Mauricio walked over to Haag's office with me and waited on the plaza while I went inside. At 8:45 a.m., Haag's assistant called me to his office. This time, he remained standing and did not offer me a seat. "I spoke with my commander. The answer is the same. Your husband will be taken to Chacabuco. Everything is already arranged."

I felt like I was drowning.

Suddenly I remembered seeing Haag's assistant on the street the night before, with his wife and a little boy about my son's age. "I know you have a child," I said, desperately. "I'm sure you love him very much, and I'm sure he loves you, too. My little boy wants to be with his father, and I want to be with him, too. Please, let me speak with Commander Oscar Haag."

Haag's assistant hesitated. He left the room, but returned a few seconds later. "I'm sorry; he can't meet you. His meeting is just starting. My commander asked me to tell you not to worry, that your husband will be fine in Chacabuco."

Sobbing, I collapsed into a chair, hating myself for breaking down in front of him. *Stop crying!* I thought. *This is exactly what they want—to see people humiliated and defeated. Stop crying!*

"Please," I said, "let me speak with him."

"Why do you want to speak with him?" asked Haag's assistant with pity. "You are going to receive the same answer. You already know it can't be changed."

"I want to hear it from him. I want him to tell me that there is no other alternative but Chacabuco. Only then would I know that I did everything in my power to protect my husband's life, that there was nothing else I could have done."

The young officer left the room abruptly. When he returned, he said, "My commander will see you for five minutes."

I scrambled to my feet and followed Haag's assistant down the hall, wiping my face and eyes as I went. He ushered me into a large conference room, closing the door behind me, and there at the center of the room stood a large man in his fifties in formal combat uniform. Commander Haag extended his hand. I did not expect that.

"I have five minutes," Haag said, pointing to a group of men in suits who were watching us impatiently through windows lining the conference room wall. "You can see I have people waiting."

I did not know how to begin but knew I could not squander my five minutes searching for the right words. "I'm Winston Cabello's sister and Patricio Barrueto's wife…"

"I know who you are," Haag interrupted. "Your husband will be transferred to Chacabuco on Saturday. In Chacabuco, he will have a place to sleep and food to eat. He is going to be just fine."

In Haag's mind, the meeting was already over. Clearly annoyed, the men in suits paced the hallway.

"I want to help my husband," I said, facing Commander Haag. "Something I can no longer do for my brother. I didn't come here to ask you why you killed my brother."

"Your brother tried to escape," Haag interrupted. "That's why he was killed."

"Don't lie to me," I snapped. "You and I know that is a lie. But I'm not asking you to explain to me why you killed my brother. I'm here because I want to save my husband's life. You didn't give Winston an opportunity, but you can give it to my husband."

Commander Haag offered me a chair, and then sat down beside me.

"I don't want you to send my husband to Chacabuco," I said, quietly. "I don't even know why you arrested him."

"Powerful people and big business demanded our involvement," Haag said. "It was the logic of money and power that dictated our involvement."

"If that is the case, why are people locked up and killed when you are already in control of the country?"

"We had to do it to save lives." Citing different reasons for the military takeover, Haag told me the armed forces had saved Chile from civil war. Hundreds of thousands of people had already died in a civil war in Guatemala, he said.

"But we were not in a war like in Guatemala. You are the one killing innocent people. You are destroying the soul of our country, fighting an imaginary war. What did my brother do? Or my husband?"

"All the people who worked for President Allende live in luxury now because they enriched themselves at the expense of all Chileans," Haag said. "Many high government officials flew to Miami, where they bought expensive mansions with stolen money."

"I want to invite you to my house, to my brother's house, so you can see how we live. We lived by honest dreams. Winston and Patricio wanted to find solutions for the inequalities of our society. Was that a sin?"

"We also care about the poor people," Haag replied. "We are building new houses, fixing some roads."

"If you care about the poor people, why is my husband locked up for caring, too?"

"Every time I walk on the street, civilians stop me angrily to say, 'Why haven't you arrested such and such person? Why is he walking freely on the streets of Copiapó?'"

Haag leaned forward, jabbing the air with his finger as if a crowd of people stood next to me, demanding answers. "The civilians of this country are the ones pressuring us to imprison people, to exercise strong authority. They want us to detain everyone who worked for President Allende or who was just a sympathizer of his government."

I did not want to hear Haag's excuses. I insisted that he send Pato to a different place so Felipe and I could be with him. Instead of responding, Haag asked what kind of work I did.

"I'm an economist like my brother and husband. I teach economics in the Social Science Department at the university here in Copiapó."

Haag asked about my son.

"Felipe is only a year-and-a-half old. After my husband's detention, I sent him to stay with my parents in Malloco. I haven't seen him in over a month."

Haag and I kept talking. Our five-minute meeting stretched into half an hour. I don't know how many times I insisted that he send Pato into internal exile.

"How are you planning to survive?" Haag asked. "You know that in Chacabuco he will have a house and food."

I grasped at hope upon hearing those words. Desperately I talked to Haag about working the land, cultivating our own food. I may have even mentioned fishing. Through the windows, I saw the men in suits pacing furiously.

Finally Haag said, "Give my assistant the name of three places where you would like to go with your husband."

I jumped to my feet and thanked Commander Haag, then quickly left the room, afraid he might change his mind. The stunned expression on his assistant's face was something to behold.

"How did you do that?" he asked.

I shrugged and said I would be back in an hour with some names.

Mauricio was waiting for me under some trees on the plaza, and when I gave him the good news, he took me in his arms and threw me into the air. Then we caught a taxi to my house and quickly spread a map across my kitchen table, choosing the three most remote Southern Chilean islands we could find. I had never heard of any of them but thought if I suggested a spot far enough from civilization, where there would be no chance of escape, Haag could more easily agree to the transfer.

Within the hour I was back at Haag's office, handing my list of islands to his assistant. The young officer promised to relay his commander's decision within two days. I never asked his name nor imagined that our paths would cross again years later, under very different circumstances.

From Haag's office, I ran to the public jail so I could see Pato during the scheduled visiting hours. The prisoners had been told that morning that they would all be transferred to Chacabuco on Saturday. Pato listened in silence as I related my conversation with Haag, and I realized that my husband would have chosen to risk his life at Chacabuco rather than break solidarity with his fellow political prisoners.

Two days later, I was still waiting to hear from Haag's office. It was already Friday, and the prisoners would be transferred to Chacabuco the following morning. I had done everything I could, and Pato's fate was now out of my hands.

I did not know how Haag's office was planning to inform me of his decision, but I was afraid to leave the house, fearing that I might miss someone coming to give me the news. At noon I rushed to the jail to deliver Pato's lunch basket, and when I got home a neighbor came over and said, "A military jeep was parked in front of your house, and they were looking for you."

I panicked. Afraid that I had missed my one chance to spare Pato from the concentration camp, I ran twenty blocks to Haag's office. Commander Haag was the most powerful man in Copiapó and could do anything he wanted. He had granted us a huge favor by agreeing to consider my request, but he could easily change his mind now just because I had not been home when the soldiers came to talk with me.

"I sent for you at the university, but you weren't there," said Haag's assistant, as I stood in front of his desk trying to catch my breath. "Then to your house. You weren't there either."

"I was at the jail bringing lunch to my husband," I said.

Haag's assistant looked pointedly at his watch. "Commander Haag wants me to ask you where you want to go, Huasco or Freirina?"

I could not believe it. Both towns were only about two hours from Copiapó. "I don't know what to say. Either one seems a dream."

"Huasco is better," he said, nodding. "It's a port and it would be easier for your husband to find a job."

"Huasco, then."

The young officer called Commander Haag at the garrison. "I have with me Patricio Barrueto's wife. She said she prefers Huasco."

I asked if I could speak with Haag and said into the phone, "Thank you so much for doing this."

"Huasco or Freirina would allow you to keep your job and visit your husband if you want to do that," Haag said. "Once in Huasco, your husband won't be able to leave the town. He will have to report to the police every morning and every evening."

"Yes, I understand that. Our son and I will be with him."

Commander Haag repeated that in Chacabuco the prisoners would have free food and housing.

"Thank you very much. I prefer Huasco," I said, quickly handing the phone back to Haag's assistant.

"Military personnel will take Patricio to Huasco on Sunday, the day after tomorrow," Haag's assistant told me, after hanging up.

On my way home, I stopped at the jail and asked a guard to deliver a message to Pato about his transfer to Huasco. All the other prisoners would be loaded into a truck to Chacabuco the next morning, and I wanted to make sure Pato knew he would not be going with them.

The moment I learned of Wito's death, I knew it would destroy my father. My parents were devastated by the loss, but I had been so consumed with trying to help Pato that I had not been able to leave Copiapó to see them for even a day. Since I could not get away, my friend Adriana had flown to Malloco to check on my parents; after spending two days at their house, she had confirmed my fears. My father was in a semiconscious state of shock and kept repeating, "They are going to kill Pato, and my Zita is going to die, and I will die with her."

It was Friday afternoon. Pato would not be transferred to Huasco until Sunday, and for the first time since the coup I saw a chance to leave Copiapó and visit my parents in Malloco. That night, I rode the bus for twelve hours to Santiago, which was near my parents' home. As the bus rolled through the desert, I gazed out the window and thought about my family.

From left to right Lito, Nano, Manuel, Elsa, Zita, Wito (kneeling)
1957

In Search of Spring

My brothers and I had grown up in Renaico, Chile, a small southern town on the bank of a river. On summer days, nearly everyone was at the river, playing in the water, picking wild blackberries, chatting in the shade of old trees. It felt like an enchanted place. Each morning my mother packed a lunch basket for our family. She watched us swim and play from a shelter of branches my father built for her on the smooth stones of the bank.

For my first thirteen years, I was the only girl and youngest child in our family, with three older brothers—Manuel (nicknamed Nano), Aldo (Lito), and Winston (Wito)—watching out for me. I was twelve years old when our parents surprised us with the news: they were expecting a new baby. A few months later we got our little sister, Karin. The day she was born, my father could not stop smiling. "It is a girl," he said, with the biggest smile I had ever seen on his face.

My mother, Elsa, a shy, devoted Catholic housewife with blue eyes and dark curly hair, and my father, Manuel, a popular elementary school principal with high cheekbones and lively honey-colored eyes, treated me like a delicate object. In their loving shelter I grew very shy, learning my "good girl" role to perfection. I learned to play alone and to love the imaginary worlds without limits that I created.

Wito, two years my senior, wanted me to experience real life. He coaxed me out of isolation and taught me to fly kites, run races, and play chess, marbles, Ping-Pong, and soccer, games that only boys were supposed to play. He invited me to play at every opportunity, but when other boys were around, I was not included in their games. Wito would ask me to sit and watch their games so we could talk about them later. This was especially true during basketball and soccer games that my brothers and their friends organized with kids from the neighborhood.

My brother challenged me and taught me to believe in myself, and as we grew up together we shared our hopes and dreams. Wito confided that when he grew up, he wanted to be in a position to find some way to help fix what he called "the sickness of the world," including the widespread poverty that we often encountered. He wanted to address social inequality in a way that would help improve people's quality of life long-term, so that charity would not be needed for temporary fixes. This made so much sense to me that I wanted to join him in that work.

Summer vacations, in the years that I was twelve to sixteen, became our special time together. We no longer lived in Renaico; our parents had moved to Malloco. We missed our enchanted river so much, that Wito and I began spending two weeks of our summer vacation at our uncle Humberto's house in the countryside near the city of Talca, about four hours from Santiago. My older brother Nano had already left Chile to study physics in the United States, Karin was a baby, and Lito, for some reason, never joined us.

This countryside near Talca was a beautiful place in the mountains. Wito and I ran after the sheep in the evenings, we ate wild berries, and most of all, we spent our time swimming in a beautiful lagoon called *La Laguna del Toro*, located in what once was my grandfather's land. This lagoon was formed by a waterfall, and nearby stood a huge tree heavy with figs, my mother's favorite fruit. My mother and her siblings had grown up in this magical place, and her fondest childhood memories were those of summer swims with her siblings in *La Laguna del Toro*.

Every day, Wito and I walked about two miles on a narrow trail from our uncle's house to the lagoon. Sometimes we rode a horse, which was an adventure. During those long walks, Wito and I talked and our topic of conversation rarely changed. It was always connected to what we saw on our way to the lagoon: extreme poverty. We talked about our childhood, when during time of emergencies, like flood, our father would walk to the countryside to bring with him entire families to stay at his school. Many times we had children sleeping in our beds at home. When the emergency ended, the families went back to their huts until another emergency hit their lives and my father would bring them back to the school to provide them with food and shelter. Wito and I, older now, talked about the need to find permanent solutions to the extreme poverty we saw while growing up and now on our way to *Laguna del Toro*. We shared ideas on how we could cure the "sickness" of the world. That was our plan.

Wito was my dearest companion. I treasured our time together.

In those days my father was very social, and his bright eyes, quick wit, and gentle nature made him a favorite in our town, especially with young people. My father loved listening to music, playing the guitar, reading literature, playing soccer, and pursuing many other interests, but above all he loved gardening, and roses were his passion. My favorite rose was the tiny pink *besitos*, or "little kisses." Knowing how I loved their delicate beauty and perfume, my father would gather these charming pink roses from his garden for me. All through high school and college I wore my father's *besitos* in my hair and on my clothing.

My father often said that poetry would save the world. Every night when I was a child, he would sit by my bed and weave profound life lessons into imaginative stories. He took me for many long walks in the country, explaining all about the interesting plants and birds that we saw, and we would carry home armloads of treasures such as branches and stones with beautiful shapes. Whenever I was afraid or needed comfort, my father would pick me up, hug me, and sing to me, planting little kisses on top of my head and trying to make me laugh. In the end, he always succeeded.

The bus jolted. Through the window I watched the sky blaze fiery red over the mountains, until soft purple bled in, and then cold gray shrouded the sky. I watched out the window as the light disappeared and darkness devoured the desert.

SEVEN

I arrived at my parents' house around ten on Saturday morning. Walking through their large grassy front yard, I saw that the fruit trees, grapevines, and flower beds my father had so lovingly tended over the years were now overgrown and neglected. The fragrance of cherry blossoms and sun-warmed roses wafted over the back fence on the warm spring air. Ever since I could remember, my father had arisen around five each morning to go out and work in his garden, where he had planted more than a hundred varieties of roses. He named his roses after people he loved—Wito's Rose, Pato's Rose, Zita's Rose—and was always giving them away.

I reached the front porch and hesitated. I had not told my parents I was coming, and suddenly I felt afraid to see them. Standing outside their front door, summoning the courage to go inside, I started noticing details of their home that I had overlooked before. Wito had spent countless hours helping my father study blueprints, hire contractors, choose paint colors, and make hundreds of other decisions about this house, and now it felt as if my brother was everywhere. My three older brothers and I had grown up in Renaico and had moved out long before my parents built their dream house in Malloco, but still, my mother and father had designed their new home with bedrooms for each of their five children.

I took a breath and walked inside. My mother was ironing, and my father was sitting in the family room with my son, Felipe, on his lap. When my parents saw me, they rushed to meet me with cries of happiness and relief. But I soon found that my father and I could no longer talk to each other.

My father was inconsolable. He cried all day long. I could do nothing to comfort him, and my presence only seemed to increase his sorrow. I had come to Malloco meaning to comfort my parents, but also desperately needing my father to comfort me, as he had always been able to before. Now I knew those days were gone forever.

At first Felipe did not recognize me. Then when he heard my voice, he clung to my neck and would not let go. He screamed every time I put him down. Over lunch, my mother and I talked at the kitchen table. My father sat with us for a while, but he could not stop crying and finally got up and left the room. My mother went after him, trying to calm him down. I saw a new strength in my mother that day: devastated by grief, she was still taking care of my father.

That night I rode the bus back to Copiapó, sure that my visit had not helped anyone. I arrived home early Sunday morning, exhausted after two sleepless nights, and quickly showered, packed a bag for Pato and me, and walked to the jail. We were always hearing about prisoners disappearing during transfers, and I wanted to make sure Pato arrived safely at his destination. I was determined to get into the jeep with the soldiers.

I did not know what time the military planned to transfer Pato to Huasco and did not want to take a chance on missing him, so I sat on a large rock outside the jail to wait. At 4:00 p.m., a military jeep with two soldiers pulled up. Adolfo was at the wheel. "I knew you were doing something when Commander Haag asked for information about Patricio," he said, smiling at my astonishment. "I volunteered today to make the transfer."

I had been waiting all day outside the jail, determined to accompany Pato during his transfer to Huasco, not knowing if I would be allowed to do that. The moment I saw Adolfo I knew everything would be fine. Hurriedly Adolfo walked into the jail to get Pato. "Wait for me here," he said. Adolfo carried with him an official document, signed by Commander Haag, instructing the jail guards to release Pato to him. Five minutes later I saw Pato coming out, accompanied by an unfriendly guard. Pato seemed a little confused; he slowly walked toward the military jeep, followed by the guard. We didn't dare to kiss or hug. Suddenly, the guard grabbed from my hands the bag I had prepared for Pato and me and started emptying it on the ground. Adolfo made him stop. "Get into the jeep," he told us. Pato said nothing; he just walked toward the jeep like nothing mattered anymore.

The military jeep was only designed for three people, but I wedged myself in between Pato and the passenger door and rode to Huasco with Adolfo's rifle in my hands. As we drove through the desert, Adolfo chatted pleasantly to ease the tension. Pato's encounters with Adolfo had been very limited, and I sensed his reluctance to say anything. After a while, Pato relaxed a bit and described the previous day's prisoner transfer to Chacabuco.

On Saturday morning, Captain Patricio Diaz had come to the jail to load the prisoners into a truck. He lined the men up on a patio and called their names as he had on the night Wito was killed. Then he started hitting prisoners with his rifle. When Diaz called Pato's name and saw that he was not going to Chacabuco with the others, he swore violently and struck Pato in the stomach with his rifle. Then he sent Pato to a different patio, away from the other prisoners.

Among the political prisoners loaded into the truck that day was Oscar Vega, a tall, gaunt man who looked much older than his sixty-seven years. Since Oscar's detention on September 19, the jail guards had repeatedly beaten and psychologically abused him, causing him to attempt suicide. I had noticed Oscar's bandaged wrists when first visiting Pato at the jail. Pato sensed that Oscar needed help, and he took the older man under his wing. They became close friends, spending long hours talking together in the jail.

"El Viejo Vega," as Pato affectionately called him, confided that his wife had passed away and his daughter never visited, so Pato asked me to start bringing lunch and interesting books for Oscar. I was already preparing daily lunches for Pato—my specialties were soups and stews—so I just doubled the recipe and packaged their meals separately. I also started experimenting with desserts so I could create special treats, such as lemon pie, flan, rice pudding, and Pato's favorite apple strudel, to help them feel better. We never told Oscar who brought the lunches. During a visit, Pato pulled me aside and whispered, "El Viejo Vega thinks his daughter brings him food. He is doing much better."

The night before the transfer to Chacabuco, Pato and Oscar said good-bye. "I want to go with you," Oscar told him. "I don't want to go to Chacabuco." For Oscar, the old desert mining town was more than a concentration camp: it was the town where he had spent his youth working as a nitrate miner, enjoying his first happy years of marriage and raising his young children with his wife. But the mining town Oscar remembered, and his cherished memories there, were long gone.

I later learned that when Oscar reached Chacabuco with the other prisoners, he went off alone to search for his old house. Twelve days later, on November 22, "El Viejo Vega" hanged himself from the living room ceiling. When I shared this dreadful news with Pato, my husband's response did not surprise me: "If I had gone with him, this would not have happened."

EIGHT

Pato was now settled in Huasco, but with my teaching job continuing at the Technical State University of Copiapó, I could not move out right away to be with him. For the rest of the spring semester, I taught economics classes in Copiapó during the week and rode the bus out to Huasco on the weekends.

One day as I was waiting at the bus stop near the university entrance, I noticed a large, conspicuous man nearby pretending to read a newspaper. He held the newspaper up very high so it covered most of his face.

A few mornings later as I was about to leave for work, I saw the same large man standing on the sidewalk outside my house, pretending to read a newspaper. He held the paper up in the same strange way, very high so it covered most of his face. *Why is he here reading a newspaper?* I wondered.

I saw the man a few more times outside the university, always standing in the same place, near the bus stop. One Friday afternoon as I was boarding a bus to Huasco, I spied the man sitting a few aisles away. He looked so familiar that I felt sure Pato and I knew him from somewhere, so I picked up my suitcase and walked down the aisle toward him. "Hello," I said, smiling, as I stopped in front of him.

The man did not answer. He turned away from me, sitting sideways in his seat, not looking at me. As the bus rattled along, he grew increasingly nervous. A few stops later, he rose abruptly and got off the bus. Soon after, Adolfo told me to be careful; he had heard that someone from military intelligence was following me around. Suddenly it hit me;

the man I had greeted in the bus was the man from military intelligence. It shocked me to think that he might have interpreted my greeting as an indication that I had discovered his identity, and that this was my way of mocking him. For days I expected some kind of retaliation. I barely slept at night, waiting for someone to get me. Everywhere I went, I kept looking over my shoulder.

During the first three months in Huasco, from December 1973 to March 1974, Pato stayed in a rundown hotel and I visited him every weekend. Our son, Felipe, was still at my parents' house, and I visited him at least twice a month. By the end of March we rented a small house at the edge of Huasco desert, on top of a hill. I left my teaching job and brought Felipe home to stay. Time had slipped by; our son was already two years old. The day I had asked my mother to take Felipe with her, I imagined it would only be for a few weeks until everything went back to normal. It took six months to finally have him back again in our lives. For nearly a year, Pato, Felipe, and I lived in that house as a family again. Felipe loved to play outside with children from the neighborhood and, under our close supervision, run a little in the desert.

Our two-bedroom house had no drapes, so I gathered leaves from the trees, glued them onto sheets of thin pink paper, and hung them on our windows to make things more cheerful. Huasco, a picturesque port with little vessels and huge rocks in the background, offered a breathtaking view. From the top of the hill where we lived, we had the loveliest view of the ocean. But for all the time we lived there, I never noticed its beauty.

Twice a day, every day, Pato went to the police station to sign his name in a logbook as required by the military to control his whereabouts. The police treated him fairly well, and very soon more political prisoners from different parts of Chile were sent to Huasco into internal exile, a practice that became quite popular during Pinochet's time. Political prisoners were released into small towns throughout Chile and placed under the supervision of the local police.

Pato soon found a full-time job in a brick-making company, spraying a long line of bricks with a hose all day to keep them wet. Eventually, management promoted him to working in the office, in charge of payroll.

I visited my parents several times, but my father was not improving, so I sent Commander Haag a letter and asked him to relocate Pato to Malloco, explaining that if my father had us nearby, perhaps he would get well. Haag impressed me as a man who seemed genuinely concerned about the families of Copiapó's victims. When I first met him, he had asked me about my entire family, especially about my parents, so I had told him about my father.

Haag approved my request. In October 1974, Pato, Felipe, and I arrived in Malloco, taking everyone by surprise. For a fraction of a second, I thought I saw my father smile.

NINE

In November 1974, Pato and I were out on an errand in Santiago when we ran into a former coworker of Wito's. I did not know Ximena de la Barra well, but Wito had always spoken so highly of her that Pato and I gladly accepted her invitation to come back to her house for lunch. Soon we were seated on Ximena's living room sofa, chatting and sipping white wine as we waited for the meal to be ready. Pato excused himself to make a phone call. The moment he left the room, Ximena turned to me and said urgently, "Do you know how Winston died?"

Stunned, I could only shrug my shoulders.

"A lieutenant named Armando Fernandez Larios killed your brother by slashing his abdomen with a *corvo*," Ximena said. "Fernandez personally confessed his crime to a friend of mine, a psychiatrist. He said that the truck carrying the prisoners stopped twenty minutes south of Copiapó, in a place called *Cuesta Cardones*. The guards had all been drinking, and they pushed the prisoners out and forced them to run in the desert. They laughed as they shot their victims down. But Winston refused to get off the truck. Your brother challenged Fernandez to kill him right there. 'I won't run,' Winston said to him. 'Nobody will ever accuse me of trying to escape.' Winston had guessed their plan. Fernandez was enraged at Winston's defiance and beat him. He then took his military knife and slashed Winston's abdomen."

I stared at Ximena, speechless. Pato walked back in but stopped in the middle of the living room, staring at me, trying to figure out what had just happened.

"I don't know why you want to know about this," Ximena said, standing abruptly. She ushered us briskly into the dining room. Reeling, I followed her to the table where, for the rest of our visit, we chatted about common friends, current events, and the weather.

I never saw Ximena again. I did not share her story with anyone, not even Pato, until more than twenty years later when we were well into our lawsuit. By that time, I had learned that a person killed with a *corvo* (a large curved knife designed to inflict excruciating pain and damage) is typically in agony for about eight hours before succumbing. Under no circumstance did I want my family to know how Wito had suffered.

But I never forgot the name Armando Fernandez Larios.

TEN

Around the time that Pato and I ran into Ximena, the US embassy called our home to say that they had visas for Pato, Felipe, and me to come to the United States. My brother Nano, who lived in California, had been working hard to obtain these special visas, which would allow us to leave Chile immediately. Unfortunately, Pato was not free to leave the country. He was not even free to leave Malloco.

Pato and I took our letter from the US embassy to military authorities in Santiago and Copiapó, requesting authorization to leave Chile. My brother Lito, an engineer and an accomplished businessman, three years my senior, traveled to Copiapó to speak personally with Commander Haag. Everyone had a similar reaction: they all said it was great that we had visas that would allow us to work in our professions in the United States, but they did not personally have the authority to approve Pato's request to leave Chile. Then they would refer us to someone else. Most said we had been given a rare opportunity and wished us good luck.

No one said yes. No one said no. Pato and I took a huge risk: we resolved to escape from Chile. Every day we heard about people being detained on the streets, in their houses, or in their places of work and their families never heard from again. Then Pato received a summon from the military prosecutors in Puerto Montt, where he had worked for a year as director of regional planning, to appear before them to answer some questions. We had no other choice but to leave the country.

To apply for passports, we needed a certificate issued by the *Policía de Investigaciones* documenting that we had committed no improprieties that would prevent us from leaving the country. This meant that the investigative police had to do a full background check and determine whether Pato had any kind of criminal record. We feared that Pato's records would include his detention as a political prisoner at the Copiapó jail and his current internal exile in Malloco, but we could not move forward without this step.

To obtain the document we needed, we had to apply in person at the *Policía de Investigaciones*. We understood that if Pato's records were not clean, we faced great risk that someone would discover that he had no authorization to go to Santiago, let alone leave the country. We decided to take the risk. It was dangerous, but Pato went to meet a private investigator we knew in Santiago who had offered to find a way to check whether Pato's records were clean. Felipe and I stayed at my brother Lito's house in Santiago, waiting for Pato to return.

Hours dragged by. Pato did not come back. With each passing moment, my terror increased that he had been caught and I would never see him again. I held Felipe tightly in my arms, cuddling him for a long time, as tears ran down my cheeks. I felt terrified to let Felipe go, so afraid at the thought that he would grow up without his father.

In the late afternoon, Pato came home carrying the document we needed to escape from Chile. I did not want him to know the terror I had felt, but unable to hold back my tears, I sat on the bed and cried. Pato held me in silence.

We applied for passports the next day, picked them up a week later, and took them to the US embassy to have the visas stamped in them. A few days later, on December 12, 1974, we packed two suitcases and then, with two-year-old Felipe in our arms, went to the airport. For safety, we could not tell anyone except our close family that we were leaving the country.

As we were about to leave for the airport, I decided to call a dear friend to tell her good-bye. Her mother, a Pinochet supporter, answered the phone. "I hope now you will behave," she told me. Her words left a mark. The realization that many Chileans considered us, not the armed forces, to be the aggressors shocked me at the time. To this day, the stigma is hard to shrug off.

Our parents accompanied us to the airport as far as the security gate, where we all waited together, too nervous to speak. An unspoken fear filled us all: Would we make it through the questioning by the international police?

Fortunately, a national register of detained people did not yet exist, and since we were flying to the United States, which had supported the coup under the Nixon administration, our destination did not raise any red flags that we might be escaping. When we walked through international police, a man took our passports and saw that we were going to the United States with visas that would allow us to work. He looked at us curiously and asked, "What kind of work will you be doing?"

Pato said, "I will be working at the University of California at Berkeley."

"Congratulations," the man said, handing us back our passports. Had we flown to Mexico or another country friendly to Allende supporters, we probably would have raised suspicion.

Pato and I said good-bye to our parents. Everyone wanted us to leave Chile for our safety—there was real fear there, as we had already lost our brother—but that did not mean they wanted us to go. Our parents wept as we hugged and kissed them good-bye. They held us very tightly. Then it was time to go. Once out of our parents' sight, we were on our own. Terrified, we walked through the airport, carrying Felipe to keep him quiet. Too frightened to speak to each other, we stood in a series of lines, holding tightly to the tickets Nano had sent. Only when we landed in Lima, Peru, did we look at each other and speak our first words. We hugged Felipe tightly. We were saved! My mother told me later that my father had fainted from shock when he saw us finally boarding the plane.

Pato had written a letter to the Chilean military authorities explaining his whereabouts and asked his brother to mail it the day after we left the country. We imagined that if Pato did not show up at the Malloco police station the following morning to sign the logbook, soldiers would go to my parents' house, looking for him. By sending this letter, we were trying to protect my parents. Years later, we decided to travel to Mexico to visit Pato's aunt and uncle who had also left Chile for political reasons. Pato's uncle, Pedro Vuskovic, had been President Allende's Minister of Economics. When Pato tried to renew his passport at the Chilean consulate in San Francisco, they stamped an *L* for "*liste*" (list) in his passport, meaning that he was on a list of about five thousand Chileans considered "enemies of the nation."

Pato could not return to Chile.

This list was modified several times, with many names removed during Pinochet's regime, but Pato's name remained until 1989, when the list was finally abolished.

ELEVEN

After escaping from Chile, we lived with my brother Nano for six months before renting a small house in the San Francisco Bay area. A week after arriving in California, Pato said that he wanted to take a walk at night around my brother's quiet suburban neighborhood. We knew it was safe to go out at night in the United States—no curfew, no military cars patrolling the streets—but still we began our walk very hesitantly. It was the most amazing feeling: there was nothing to worry about. Suddenly we heard a car approaching, and when the headlights shone on our faces, we panicked and froze. The vision of soldiers driving up in a military car and grabbing us was so real that Pato and I could not walk. Trembling violently, we went back inside the house.

It took us some time to feel safe after coming to the United States. Many wonderful people made us feel welcome, and these kind souls encouraged us to talk about our life under military rule, making it clear that we no longer had to hide who we were. Unfortunately, more often than not we were reminded of the brutal country we had left behind.

When Pato and I came to the United States, we only knew the little bit of English we had learned in high school, so a few months after arriving I began taking English language classes at the Berkeley Adult School. One day the teacher asked us to describe our reasons for emigrating. "After losing a dear brother at the hands of military personnel," I wrote, "we escaped Chile to protect my husband's life."

The teacher asked if she could read this aloud. Before she finished the sentence, a Chilean man stood up shaking with rage. "They deserved what they got!" he shouted, his face turning an ugly red as he pointed at me. "Do you know what happened to me one day? I was in line buying bread. I had the bread in my *hands*, and a man snatched it from me. *Yes*, he *snatched* the bread from my hands!" The man glared at me, and in his eyes I saw the same intense hatred I had seen in Captain Patricio Diaz and Lieutenants Ojeda and Marambio. Trembling, I remained silent.

Pato and I soon found our first job, working as janitors cleaning a ten-story office building in Oakland. Every night for six months, we hired a sitter for Felipe and worked from midnight until early morning. A year later, Pato found a job with Catholic Charities in San Mateo, and I began work with the San Mateo County School of Education. By mid-1977 we were renting a house in San Mateo, and in May 1978, our son Roberto was born.

Roberto's birth marked a new beginning for Pato and me. It had been three years since our escape from Chile, but we had been living in the past ever since. We had thought the military would remain in power for a year, maybe two, and then we could return to Chile once things normalized. Believing our absence would be brief, we did not want to put down roots in the United States. With Roberto's birth, however, I realized we had done just that. The United States, which we thought would be a temporary refuge, became our home.

A month after Pato and I made a down payment on a house in a working-class neighborhood, our employment contracts ended due to lack of funds. We called our friends who owned a janitorial business, and after a week of intensive training, we went to work for them, painting, steam cleaning carpets, and cleaning bathrooms, kitchens, and apartment windows. Soon we were running our own janitorial and painting company. For the next five years, our business supported us financially. Those were years of total isolation from our hopes and memories: no past, no future, just long days of hard work. But our business gave us the time and security we needed to be able to nurture and care for our family. Our new life was a gift, and we used it well.

In November 1978, my parents came from Chile to live with us. With my two brothers and sister living nearby, Felipe in elementary school, and Roberto still a baby, my parents had an active family life in the United States. But six months after they came, my parents longed to move back to Chile. Unable to speak English or easily adapt to the many cultural differences, my mother, sixty-one, and father, sixty-seven, felt uncomfortable in California.

Nano did not think we should let my parents return to Chile. "When they go, they will probably want to come back again because we're all here," he said.

"Let them go back," I told my brother. "I'm sure you are right, but that's not something we can tell them. They have to feel it for themselves."

My parents moved back to Malloco, but once there, they realized their friends all had their own busy lives in Chile, while their own children and grandchildren were back in the United States. A few months later, my parents returned to California, and this time my mother brought family treasures from home.

My mother and father lived with us for a while before moving to a one-bedroom duplex about two blocks from our house. My mother, who had always been quiet and shy, began to join all kinds of activities offered in Spanish by the Catholic Church—special masses, social events, bingo games—and she developed a beautiful group of friends. My father did not join in, and as my mother took a more active role in our community, my father became increasingly isolated. He grew very thin and sat at home playing backgammon against himself, the right hand playing against the left. Every morning, my mother struggled to get him out of bed.

Our entire family tried to draw my father out. My brother gave him a guitar for his birthday, but he never played it. Pato went often to my parents' duplex to play backgammon with my father. The more I think about my father, the more I think he was waiting to die. But Felipe and Roberto fascinated my father and brought him out in ways that no else could. Every weekend, Pato took my father to Felipe's American Youth Soccer Organization (AYSO) games, and he videotaped all the World Cup soccer games so my father could watch them throughout the year.

Roberto began singing in the Golden Gate Boys Choir when he was eight years old, and my father attended every performance.

I saw my parents at least once a week. My mother loved to make dinner with all the children in the house, and every Sunday we shared a big family lunch at my home or theirs. My father was always there when we celebrated holidays, birthdays, and special occasions, but he sat apart from everyone, staying out of the conversation.

Sometimes my father would connect for a little while. He liked reading Latin American literature, so we kept him well supplied with books; whenever I drove past my parents' home I saw my father sitting outside on the duplex stairs, smoking cigarettes and reading.

My father had lost all interest in gardening, but as my mother blossomed in her new life, she began caring for the plants and flowers in the little strip of earth outside their duplex. Sometimes she cut roses and brought the beautiful blooms inside, brightening their home with rich color and fragrance.

TWELVE

In January 1987, I returned to Chile for the first time. Pinochet was still in power, and with Pato on the *L* list he could not travel to Chile to see his mother, who had recently been diagnosed with cancer. In his place, I took eight-year-old Roberto to visit his grandparents.

On our first day in downtown Santiago, Roberto and I ran into an anti-Pinochet street protest as we exited the subway. "*Pinocho, escucha, andate a la chucha!*" the crowd chanted as it marched by. (Loosely translated, that means, "Hey, Pinochet, go fuck yourself!")

That takes guts, I thought, smiling.

Suddenly the protesters screamed and scattered. Police officers were throwing tear gas into the crowd. I grabbed Roberto and rushed back into the Metro station. As we stood at the entrance watching the chaotic scene, a woman next to us remarked, "*Estos comunistas desgraciados, los debimos haber matado a todos.*" ("These disgraceful communists, we should have killed them all.")

"*We*," I told Pato's parents when Roberto and I finally reached their house. "She said *we*."

"It shows that you haven't been living in this country for over a decade," Pato's mother calmly replied.

No one reacted passionately to what I considered an abomination. *How in the hell does the abnormal become normal?* I kept thinking.

While in Chile, I learned that the Vicariate of Solidarity—a human rights agency offering legal advice to Pinochet's victims and their families—was investigating General Arellano's crimes. The Vicariate's lawyers were taking testimonies from victims' families, hoping to gather enough evidence to prosecute Arellano for the Caravan of Death killings. I decided to give my testimony.

My cousin Irene Rojas, a human rights lawyer, warned me not to go alone since the military had the Vicariate under surveillance. So on January 17, Irene and Roberto accompanied me to the Vicariate, where the lawyer promised that my testimony would be strictly confidential.

I told the lawyer everything I knew: about Adolfo, about Wito's refusal to get off the truck in the desert, about Fernandez, about the *corvo*. Roberto already knew that his uncle Wito had died, but he had never heard the details. For the entire two-hour meeting, eight-year-old Roberto sat listening on Irene's lap and did not speak or move. On the bus, however, my son began asking questions: "Zita, why did the military kill *tio* Wito? Why did Pinochet kill people? Why did they say he tried to escape? What is a *corvo*? Tell me, Zita."

Pato and I had always encouraged our boys to ask anything they wanted to know, but Roberto's questions were not safe here: not in public, not in Pinochet's Chile, not in a country where you had to hide who you were and could not speak the truth. Everyone on the bus was listening. Desperately I tried to distract Roberto, but, confused by my reluctance to answer, he asked more questions. Finally for safety, I took him off the bus and caught a taxi instead. "I will answer all your questions when we get home," I told him. "I just need to think."

When Roberto and I returned to the United States, I told my family about my experience testifying at the Vicariate.

"You are just wasting your time. The only crime that will ever be prosecuted in Chile is the 1976 car bombing in Washington, DC," Lito said, referring to the *Dirección de Inteligencia Nacional* or DINA (National Intelligence Directorate) car-bombing assassination of former Chilean ambassador Orlando Letelier and his US assistant, Ronni Moffitt, on Embassy Row.

"I don't think you should go back to Chile again," Nano told me.

Pato was silent.

The Vicariate's lawyer had assured me complete confidentiality, but I already regretted disclosing Adolfo's full name. What would happen to Adolfo if military authorities got hold of my testimony?

"Don't worry," the lawyer had promised. "Nobody would ever know about him. Your testimony is confidential. Just tell us everything you remember."

THIRTEEN

Three years later, in January 1990, I traveled alone to Chile. With Pinochet newly out of office, the country was preparing for its transition back to democracy. On my first afternoon in Santiago, I was strolling the crowded main avenue when I saw a photograph of a helicopter on a book vendor's cart. Moving closer, I read the words "Caso Arellano" on the cover of a book: *Los Zarpazos del Puma* (*The Claws of the Puma*) by the Chilean investigative journalist Patricia Verdugo, whose father was tortured to death after the coup. I stood at the vendor's cart for a long time, holding the book in my hands, forgetting the crowds and the noise around me. Then I bought the book and returned to my in-laws' house, where I went to my upstairs bedroom and began to read.

In her book, Verdugo described the Caravan of Death's atrocities in Cauquenes, La Serena, Copiapó, Antofagasta, and Calama. A few pages into the chapter "Copiapó y la 'Comisión Especial,'" I read:

> Regarding Winston Cabello Bravo…He was detained the day after the coup, on September 12, when he attended a meeting between government officials and Commander Oscar Haag. Haag detained him while everybody else was leaving the meeting…He was the first political prisoner of the region…Later on, on September 27, his brother-in-law, the economist Patricio Barrueto Cespedes, was detained…As Zita Cabello stated, "My husband was able to call my mother that night"…And the dramatic account of Zita Cabello continues: "a few minutes after 1:00 a.m. on October 17, Adolfo Gonzalez came to my house…"

Adolfo. What had I done? Somehow my confidential testimony from the Vicariate, with many mistakes included, had found its way into Verdugo's book. I began to cry.

"What's happening?" asked Pato's parents, opening the bedroom door.

I held up *The Claws of the Puma*.

"We didn't see you had that book," said Pato's mother, trying to calm me down. "I don't think you should read it anymore."

Pato's parents asked me to come downstairs for tea, but I told them I had to go out immediately.

"You just arrived today," my father-in-law said. "Whatever it is, it can wait."

"No, it can't."

I left the house, searching for information about Adolfo. I could not learn a thing. Two weeks later, I returned to California with a tremendous sense of guilt. All I could think was that I had placed my friend's life at risk.

Was Adolfo dead because of me?

FOURTEEN

My parents' fiftieth wedding anniversary was approaching. My mother bought a beautiful pink dress and hat and was excited about having a big celebration. My father was beyond caring, but we rented him a tuxedo, and when he tried it on, he looked so handsome.

On July 27, 1990, as I was planning my parents' anniversary party, my home phone rang. A stranger from Copiapó was calling to say that the court had given authorization to begin searching for victims' remains from the Caravan of Death killings. I asked if they could wait a week so my siblings and I could be there, but they did not want to delay.

My siblings and I struggled with whether to tell our parents. My father was so physically and emotionally fragile, and my mother was so happy about their anniversary party, that we decided to keep it secret and continue with the celebration. On the morning of my parents' anniversary party, another call came from Copiapó: Winston's body had been found.

That afternoon, my mother glowed with happiness as all our friends came to witness my parents' renewal of vows at the church. Roberto's choir sang at the service, and it was a memorable, wonderful day for our family.

That night after the party, Lito flew to Chile in time to attend Copiapó's church service and community funeral for the Caravan of Death's victims. Lito was able to accompany Wito and the twelve other victims to the cemetery. The whole town was there to say good-bye.

A few years later, while visiting friends in Chile, my mother learned that Winston's remains had been discovered during the exhumations. My father never knew that Winston had been found.

My father's heavy smoking had been worrying us for years. We talked with his doctor about our desire that he quit, but the doctor recommended against it saying that smoking was about the only pleasure my father had left. We watched helplessly as my father began developing emphysema. He could not walk much because breathing was difficult, so he spent more time than ever sitting outside on the duplex stairs, where he smoked cigarettes and read.

One day at age seventy-nine, my father became so ill that my mother took him to the hospital. I visited him twice a day, holding his hand as I caressed his brow, and that seemed to comfort him. My father did not say much in the hospital. When he did, he was not always lucid, but he liked having my hand to hold.

One day my father pulled out all his tubes. He kept telling my mother, "Take care of Zita." He was not fighting to stay alive, and I think he knew he was going away.

At the time, I was teaching economics and other subjects in the Latin American Studies Program at the University of California, Santa Cruz, and I got so run down and exhausted that I fell ill. On the morning of February 4, 1991, I went to visit my father at the hospital. He did not talk at all. I was so sick that I went home and went to bed, and when Pato stopped by the hospital later that day, the nurse told him my father would probably not last through the night. Pato did not share this with me; I think he was worried about my being so sick and exhausted. That night I stayed home and slept, and sometime around midnight my father passed away. No one in our family was with him.

Roberto sat with me at my father's funeral. As the choir sang a beautiful requiem, my twelve-year-old son took my hand and cried harder than I had ever seen.

FIFTEEN

In 1995 I flew to Chile to work on a low-budget documentary film called *Never Again Shall We Say Never Again*, which explores the social origins of the crimes committed under Pinochet, as well as how those crimes were dealt with in the post-Pinochet era. I received a small grant from the University of California, Santa Cruz (UCSC), and we funded the rest from our personal savings. I gathered an amazing team: my son Felipe and one of my students from UCSC, David Silverman. In Chile, I hired two recent film school graduates who did the filming and helped me rent a video camera at low cost. I returned to the United States with more than twenty hours of filmed interviews. I immediately wrote the script and worked with Felipe to do the editing.

Before leaving for Chile, I called a friend in New York to ask if he could help arrange some interviews. "Why don't you interview Armando Fernandez?" my friend asked casually. "He's here in the US."

A chill ran through me. I had not heard Fernandez's name since 1974, the day Ximena told me how he had killed my brother. I made the documentary without attempting to interview my brother's killer. I did not know what to do with the information I received from my friend.

I was so determined to make "sense out of nonsense" that I asked questions everywhere I went in Chile, following leads that might better have been left alone. I now realize that in working through my own questions, I have unintentionally brought pain to others. One experience particularly haunts me.

When Wito became head of the Copiapó Regional Planning Office in 1971, he "inherited" a couple of employees from President Eduardo Frei's previous administration. One of these, a middle-aged administrator named Mr. Raúl Gallo, was highly critical of President Allende's new government. As the only ORPLAN employee unsympathetic to the Allende administration, Mr. Gallo had not lost his job after the coup. Wito and Pato were always coming home with stories about Mr. Gallo's poor performance at work: messages never taken, information misfiled, deadlines missed. Wito worried about the atmosphere of uncertainty that these mistakes created in the office but would always just smile and say, "What is *Señor* Gallo going to do today?"

I had never met Mr. Gallo, but for some reason his name kept playing in my mind. Over the years I had wondered if he'd been one of the civilians pressuring the military to detain people who had worked for the Allende government before the coup. Finally this nagging question spurred me to look for him.

In 1995, while filming my documentary in Chile, I knocked at Mr. Gallo's apartment. Slowly the door opened to reveal a frail old man leaning on his cane. He could barely hold his body upright.

As soon as I saw Mr. Gallo, my mind went blank. I had convinced myself on the way over that I had a good reason for wanting to see him. But standing on his doorstep, I wondered if I really did. Hesitantly, I introduced myself as Winston Cabello's sister and Patricio Barrueto's wife.

Mr. Gallo invited me in. Moving with great difficulty, he led me slowly through the small room where he lived alone, past a table, a bed, and a couple of chairs. He lowered his fragile body into a wheelchair, wincing with pain, and asked me to sit down. As I faced him, I already knew I had nothing to say.

For a few minutes, Mr. Gallo reminisced about the planning office. Then he began talking about Wito. "Señor Cabello was the best boss I ever had," he said, his frail voice breaking. "He was kind, honest, and generous. His death was the biggest crime of all. These criminals…"

Mr. Gallo bent forward, sobbing. He almost collapsed in on himself. He wept for a long time, his head nearly touching his knees. Finally he looked up. "Please leave," he said. "And don't ever come back to see me again."

As I left Mr. Gallo's apartment, an intense sadness filled my heart. Had I been wrong to seek him out? Had I really expected him to clarify my doubts?

Before flying home, I visited my parents' old house in Malloco. It was early spring in the Southern Hemisphere, and the hundreds of beautiful roses my father had planted over the years were all in glorious bloom. I found my favorite—the tiny pink *besitos*—and broke off a single branch, which I wrapped in a wet paper towel and placed between layers of clothing in my suitcase. As soon as I got home to California, I planted the branch in a small pot and placed it outside on our deck. Through late autumn and winter I occasionally watered the branch, not expecting it to survive but wishing it would.

At the beginning of spring, the *besitos* came alive. Tiny green leaves unfurled from that dead-looking branch sticking out of the dirt. From that moment, I began to take special care of it, feeling that if it died now it would be my fault.

One spring day, a tiny pink rose appeared at the top of the branch. This *besitos* branch became a symbol of hope, love, and beauty for me. The following year when the little rosebush was established, I made cuttings for all my family. Today my father's *besitos* grow in all our gardens, and each time I see them, they feel like an expression of his love for us.

We are grateful for this special rose, this final gift of hope from our father.

SIXTEEN

I did not try to contact Fernandez in 1995 as my friend in New York suggested, but three years later something happened that changed our lives forever.

On Sunday morning, October 17, 1998, Pato held up the front page of the *San Francisco Chronicle* so I could see the news. General Pinochet had been arrested in London at midnight on October 16—the twenty-fifth anniversary of Wito's death—in connection with the Caravan of Death killings. On that day, thousands of Pinochet's victims and their families emerged from a quarter century of darkness. Around the world, people danced in the streets. Justice was finally closing in on a man with blood on his hands.

Suddenly I realized that if Pinochet could be held accountable in England for crimes committed in Chile more than twenty-five years ago, perhaps Winston's murderer, Armando Fernandez Larios, could be brought to justice in a US court of law. This captivating vision was swiftly replaced by dread when I realized that to file a lawsuit, I would have to reveal the secret of how Wito had died.

I had tried to talk to my brother Lito about it once, shortly after Ximena gave me the news. "I heard they used *corvos* to kill the prisoners," I had said, tentatively.

"People say so many different things," Lito had snapped.

I should have known Lito would not want to hear it. Even as Ximena was giving me the news in her living room, I remember thinking, *Why is she telling me this? Why would I want to know how Wito died? Isn't it painful enough to know that they killed him?* I am, however, forever grateful that she told me.

About ten days after Pinochet's arrest, Lito called to say that human rights lawyers from the Center for Justice and Accountability (CJA) in San Francisco were taking testimonies from Chilean victims and their families to help support proceedings against Pinochet. Lito's friend had already testified, and my brother urged me to talk with CJA's legal director, Shawn Roberts, about including Wito's story in the package they were compiling to send to England. That afternoon, I left Shawn Roberts a message.

I had no idea what I was starting.

On November 11, an attractive blond lawyer named Beth Van Shaack arrived at my home in Foster City. Excited about the international law movement against Pinochet, Beth explained that CJA was a nongovernmental organization whose role was to hold human rights abusers living in or visiting the United States accountable for crimes they had committed outside the country.

Through my living room window, I watched the sun sparkling on the lake behind my house as I gave Beth my testimony. A few times, I saw Beth's eyes fill with tears. As we were talking afterward, Beth mentioned a case that CJA was working on. Two Salvadoran generals living in Miami, Florida, were being held responsible for the killings of two nuns in El Salvador. "The plaintiffs in this case are family members of the nuns," Beth explained. "It will probably go to trial next year."

"I have a case for you," I said, suddenly.

"You do?"

I shared what Ximena had told me, adding, "I know in my heart it is a truthful story. I don't need evidence to prove it. I knew my brother well. It didn't surprise me to learn that he chose a painful death. He stood his ground and wouldn't run.

"In 1995 a friend of mine told me that Fernandez had been in the United States since 1987, when he made an agreement with the US government," I continued. "My friend said that Fernandez provided information regarding his role and the roles of his superiors in connection to the 1976 car bombing in Washington, DC, that killed Orlando Letelier and Ronni Moffitt. He also said that Fernandez pled guilty to being an 'accessory after the fact' in the bombing and served a few months in a federal prison."

I told Beth that after I had spoken with my friend Ronnie in 1995, I came across several magazines, one of them *Analysis*, a weekly Chilean publication that carried several articles describing Fernandez's desertion from the army and his trip to the United States in connection to the Letelier criminal investigation.

"It doesn't ring a bell," Beth said. "I only knew about Michael Townley, who now lives under the witness protection program. Are you really sure this is what your friend Ronnie told you?"

"Would it help if I tell you that my friend Ronnie is also the stepson of Michael Townley?" Michael Townley was a Central Intelligence Agency (CIA) agent and Chilean secret police (DINA) operative convicted for the 1976 car-bombing assassination of former Chilean ambassador Orlando Letelier in Washington, DC.

It helped.

Beth explained that lawsuits against human rights violators living in the United States are possible under the Alien Tort Claims Act and the Torture Victim Protection Act, which provide jurisdiction in US courts for human rights abuses committed overseas. Since these were civil rather than criminal actions, the perpetrator would be fined if found responsible.

"So he won't go to prison?" I asked, disappointed.

"No, he won't."

"So you are telling me that there is no existing law that would allow us to bring a criminal action against Fernandez for Winston's death?"

"Not that I know of," Beth said. "But I can look into it. Actually, we rarely collect money. It's a symbolic action that sends the message that we won't accept criminals in this country. And if they insist on coming, we will make their lives miserable."

The thought of accepting money for Wito's death disgusted me. I wanted justice, not financial compensation. "I have to think about this," I told her.

Beth offered to look into Fernandez's legal status in the United States, explaining that if he was in the witness protection program, we would not be able to bring legal action against him. In the meantime, I agreed to contact my friend Ronnie to see if he could help CJA locate Fernandez.

Just the idea of a lawsuit was enough to take me back to the horror of those dark years in Chile. I knew my family would probably never collect any money from Fernandez, but the idea of a financial settlement still troubled me. Was this the right way to deal with wrongdoings? As an economics teacher, and knowing the kinds of situations that Wito and Pato had had to deal with as economists in Chile, I already knew that the worst of human passions are often linked to money. I know what people are willing to do in its name.

Whenever I teach about the coup and the years of violence that followed, money is always at the core of our discussion. "The underlying basis for the horror of Pinochet's years was nothing more than the protection of the economic interests of a handful of people," I tell my students. "In its name, and at the expense of peace, freedom, and democracy, the Chilean armed forces destroyed lives, honor, and human feelings." Immediately after President Allende came into office, President Nixon gave the order to place pressure on the Allende government to prevent Allende's nationalization of several US corporations and the copper industry. In 1970, the US manufacturing company ITT Corporation owned 70 percent of Chitelco, the Chilean Telephone Company.

I was facing a moral dilemma. Soon after my conversation with Beth, I was lecturing on economic globalization and global governance, when I asked my students, "What is justice?"

The class discussed truth, reconciliation, forgiveness, forgetfulness, revenge, and punishment. Then a student said, "I believe a civil action is an important tool as a punishment and as a deterrent to future criminals."

"It also brings the truth," I said, surprised to be suddenly defending the value of a civil case. "It doesn't matter where the truth comes from. It could be either from a criminal or civil investigation. It is the truth that matters. With it, we can restore dignity to the victims' lives and honor them with respect and pride."

Driving home from UC Santa Cruz that afternoon, I had a revelation: it did not matter whether we filed a criminal or civil case. What mattered was the truth. Suddenly I understood that a civil action *would* bring out the truth, and through it, Wito's voice, dreams, and example would be able to endure. In a way, my brother could become immortal.

Still, something was holding me back, and it was powerful enough to make me retreat. Three weeks after meeting with Beth, I told a good friend that we were considering a lawsuit. My friend was thrilled. "What is his punishment?" he asked.

"This is a civil lawsuit. If found responsible, his punishment would be a judgment set by the court."

"You mean he will have to pay money," said my friend, looking skeptical. "Of all the people I know, Zita, don't you feel bad about that?"

I knew then that fear was holding me back: fear of being misunderstood, fear of being judged. I had been raised to always consider what others would think of my actions. If it ever even *seemed* like I was not meeting people's expectations, I felt deeply ashamed. If my friend who knew and loved me was already assuming that I had compromised my moral beliefs by pursuing a civil case—which was my only option for learning the truth, but by definition, would ultimately result in financial compensation—how could I possibly convince everyone else that all I wanted was to tell the truth?

In December 1998, I discussed Pinochet's arrest in a radio interview with CJA's executive director, Jerry Gray. As we were talking afterward, Shawn Roberts, the legal director of CJA, came up and introduced herself. She asked me to speak at an upcoming press conference urging the Clinton administration to support Pinochet's extradition to Spain and to declassify US documents on the regime's human rights violations. When I told Jerry that I had decided to pursue the lawsuit, he scheduled a meeting for the following week and urged me to contact my friend Ronnie immediately.

Ronnie came to Capitol Hill to see me at the press conference. Afterward over dinner, he said that he was not sure of Fernandez's legal status but believed he lived somewhere in the United States.

When I got back to California, I gathered all the information I had collected over the years identifying Fernandez as a member of the Caravan of Death or relating to his role in the Letelier car-bombing assassination in Washington, DC, and wrote a summary of the materials. I brought everything to my meeting with Shawn and Jerry, who advised me not to share my plans with anyone. "We don't want him to flee," Jerry said.

Shawn called the State Department to ask about Fernandez's legal status, but was told that they would not release any confidential information. A few days later, however, Shawn received an anonymous envelope in the mail containing a copy of the agreement Fernandez had signed with the State Department in 1987. We still don't know who sent it. According to this agreement, the US government had offered Fernandez the opportunity to enter the Federal Witness Protection Program after his release from federal prison, but he had chosen instead to live openly in the United States. Included in the signed agreement was the US government's promise that it would not allow Fernandez to be extradited to Chile on charges associated with the Letelier assassination.

Fernandez was not living under an assumed name, so we would be able to file a lawsuit against him in the United States.

But we had to find him first.

SEVENTEEN

A few weeks later I told my brother Lito that a member of the Caravan of Death, Armando Fernandez, was living in the United States and I needed help finding him. "We can hold him responsible for Wito's murder."

Lito searched the Internet without success. (This was in the early days of the Internet, and there was much less information freely available on it than there is now.) Lito then decided to e-mail his old college friend Victor Canales to ask for help. The next day Victor responded with a four-page e-mail saying that he had contacted Eduardo Contreras, the human rights lawyer who filed the first criminal lawsuit against Pinochet in Chile, and that Contreras had immediately offered his unconditional support. Contreras urged us to contact Judge Juan Guzmán, who had gained international recognition for being the first to prosecute Pinochet on human rights charges, believing that he would be very supportive of our action.

A few days later, Victor sent a five-page e-mail detailing Fernandez's background, from his days at the military academy to his part in the assault on *La Moneda* during the coup, as well as his involvement in a number of unlawful activities. Victor's generosity overwhelmed me, as our only prior contact had been the following e-mailed response to my documentary:

> Thanks for the reflection that your work invites us to do. I have asked myself where was I when Aldo and all of you

finally buried Winston, and why did I not accompany you at that moment. Part of the answer is simple; I was out of the country working somewhere. Another part is more complicated. We were in close contact with so much suffering for many long years, covered by a mantle of so many terrors that I believe I was not informed about you on time. But now, at least, believe me that I would have liked to be near you during those moments, for your brother, for my parents, for my wife and my children, for all of us. For better times that should arrive. Soon. It is never too late.

A warm hug,
Victor Canales

Victor e-mailed to say that Fernandez might be working in an art gallery in Miami, Florida. In January 1999, CJA hired a private detective, and a few weeks later our kitchen phone rang.

"We found him," said Jerry.

I stood for a long time with the receiver in my hand, gazing out our kitchen window at the bright winter morning. Suddenly I had to get out of the house. I ran through our front yard and down the street, as years of pent-up emotions and questions raced through my mind. *Is this what Wito would want me to do? Will Fernandez tell us why he killed our brother?* We had waited so anxiously for someone to locate Fernandez, afraid that he had already left the country and we had missed our chance to pursue justice.

I ran as fast as I could through the streets of our neighborhood until I was exhausted. Then I walked home and called Pato at work. "They found him."

Ten minutes later, Pato walked through the front door. I knew he would come. As we stood together in our living room, holding each other in silence, all I could think of was a time when cruelty beyond imagination had torn our lives apart. I clung to Pato for a long time before, finally, I realized he was crying.

EIGHTEEN

News of Fernandez's discovery shook us to the core. Pato and I often sat in silence, thinking of the night that Captain Diaz and two unknown officers had burst into the garrison sleeping quarters to take Wito away. We rarely spoke about the events surrounding Wito's death, but that did not mean our memories had faded. "The smile of that very young officer lingers in my mind," Pato said. "A smile full of spite. It's an unsettling feeling to know that man lives in Miami."

We now knew that the two officers from the helicopter were Armando Fernandez and Marcelo Moren. Fernandez, twenty-two at the time and the youngest officer in the squad, gave Moren away when he said, "Look, Marcelo, these sons of bitches even have cake."

Pato warned that frustration and humiliation were almost certain if I chose to pursue a lawsuit. But I was not alone. Our family history was giving us an opportunity to do something good, and we hoped the results would also be meaningful for others.

Now that CJA's private detective had found Fernandez's home address, we could seriously consider moving forward. Up to that point, we had been unsure as to whether Fernandez was even still living in the United States or perhaps hiding somewhere protected by the State Department.

A week after the detective found Fernandez's address, Shawn Roberts from CJA came to my home and said, "We now can file a lawsuit on your behalf for Winston's death. If you want—*only* if you want—you can invite your siblings and your mother to join you."

I talked with my brothers and sister, advising them to consult their families before answering. Lito called the next morning, sounding as if he had not slept at all. "Yes," he said. "My daughters were very supportive." Karin's husband and daughter were also happy that she would be part of this journey. Even though Karin was fourteen years younger than Wito, the two of them had shared a special bond. When Wito was initially studying to be an elementary school teacher, he practiced with Karin teaching techniques, games, and especially new puzzles developed for preschoolers and kindergarteners. Karin will never forget the day that Wito took her to Santiago when she was twelve years old. They had walked into a bicycle shop and my brother asked her, "Which one do you like?"

"This one," Karin had said.

Wito had reached into his pocket, produced his checkbook, and bought her the bicycle.

Nano, as head officer of a student exchange program, regretfully declined to be part of the lawsuit. "I spoke with my wife last night. We think that if I get involved in this lawsuit, the US embassy in Chile might not be very happy. It could potentially create a problem to get visas for our students."

I did not know how to approach my mother about the lawsuit. Over the years she had wanted to talk about Wito many times, but I had never been able to bring myself to do it. "Why was he killed?" my mother would ask. I had no answer.

At the time of Pinochet's arrest, my mother had closely followed the news. She said, "I'm glad that man has been arrested. Pinochet...such a bad man...he killed my little son." Now that she was eighty-two, my mother's memory was failing but she had never forgotten Wito.

"You know, Mom," I began, "there is this man in Miami who was responsible for the killings of many people in Chile during Pinochet's time. We want to file a lawsuit against him. I would like for you to help me do it."

My mother began to cry. As I explained about the lawsuit, I never mentioned Wito, but my mother knew all the time that I was talking about him. "Yes," she said when I had finished. "I want to do this with you."

Karin, Lito, and I agreed that if *any* money were to be awarded for our lawsuit, every penny would go to a nonprofit working to advance human rights. Absolutely no money would come to us. We all felt very strongly about this.

I began helping the legal team gather information, calling human rights lawyers in Chile, translating documents, and doing anything I could think of that would help move the process forward. For our case, CJA teamed up with the Palo Alto law firm of Wilson Sonsini Goodrich & Rosati (WSGR), and both organizations generously agreed to work pro bono. I spoke daily with Shawn Roberts at CJA, as well as WSGR lawyers David Sloss or Adam Safwat. David, a kind, patient man, showed great respect for my family's loss. Adam was different, like a little boy holding a fascinating new toy in his hands, examining it from every angle as he reviewed each detail of our case and worked to absorb the story's complexity. This legal team was a tremendous gift to our family.

David and Adam understood my reluctance for a civil trial and searched for legal alternatives. But after talking with the State Department to evaluate the legal possibility of a criminal action against Fernandez, David confirmed that a civil trial was our only option. In the meantime, Lito and I were talking with Victor Canales, Eduardo Contreras, and the tremendous network of legal professionals that Victor had assembled in Chile, who generously offered their expertise and clarified our lawyers' questions.

CJA's private detective had already gone several times to the gated community in Miami where Fernandez lived, but after two months of trying, the detective had still not been able to physically locate Fernandez to serve him a subpoena. Finally, on the morning of February 28, 1999, the detective got inside the gated community and served Armando Fernandez with legal papers at his front door.

"What do I do?" asked Fernandez, astonished.

"Find a lawyer," the detective replied.

NINETEEN

Our lawyers needed a photograph of a *corvo*, so I took an image from my files to our local camera store for reprinting. As I waited at the counter, I noticed the man next to me staring at my photograph. *What the hell are you doing with such an awful thing?* his eyes seemed to ask. Finally he said, "That's a killing knife. This knife is used to make victims suffer, not to kill them instantly. That's why the knife is curved, as opposed to the knife I carried when I was in the Marines: a straight, extremely sharp knife on both sides, which is made to kill instantly. But the knife in your picture is used by soldiers to cut their victims' insides, usually the abdomen, so that they're in agony for hours."

No one had ever described Wito's death so bluntly to me. I closed my eyes and gripped the counter for support, trying to dislodge the hideous images that sprang to mind. Of course, I had read about the *corvo* in history books; in school we had all learned about the Chilean soldiers' first use of this cruel weapon in the nineteenth-century war against the Peruvian-Bolivian Confederation, which had made them widely feared among their enemies for their brutal acts with the *corvo*. But that had felt so distant, so unrelated to my life at the time.

If I could not bear to imagine a *corvo* being used on my brother, how could I possibly share Ximena's story with my family?

In March 1999, Adam phoned me the night before Karin, Lito, and I were due to give our testimonies at WSGR. "Have you told your siblings how Winston died at the hands of Fernandez?" he asked.

"No, I haven't yet."

"You have to tell them tonight," said Adam. "Otherwise, I will do it myself tomorrow."

I paced in my living room, trying to think of the right words to tell my family what I knew. I called Karin first. "I need to tell you something before our meeting tomorrow."

When I finished, Karin was crying. "One day, I locked myself out of your house," she said. "I forced my way in through your bedroom window. I saw a book on the nightstand. I read it. I know how much the truth has tormented you all these years."

I tried to speak, but my voice caught in my throat.

"I understood why you didn't want us to read the book," Karin continued. "You wanted to spare us the pain. That's why I never asked you any questions. But it's good we are finally talking."

"I have to call Lito now," I managed to say.

My brother had also read *The Claws of the Puma*. "I don't remember exactly how or when I learned the story of his death," Lito said.

"It had to be the book. I only told the story once before, to a lawyer from the Vicariate. Somehow my testimony got into the book." I completed the story for Lito and waited for him to respond, but my brother remained silent. Finally he said good night and hung up.

The next morning at WSGR, Karin gave her testimony to Beth, Lito gave his to David, and I told my story to Adam, Shawn, and a few other lawyers. That afternoon, Beth and David joined the meeting. My entire life came under scrutiny. I had only prepared myself to talk about Wito's death, so Adam's barrage of personal questions took me by surprise. "Would you say your family was middle class or upper middle class?" he asked.

"Growing up we never talked about being poor," I replied. "My father was a school principal and earned a very modest salary. That was the only source of income for the family. My mother dedicated her entire life to taking care of us. She made all our clothes, knitted our sweaters, prepared our food. I believe we were the best-dressed kids at school because of her. Looking back now, I can easily see the tremendous sacrifices our parents made for us. So I would say we were poor but unaware of it. I couldn't have imagined having more."

Adam did not seem very interested, but he let me finish and then asked about Pato: how we met, when we married, why he was working with Wito at the time of the coup. As he interrogated me about our escape from Chile and our new lives in the United States, his questions kept coming back to our financial situation: our jobs, whether we had ever applied for welfare, and the details of our living expenses in the United States.

I tried to explain my reasons for earning advanced degrees at UC Berkeley. In 1984 I began having recurring nightmares in which I was trying to get to my old classes at the School of Economics of the University of Chile. Every time I tried walking up the stairs, they flattened suddenly and I fell to my knees, unable to reach the top. In these dreams, I kept hearing Wito's voice: "What are you doing with your life? You are really wasting your life, Zita. Do something about it. You have questions that need answers." I left my janitorial job to earn a PhD in Latin American studies at UC Berkeley, and two years later I also enrolled in the behavioral science master's program in the UC Berkeley School of Public Health. By spring 1989, I had completed both degrees and soon began teaching in the UCSC Latin American Studies program. "I've been teaching there ever since," I said, smiling.

"How did you pay for your studies at UC Berkeley?" Adam asked.

When people learn that my brother was killed by the Pinochet regime, they inevitably ask why he was killed. I try to explain that there *was* no reason: Wito was arrested without charges, and the military prosecutor had already decided to release him. Wito was no threat to the military regime. He was not even very political. He was just a public official appointed by President Allende, and after the coup everyone associated with the deposed administration fell under suspicion.

"But what did he *do*?" people would ask.

I soon realized that my answer did not make sense to people who had never lived under political repression. Today I understand that when people ask why Wito was killed, it is because they are trying to make sense of the senseless. There was no reason for the military to kill my brother. There is no justification for what happened to Wito and thousands of other innocent people under Pinochet's rule. From the day of the coup until the day Pinochet left office in 1990, arbitrary detention, torture, summary executions, disappearances, and killings became a way of life in our country.

"Why was Winston killed?" Adam asked, as the interrogation continued.

I tried to explain in every way I knew how.

"But what did he *do*?"

I told Adam about Wito's job. I explained that in 1964 President Eduardo Frei created the Ministry of National Planning to promote economic development throughout the country. When President Allende took office in 1970, he gave greater priority to economic planning to coordinate economic decisions at the national and regional level. To this end, the country was divided into twelve regions. Each region had a planning office (ORPLAN). Wito was appointed director of the Atacama-Coquimbo region in 1971 to assist the president in setting guidelines for development policies for the region. The office was located in the northern city of Copiapó, so by the end of 1971, Wito had been transferred from the national planning office in Santiago to the regional planning office in Copiapó. This region shared similar characteristics with others throughout the country: low quality of life, high unemployment levels, and low productivity. Wito's responsibilities were quite technical. He had to identify and evaluate investment projects to achieve the stated social and economic objectives of the government: reduce inflation, decrease unemployment, and improve quality of life. Wito wrote a long-term perspective plan, supplemented by a medium-term plan document and annual plans.

I also told Adam about Wito's qualifications for the job. My brother had graduated from the school of economics of the University of Chile in 1969. As a student he excelled in all subjects, particularly in statistics and econometrics. He chose to specialize in economic planning. During his last two years at the school of economics, he taught accounting system analysis and wrote a thesis on the role of private capital in promoting regional economic development. His thesis advisor, Juan Cavada, who worked at the national planning office (ODEPLAN), recommended

Wito for a job at this prestigious government organization. My brother was fortunate to be selected for the job, and at the beginning of 1969, he began his professional career as an economist at ODEPLAN.

What else was there to say?

"Director of Regional Planning," Adam said, watching me steadily. "A lot of power for a twenty-eight-year-old young man."

Adam's words hung in the air like an accusation. The way he said "power" and the way he looked at me as he said it really troubled me. *Is he trying to find reasons to justify Wito's death?* I wondered. *Does he believe my brother did something to deserve his fate?*

Finally the interrogation ended. I felt hopeful as I left WSGR, sure that something noble was developing. Our lawyers' enthusiasm was unmistakable. But once home, I gave in to exhaustion. Adam's questions had confused me: I had nothing to hide, but escaping from Chile and living for decades in political exile had been emotionally draining. Adam's interrogation had brought it all back.

That night, I could not sleep as Adam's questions haunted my mind: "Why was Winston killed? What did he *do*?"

Why ask? I thought as I lay awake. *Do we ask victims of genocide what they did to deserve their destruction? Isn't it enough to know that he was murdered by a cruel, repressive dictatorship?*

Unable to sleep, I kept thinking, *Why would people believe me, Wito's sister, when I say that my brother was good and kind, a loving and caring young man? Maybe if someone else talked about him, the question "But what did he do?" would finally end.*

This is what a friend, Roberto Pizarro, an economist, said on October 20, 2001, during a memorial to honor our brother's life:

> All the crimes committed under Pinochet's dictatorship were unjustified and atrocious. There was no just cause, there was no trial, there was no right to a defense, there was no war. These acts were committed against unarmed civilians. But the greatest of all the crimes was the assassination of Winston Cabello. He was not a political activist. This is known by all of us who knew him during his short life as a student, professional, and family man.

During the many years of our exile, my wife, Alicia, and I, both friends of Winston, remembered him fondly—as I believe that all those who spent time with him in the school of economics remember him—and we do not hesitate in classifying this assassination as one of the most cowardly acts that was committed during the regime of the disgraceful.

I have memories of the courtyards of the school of economics, of Winston with his sweet, slanting eyes. He did not participate directly in politics, although he probably had his heart set on the left during moments where Chile dreamt of building a greater society. He was an active member of the school's folklore group, together with Pato Barrueto, his brother-in-law, and Zita, his sister—his dear sister. He sang songs by Violeta Parra and Victor Jara. He showed us the typical dances of our land from the extreme north to Punta Arenas.

Winston's professional work began in the planning office in Santiago. Later, because of his own merits and interests in the north of Chile, he became the regional director for the planning department in Copiapó.

Although I did not follow Winston's professional endeavors between 1970 and 1973, I am sure that as director of ORPLAN he was professional and completely dedicated himself to public service. And I have no doubt that this fine man could never have created hate nor had any enemies.

Therefore, someone who did not know him could only have committed Winston's assassination. Anyone who ever looked into his tender eyes could not have fired; their hand would have trembled. So the assassins came from Santiago, and it could not have been any other way. They were from the Apocalyptic Caravan of Death, and Fernandez Larios was responsible for the execution.

Those of us from the school of economics on Republic Street render our heartfelt homage toward Winston Cabello. We unite with his family, for their pain, for the efforts that they have made to look for and find the truth. They deserve it.

I know Adam was not looking for reasons to justify my brother's death. Perhaps my emotional reactions after his questions were connected with experiences I had encountered with people from my own country. For some Chileans, Pinochet's human rights violations of murder, torture, and forced disappearances pale in comparison to the humiliation they felt having to stand in food lines under President Allende. To these people, any punishment seems justifiable to avenge that humiliation.

During one of my seminars at UCSC, "Chile: From Allende to the Present," a Chilean exchange student asked if she could share some reflections with the class. "I was raised and educated under Pinochet's dictatorship," she said. "During my elementary and high school years, never did our teachers, nor our history books nor my parents talk to me about the three years of Allende. For my generation, those years do not exist. The saddest part is that we never heard of the horrendous human rights violations committed under our noses. So last week I confronted my parents for their silence: 'Why did you never tell me about the crimes Pinochet committed?' My parents were surprised by my question and just said, 'You have no idea how much we suffered during Allende. We had to stand in long lines to buy food. It was a chaotic time.'"

TWENTY

In drafting the complaint, our lawyers used the information I had gathered about Fernandez's criminal actions, including his involvement in the Caravan of Death. They also drew from the *Rettig Report* (1991)—a document produced by the Chilean government's Commission on Truth and Reconciliation—and Patricia Verdugo's book, *The Claws of the Puma*. My testimony as it appeared in *The Claws of the Puma* posed some legal challenges. "How did Verdugo obtain your testimony if you say you never spoke with her?" our lawyers asked. Finally, we agreed that Verdugo must have obtained my testimony from the Vicariate of Solidarity, confidentiality notwithstanding.

Trying to explain the difference between my current testimony and the testimony in Verdugo's book was also difficult, but after reviewing my lawyers' interrogation notes, this became easier. Whenever I testified at WSGR, the lawyers asked me to review their notes, and I always found discrepancies. At the Vicariate, I had never had a chance to review the lawyer's notes.

Finally, it happened. On March 19, 1999, our lawyers filed a lawsuit against Armando Fernandez Larios in the Federal District Court of Florida for "extrajudicial killing, torture, crimes against humanity, and cruel and inhuman treatment."

Things started moving very quickly. CJA organized a press conference at the Amnesty International office in San Francisco. "We want to inform the public about your lawsuit," Shawn said. "You will be allowed to read a statement preapproved by the legal team."

I spent the weekend thinking about my personal statement. When Pato and the boys took me to dinner Saturday night, Felipe asked, "Will Zita be in some kind of danger as a result of this?"

"No," I said quickly.

"Maybe," Pato replied. "We don't know. There are thousands of reasons why that might be a real possibility."

Over dinner, Pato and the boys devised a plan to protect me. Suddenly, I needed a new scanner, tape recorder, camera, and a new computer with the latest technology to protect documents and e-mails. It's amazing the things I *need* when the boys get involved.

On Monday morning at the Amnesty International press conference, in a room packed with reporters, I read this statement with Felipe at my side:

> My brother, a dreamer, an idealist, a loving parent, a wonderful son, and an unforgettable brother, was a young economist, twenty-eight years old, working for the Allende government as director of economic planning for two northern regions in Chile. He was killed on October 17, 1973, in the northern city of Copiapó, by members of the Chilean army. We were never given an opportunity to bury him, left without a sense of closure, and no chance for justice to be served.
>
> For the past twenty-five years, my siblings and I have dedicated our life to give meaning to our brother's death, to give meaning to suffering. How could I look into my parents' eyes when they asked me, "Why was Winston killed?" I didn't have an answer then, and I still do not have it today, but what I learned in these twenty-five years is that if we want to prevent these atrocities from happening all over again, justice has to prevail. For the first time in twenty-five years, my family has the opportunity to see that justice is served and to learn the whole truth about what happened to our brother Winston.
>
> This lawsuit against Fernandez Larios is an opportunity not only for my family, but also for the international community itself, to seek justice. Impunity is the greatest threat to our

individual freedom. Without justice served for human rights violations there is no weight behind the rhetoric of defense of these primary rights.

On behalf of my family, I want to express my greatest gratitude to the Center for Justice and Accountability of San Francisco, and to the attorneys at Wilson Sonsini Woodrich & Rosati of Palo Alto and Concepcion & Sexton of Coral Gables, Florida.

The next day, Adam and Shawn explained the process of creating an estate for Winston: a legal recourse offered by the US system, which enables a deceased person to bring a lawsuit against the party responsible for his or her suffering. "It would be Winston himself joining you, your mom, and your siblings in seeking justice for his death, his torture, his suffering," Shawn said. "Winston's estate doesn't exist. No money, no physical assets, no debts. But for the purpose of the lawsuit, we create the estate, a little box to put Winston's assets in, and you as his representative will receive the key to that box. If you win the case, the money allocated to the estate will go to that empty box. At that point you will become the 'executor' of your brother's estate."

"It will be an honor to be my brother's voice," I said.

I began to spend every free moment outside of teaching searching for new information on the Caravan of Death. At the same time, legal proceedings against Pinochet were fueling international efforts to discover the truth about thousands of human rights atrocities committed under his rule: secrets that had been closely guarded for more than twenty-five years. Through it all, our lawyers' interrogations continued: "Once you read of Wito's death in the newspaper, what did you do? Did you go to the military for explanations? Did you hire a lawyer? Did you take any legal action? Did you demand to know where he was buried?"

"No," I answered regretfully each time. "I did nothing."

On April 7, 1999, our lawyers filed the final copy of our amended complaint against Armando Fernandez. It read:

On information and belief, except where otherwise indicated, the plaintiffs allege as follows:

Winston Cabello received a graduate degree in economics from the University of Chile in approximately 1968.

Prior to the coup d'etat on September 11th, 1973, Winston Cabello worked as an economist appointed by the Allende government to serve as the Director of Regional Planning Office for the Atacama-Coquimbo region in northern Chile; the Office was located in Copiapó.

The Copiapó Office was one of twelve regional offices that Allende's government created to promote its economic reform program. Winston Cabello exercised significant control over government expenditures in the Atacama-Coquimbo region. In addition, he helped organize local industry groups and community organizations.

Over the course of the Allende Presidency, conservative elements in Chile, including the military, became increasingly hostile to the Allende government. Winston Cabello's implementation of Allende's economic agenda made him a target of the conservatives.

On September 11, 1973, Chile's armed forces staged a coup d'etat that ousted the democratically elected government of President Salvador Allende...Military authorities throughout Chile, including the defendant and his superior officers, immediately launched a systematic assault on those perceived to be potential opponents of the new regime...

On September 12, 1973, the day after the coup, General Oscar Haag, the local military official responsible for Copiapó, summoned public officials, including Winston Cabello, to a meeting. After the meeting, Haag refused to allow Winston Cabello to leave with the other officials. Haag told Winston that he was being detained because his vehicle from the Office of Regional Planning had been seen in "suspicious places" on the day of the coup. That same day, General Haag imprisoned Winston at the local jail in Copiapó. Winston Cabello is believed to have been the first political prisoner to be held in the region of Copiapó following the coup d'etat.

Some time within the first two weeks after he was detained, Winston Cabello was transferred from the local jail to the Copiapó military garrison...

During October 1973, the defendant and the other members of General Arellano Stark's unit, acting under official orders from General Augusto Pinochet, carried out a common plan to torture and execute at least 72 political prisoners held at the Cauquenes, Copiapó, Calama, La Serena, and Antofagasta detention facilities in northern Chile (the "Caravan of Death.")

At the time of his resignation from the Chilean army, the defendant publicly admitted that he had been a member of Arellano Stark's unit.

On or about the 16 of October 1973, Defendant Armando Fernandez Larios, and the other five members of General Stark's unit arrived at the Copiapó military garrison by helicopter.

After their arrival, the defendant and other members of General Stark's unit instructed local military officers to provide them with the files of the political prisoners held in the Copiapó jail and garrison. After searching through the files, they selected thirteen political prisoners to be executed, including Winston Cabello.

The selection of thirteen prisoners in Copiapó for summary execution was part of a common plan of the defendant, other members of the Stark unit, and local military authorities to eliminate political opposition to the Pinochet regime...

The defendant and other members of Stark's unit then began to drink Pisco, a Chilean "moonshine," they became intoxicated. One of the members of the Stark unit asked one of the local military officers if he wanted to join them for a "party."

The military officer understood that he was being invited to participate in the torture and execution of the thirteen political prisoners selected that evening...

During the night, the thirteen designated political prisoners were removed from the facilities where they had been detained…

Sometime between midnight and 2:00 a.m. on or about October 17, 1973, the defendant and other members of Stark's unit, accompanied by Captain Diaz, and Lieutenants Marambio and Ojeda, drove the truck on the main highway toward the city of La Serena. About ten minutes outside Copiapó, in a secluded area of the highway, the truck stopped; the defendant and other members of the Stark unit ordered the prisoners to get off the truck.

The defendant and some of the other military officers were armed with *corvos*. A *corvo* is a short, curved knife traditionally carried by members of the Chilean military. It is designed to inflict wounds that, although ultimately fatal, cause a slow and painful death.

As the prisoners were forced off the truck, the defendant and his co-conspirators sprayed some of the prisoners with bullets and fatally stabbed the others with their *corvos*.

Winston Cabello refused to get off the truck. Winston told the defendant that the defendant would have to kill him on the truck. The defendant then slashed Winston Cabello with a *corvo*.

In furtherance of the co-conspirators' common plan to eliminate political opposition to the Pinochet regime, the bodies of the victims were buried in an unmarked mass grave.

On October 18, 1973, an announcement (a military "bando") was published in the local newspaper indicating that thirteen prisoners had been killed "while trying to escape" as they were transferred out of detention from Copiapó to La Serena prison. The military account in the newspaper was false.

Shortly after Winston Cabello was killed, his family was provided with a death certificate that indicated that his death was caused by "ejecución militar" (military execution). Several years later, in 1985, the Cabello family received a revised death certificate, which identified the cause of death as "herida de balas" (a gunshot wound.) Finally, in or around 1991, the Cabello family received yet another revised certificate, which omitted any reference to the cause of death.

From 1973 until 1990, the military authorities in Chile deliberately concealed from the Cabello family and the families of the other victims the burial location of the thirteen corpses.

From 1973 until 1990, the military authorities in Chile purposefully refused to allow the Cabello family to provide a proper burial for Winston.

In July 1990, after the transition from the military government of General Augusto Pinochet to the civilian government led by Patricio Aylwin, and in response to a petition submitted by the families of the deceased political prisoners in Copiapó, an exhumation of a mass grave was undertaken. Thirteen bodies were ultimately exhumed; the remains were very well preserved despite the passage of years, due to the desert climate and the composition of the soil.

There was no indication that the victims had been killed during an escape attempt; many of the deaths are believed to have resulted from knife wounds, not gunshot wounds.

Our amended complaint included an explanation of the legal basis for our allegations and an exhaustive description of the laws Fernandez had violated, including the Torture Victim Protection Act, the International Covenant on Civil and Political Rights, and Customary International Law. Here the lawyers wrote:

> Defendant Fernandez Larios actively participated in the extrajudicial killing of the decedent, Winston Cabello. The extrajudicial killing of Winston Cabello was not authorized by any court judgment, and was unlawful under the laws of Chile that existed at that time. The decedent, Winston Cabello, was never charged, convicted or sentenced for any crime...
>
> The defendant and his co-conspirators specifically intended to inflict severe pain and suffering on Winston Cabello.
>
> The acts of extrajudicial killing, torture, and other inhumane acts alleged herein constitute crimes against humanity. These acts were committed in a systematic manner and on a large scale; they were instigated and/or directed by the government of Chile against a civilian population.

The acts described herein—including, but not limited to, the act of cutting Winston Cabello with a *corvo* knife while he was still alive—constitute cruel, inhuman or degrading treatment or punishment of Winston Cabello.

Our lawyers' commitment to Wito's case was a tremendous gift to my family. David brought a kind of calm to the proceedings. Shawn patiently explained the intricate steps. Adam, young and visibly enthusiastic, was extremely anxious about "facts," "truth," and "evidence" in a way that was contagious. "Can we prove this?" he would frequently ask.

"I don't know," I would reply. "Isn't it our job to find the evidence to prove it?"

Armando Fernandez was already a notorious figure in Chile, and stories of his cruelty had been circulating for decades. While it was true that each time I looked into one of these stories I found some kind of factual basis behind it, we could not use stories as testimony in a court of law. We needed solid evidence.

I realized that the best way to help my lawyers was to go out and personally verify the stories about Armando Fernandez. I needed to find people who could actually say, "I saw that."

TWENTY ONE

"Promise to tell us the whole truth, nothing but the truth."

"Yes, of course," I told Adam each time. I don't think my lawyers realized how profoundly committed I was to "the whole truth, nothing but the truth."

My determination to find the facts about Wito's death sometimes became a source of conflict with our lawyers. "Most probably, the entire truth of the case will not be possible to establish," they would say.

"But that doesn't mean we should surrender our aim to first and foremost establish the entire truth," I would insist.

We agreed to treat each obstacle as a challenge to overcome, and to only exclude a claim from our story if several attempts to find supporting evidence failed. Unfortunately, one of my family's most cherished memories fell casualty to this process. At lunchtime on October 16, 1973, just hours before Wito was killed, he had called my parents from the military prosecutor's office. In the United States, people can typically make phone calls after they are arrested, but this was not normal in Pinochet's Chile.

"How are you doing, little sister?" Wito asked thirteen-year-old Karin, when she answered the phone. "Is Mom home? I want to tell her that I will be released on Sunday."

"Just a few more days," Wito told my mother when she picked up the phone. "I will go home, and Pato, too. So tell my dad not to worry."

"He sounded so happy," Karin often recalls.

Pato's testimony to our lawyers corroborated what Wito told my family on the phone that day, and what he said during our last visit at the garrison.

"It's all hearsay," my lawyers said. "Winston told your mother; that's hearsay. He told you; that's also hearsay. And Pato never got the chance to speak with the military prosecutor Carlos Brito."

"Well then, let's go find this guy," I replied.

Intellectually I understood the concept of hearsay. But it felt wrong that my lawyers did not believe in the possibility of proving that Major Brito had decided to release my brother. *Why not at least try?* I thought. *What if we could find Carlos Brito? What if we could find documents testifying to Wito's imminent release?*

But my lawyers had no room for this important story in their case.

TWENTY TWO

"This is going to be our biggest nightmare," our lawyers said of the US Torture Victim Protection Act, which provides for a ten-year statute of limitations, meaning that rights could not be enforced by legal action or offenses could not be punished after a designated amount of time had passed (in this case, ten years). Twenty years had passed since Wito's death, so we fully expected a motion to dismiss our case due to this restriction.

Our lawyers worked tirelessly through April and May, preparing to rebut expected arguments from Fernandez's lawyer. Fortunately, during this time, the Chilean courts were studying the validity of the "permanent kidnapping" crime argument, which defines "enforced disappearance" as an ongoing crime until the victim's remains have been recovered or the fact of death established. This made all the difference.

"From 1973 until 1990, the military authorities in Chile deliberately concealed from the Cabello family and the families of the other victims the burial location of the thirteen corpses," our lawyers stated. "In July 1990, after the transition from the military government of General Augusto Pinochet to the civilian government led by President Patricio Aylwin, and in response to a petition submitted by the families of the deceased political prisoners in Copiapó, an exhumation of a mass grave was undertaken in Copiapó. Thirteen bodies were ultimately exhumed."

Since we had filed our case in 1999, we were just within the ten-year statute of limitations based on when Wito's body had been found. For the court to rule in our favor on this issue, however, we needed strong evidence to prove that for seventeen years we had not known "Winston's whereabouts."

"Did anyone in your family know where Winston was buried?" my lawyers kept asking.

"No," I answered each time.

"How can we prove then that the burial site was unknown to the families when it was found the same day they began searching for it?" Adam asked. "Maybe your family didn't know, but that doesn't mean the information wasn't out there for you to have it. Did you ever ask?"

"Nobody knew," I replied. "The military never disclosed that information. We had an inkling that they had been buried in the local cemetery because some family members visited the cemetery the same day we learned of their deaths. They identified a place that showed indications of earth recently removed, and nearby they found a shoe that belonged to one of the victims. All I can say is that for seventeen years, families of the victims placed flowers on that spot, hoping it was their resting place. I visited it myself a few times. It was the place."

"So you all knew."

"No. We wanted to believe that that was the place, but it was never confirmed. No, we didn't know. But it would be easy for you to prove that we didn't know. I can show you how."

"We are waiting," said Adam, impatiently.

In late May 1995, a person who had filmed the exhumations mailed me four VHS tapes with the following message: "These are tapes of Copiapó's exhumations. We are placing them into your hands because we believe you will find a dignified way to use them in your teaching. So that Never Again." A month later, I had sat in my living room watching the videos from beginning to end, my heart racing when I thought I saw fragments of the green sweater my mother had knitted for Wito. I kept searching for a sign that my brother was there, that Wito had finally been found. As I watched the exhumations on our television at home, I finally let myself feel the tremendous pain of losing my brother.

"The exhumations lasted for two days," I explained to our lawyers. "Forensic doctors and anthropologists directed the entire operation, assisted by a group of diggers. For almost all of the first day, the group excavated unsuccessfully in different locations of the cemetery. It wasn't until late afternoon when they finally stumbled onto the first signs of bodies buried in a mass grave."

Adam began tapping his fingers on the table.

"One member of the group had a video camera," I continued, ignoring him. "He videotaped the entire two days' work. Everything. So if you want, I can give you copies of the videos. I have them in my house. They give proof, you *will* see, the long hours of frustrated efforts to find the remains of the thirteen victims."

"When can we have copies of the videos?" asked Adam.

The next day, I brought the videotapes to our lawyers. I later learned that the entire legal team had watched the exhumation footage together in awe.

As expected, the statute of limitations turned into a major headache, which lasted through the end of the trial. Fortunately, the court never upheld motions filed by the defendant to dismiss our case; instead the court always ruled in our favor, accepting our lawyers' arguments that since Wito's body had not been found until 1990 and we had filed the lawsuit in 1999, the ten-year statute of limitations had not yet run its course.

"Exhaustion of remedies" presented another major challenge. David asked if anyone in our network of human rights lawyers could provide a declaration documenting unsuccessful efforts to pursue judicial remedies in Chile for human rights abuses of the 1970s, explaining, 'To obtain a favorable outcome in the lawsuit in the United States, we must persuade the court that it is impossible to obtain a judicial remedy in Chile."

About two weeks later, Victor Canales forwarded a letter from two prominent Chilean human rights lawyers—Eduardo Contreras and Carmen Hertz—who wrote:

> Our efforts were largely thwarted by a legal system unwilling to prosecute anyone responsible for the crimes committed under Pinochet's regime. In addition, the climate of repression, reprisal and intimidation that existed during Pinochet—and carries on

well into present times—makes it impossible to expect families of the victims to run the risk of presenting criminal complaints and seeking punishment for the atrocious crimes of the 1970s.

To make matters even worse, Chile's Supreme Court in 1990 upheld the 1978 Amnesty Law, thus precluding any prosecutions of pre-1978 human rights violations, which is the case of the Caravan of Death crimes.

Amnesty laws such as these are a primary reason that justice remains obstructed in Chile and in other countries that have suffered major human rights violations. In Chile, the Pinochet regime protected itself by enacting a 1978 amnesty law, giving legal impunity to the perpetrators of all crimes committed from 1973 to 1978. In this way, people like General Pinochet and General Arellano legally forgave themselves and their men for the atrocities they committed. The rest of us are expected to follow suit. Unfortunately, Chile's democracy seems willing to uphold these amnesty laws.

In the words of Helmut Franz, "By not fully accepting its complicity in past tragedies, a country will inevitably re-create them."

Nine years had passed since Pinochet's abdication of power, yet by 1999 Chile's democracy still had made no progress in creating the kind of security or confidence in the Chilean judicial system needed for people to feel safe in seeking redress for past human rights abuses. As our lawyers worked to establish "exhaustion of remedies" in Chile, this was the core of their arguments. This was something my family understood personally; as Veronica, who has continued to live in Chile since Wito's death, told me, "I've never attempted—to this day—to take any legal action for Wito's death because of fear."

The issue of fear was pivotal to our lawyers' arguments. Unfortunately, it was not sufficient to prove what Fernandez and his lawyer demanded: that we had exhausted all judicial remedies in Chile and all our actions had been unsuccessful. How could we prove that all legal actions had been unsuccessful when we were arguing that fear had prevented us from taking any legal action in the first place?

Meanwhile, the interrogations continued.

"Have you, in the past twenty-five years, taken steps to hold military officers accountable for your brother's murder? Have you ever demanded, in the last twenty-five years, an explanation as to why he was singled out to be killed?"

With each question, my family agonized: Had we done enough for Wito?

"I was only thirteen years old. I was only a kid," Karin told me, fighting back tears after her interrogation. "They asked me if I filed any legal action for Wito's death. How could I? I didn't even tell my best friends in high school that they had killed my brother."

"These are just lawyers' questions," I said, trying to reassure her.

"We were so afraid, Zita," Karin said. "I remember when the military came to our house to bug our phone lines. And Mom and Dad, their sorrow so deep that they cried all day long. After we left Chile in 1978, do you know something? Do you realize that among ourselves, during all these years, we still don't even pronounce our brother's name?"

A few days later, Lito phoned me. "I told them that before leaving Chile with my wife and two daughters in 1978, it was impossible to do anything. Then they also asked me if, after I left Chile, I had done anything to pursue justice for Winston. I told them that during all these years, our lives have been consumed with figuring out how to make a living in this country."

Rarely have I heard such pain in my brother's voice.

David asked for a copy of my testimony to the Vicariate of Solidarity, explaining that it would help establish that my family's efforts for justice had not made it through the Chilean legal system. (By this, he meant the effort of giving my testimony so it could be included in the Vicariate's broader prosecution of Arellano.) I asked my cousin Irene for help, since she had once worked at the Vicariate and had gone with Roberto and me the day I had given my testimony. Soon a package arrived from Chile, containing my testimony and four hundred pages of documents that Irene thought would be helpful. Most were from 1973, gathered by Chile's Truth and Reconciliation Commission during its investigation. Suddenly we had classified papers from Copiapó's garrison, jail, and cemetery, all chronicling the military's plan to execute the thirteen prisoners and make it look like an escape attempt. Reading these documents I felt sick to my stomach. The lies were so bold that I as read I kept wondering, *Did they really think people would believe what they wrote in the documents?* I found so many inconsistencies in their "story." The documents described an escape plan that the "thirteen most dangerous political prisoners" had devised. *How could they have planned to escape when the victims were detained in different facilities, some of them in isolation at the jail, like Leonello Vincentti, and others like Manuel Cortazar, who was arrested the day he was killed?*

That summer, David left WSGR to accept a teaching position on the East Coast. This fine lawyer had been a driving force in our planning process, and we were not sure how to proceed without him. A few weeks later, I met with Adam, Shawn, and Nicole—a new lawyer at WSGR who was replacing David on our case—to discuss our strategy going forward. During the entire meeting, Nicole conducted herself with a certain degree of authority and command about my brother's case that produced in me the opposite impression: that she did not understand but wanted me to know that she was now in charge.

"Discovery phase ends by the end of November, and we still don't have solid evidence to connect Fernandez with Winston's murder," said Adam. "We need to locate Adolfo. He is our only witness."

"I need to explain to him how his name got into Verdugo's book." I reminded the lawyers of our agreement that I must speak with Adolfo first. "I need to apologize for any wrong I might have caused him."

Since the beginning, our lawyers had placed their highest hope in Adolfo's testimony, saying that if Adolfo saw Armando Fernandez in the truck or in the vicinity of the truck with the prisoners, that this would be enough to support our allegations against Fernandez. I understood the lawyers' rush to find Adolfo but disagreed with placing all our hope in one person.

"Why don't we look into the long list of potential witnesses I gave you last week? Some of them might provide us with powerful testimony," I said.

"What other witnesses?" Adam asked.

"In the *tomos* we received…" I began. The lawyers looked confused.

Two weeks earlier, Victor Canales had mailed us seven large volumes (*tomos*)—about nine hundred pages each—from Judge Guzmán's investigation on the Caravan of Death. Hugo Gutierrez, a well-known human rights lawyer in Chile, had given Victor access to every piece of information the judge had gathered since initiating the investigation in 1998. It had taken me a full week to read through all the *tomos*, placing yellow stickers with notes on each page with information about Fernandez, Copiapó, or the Caravan of Death. I had given the stack of *tomos* and all my notes to Adam, explaining what everything meant, and he had offered to make copies for me.

"Oh, Zita," Adam interrupted, "here are your copies."

I walked over to the stack of *tomos* to select some potential witnesses for my lawyers, but all my notes were gone. "Where are my notes, the yellow stickers?"

"The people who made the copies probably took them out," said Adam. "We had to make copies for the defendant's lawyer, too. We are required by law to send all the information we come across during discovery phase to the other party. It will force Steve Davis to go over the thousands of pages if he wants to know what is in there. What is in the *tomos*?" asked Adam, smiling.

Don't you remember the day I brought you the tomos and explained what we had? I felt like screaming. Instead I replied, "They include testimonies from military personnel and political prisoners who witnessed the events that took place in the different cities visited by General Arellano and his death squad. From what I read, the judge let the witnesses speak freely about their experiences."

Nicole narrowed her eyes. "So the judge doesn't ask questions about Fernandez Larios."

"No," I said. "His investigation is not about Fernandez; it's about Pinochet and his connection with the Caravan of Death killings. A considerable number of people have already mentioned Fernandez to the judge, like Lieutenant Enrique Vidal, for example, even though the judge didn't ask specifically about him. I believe we should be contacting these people so we can ask them *our* questions. They might surprise us."

The lawyers just stared at me.

Nicole left early, saying she had another meeting to attend. With a toss of her red, curly hair, she said, "Nice meeting you."

Adam asked me to watch the exhumation tapes again. I already knew it would be impossible to identify Wito, but I sat down a few days later and forced myself to watch them all over again. Buried in a mass grave for over fifteen years, the thirteen skeletons were unrecognizable. Still I scrutinized each image, watching especially for familiar clothing. Again, I thought I saw fragments of the green sweater our mother had knitted for Wito.

In late August, I met with Adam and Nicole to share what I had found. It was not much. A few times during our meeting, I mentioned Wito's green sweater.

"What's so important about the sweater?" Adam demanded.

"Nothing really," I said, quickly. "I'm sorry about that."

Nicole surprised me by announcing that she would travel to Chile on September 7. She said, "We have two lawyers in Chile working with us on Winston's case. Mr. Gonzalo Figueroa and his son."

I had never heard of them.

"Just for you to remember, they are your lawyers in Chile now," Adam told me.

Something felt wrong. I was perfectly happy with the human rights lawyers that Victor had already engaged for us in Chile. Not sure what to do, I just nodded.

"I hope you'll have time in Chile to meet the lawyers who've helped us so much in our case," I told Nicole. "And of course, I hope you will meet Victor. It would be good if the new lawyers could help you arrange meetings with some of the witnesses from the list I prepared from the *tomos*."

"Thank you for the suggestion," Nicole said.

Shawn called me at home that night. "Do you know Nicole is going to Chile? I think you should go."

The next day, Shawn told Nicole, "I think Zita should go with you."

"If she wants to go, she can go," Nicole said.

It seemed obvious that Nicole did not need or want me to accompany her, and I saw no reason to force the issue. "Under those conditions, why should I go?" I asked Shawn the next time we spoke. "There's no reason for me to go."

A few days before Nicole's trip, I suggested that she meet Wito's widow, Veronica, who was caring for her ailing father in Putaendo, Chile. Veronica had already made it clear that she did not want to be involved with the case, and my lawyers and I understood this. Nicole had shared some names of people she planned to meet, and I just thought it would be a respectful gesture for her to call on Veronica while in Chile. When I asked my sister-in-law if this would be all right, Veronica repeated that she did not want to be involved with the case, but said, "If she wants to come to Putaendo, yes. Why do you want me to meet her?"

"It's just a social visit," I said, assuring Veronica that she had nothing to worry about. I explained that a lawyer named Gonzalo Figueroa would call to arrange the time.

The day Nicole arrived in Chile, she and Gonzalo Figueroa went to see Veronica. Later that day, I called Veronica from California to ask how the visit had gone.

"You told me Nicole was coming to meet me, not to interrogate me," Veronica said, angrily. "Nicole walked into my house and began questioning me about the night Wito was killed. This is not exactly what we had agreed."

"I'm as surprised as you are," I faltered.

"When she finished with her interrogation, she just said, 'Nice meeting you,' and left. I wasn't prepared for this," said Veronica, beginning to cry. "I'm taking care of my dad, and I'm still afraid of talking. She had no right to come to my house to interrogate me. Just before leaving, Nicole asked me if I could testify in Miami. I said yes."

"Why did you say yes if you don't want to do it?"

"Because I don't want to mess things up for you, Zita. Nicole said that my testimony would be very important. Can you imagine that you might lose the case because of me?"

"Probably there was a miscommunication between Nicole and me," I told her, anxiously. "Nicole is a new member of the legal team. You have to believe me. I just wanted her to visit you. I never expected she would go to your house to interrogate you."

I should have known better. Nicole had gone to Chile to work, not to make social calls.

Apparently, Veronica talked to Lito. "Why is Veronica's name listed as a witness?" my brother asked Nicole when she returned from Chile.

"Well, we included her so the defendant's lawyer won't include her as one of their witnesses," said Nicole, explaining that the prosecution and defense could not both have the same witnesses. "Steve Davis cannot call any name from our list. We did not want to put Veronica through the pain of being contacted by Fernandez's lawyers."

"If you don't include her name, does Veronica have to testify if Fernandez's lawyers ask her to do it?" asked Lito.

"No. These are voluntary testimonies."

"Then I will let her know that," Lito said. "That she doesn't have to testify."

"Please don't do that."

I heard later that Nicole was not happy about Lito telling Veronica that the testimonies were voluntary and she was not legally obligated to testify.

As soon as I hung up with Veronica, my phone rang. Victor Canales was calling to say that Gonzalo Figueroa—my new lawyer in Chile—had located Adolfo and had already booked a flight with Nicole to go out and meet him.

I was furious. I called Pato at work, so angry I could hardly speak. Pato calmed me down and suggested I call Adam immediately.

"I heard you found Adolfo, and that Nicole is planning to visit him on the thirteenth," I said, when Adam answered the phone. "I thought we had agreed that I would speak with him first."

"You can write him a letter, if you want. Nicole can deliver it for you." Adam hung up.

Without Adolfo's phone number or e-mail address, I had no other option. I spent the next day writing him this letter:

September 9, 1999

Dear Adolfo:

I hope you remember me. I'm Zita Cabello, we met many years ago, in the city of Copiapó. I have been living in the United States with my family since 1974.

In my mind, I've been writing this letter to you for over 20 years; and now, when I finally sit down to do it, I realize I don't know how to begin. I will begin by recounting a story to you. In 1986, after twelve years of being away, I returned to Chile. This trip was filled with emotions and memories; and in my need to confront the past, to find answers regarding the events of October 17, 1973, I approached the Vicariate of Solidarity in Santiago. Some friends had told me that lawyers from the Vicariate were gathering information to file a criminal lawsuit against General Arellano Stark. The lawyers assured me that every piece of information I would provide them would be highly confidential, and that it would never be leaked to the public. Given that understanding, I related to them everything I knew regarding the events of '73. Events that I have never been able to forget.

I was in Chile for two weeks, and I returned in 1989, also for two weeks. During this last trip I stumbled upon the book *The Claws of the Puma*. I began reading it, and as I kept reading it, I realized that the book re-created our story. It was an emotional moment for me because finally somebody had had the courage to speak the truth that surrounds the painful events that took place in northern Chile in October 1973. I was anxiously reading the chapter on Copiapó when all of a sudden I saw my name beside your name, and an immense rage came over me. I felt betrayed, not only by the lawyers from the Vicariate, but also by the author of the book, whom I had never spoken with. I couldn't finish the book, and for the few days I stayed in Chile, I looked for you. I went to Copiapó but no one was able to provide me any information about you. I feared the worst. For years I kept searching for you, and it wasn't until 1995 that I learned you were doing well. I felt a great relief. Since then, I have harbored one wish, that you will give me the opportunity to ask you in person for your forgiveness, and above all, to express to you the affection and profound gratitude my family and I feel toward you.

You've always been in our memories. My two sons grew up knowing and respecting your name, knowing that in great part you made it possible for them to grow up with their father at their side.

Adolfo, I hope you will give me the opportunity to speak with you. Especially now that our family has filed a lawsuit in the United States against Armando Fernandez Larios for the death of Winston. I need to explain to you certain details concerning what is happening. Your name has come up in conversations with my lawyers, as well as the names of others like Vidal, Morales, and Brito, and of course Haag. Vidal already provided a powerful testimony regarding the events of October 17th. He also described in detail some of Fernandez's actions.

Adolfo, if you allow me, I would like to visit you so we can talk. Nobody needs to know about our conversation, I would respect your wishes, but please, give me that opportunity. Unfortunately I don't have too much time, I need to go back to work in two weeks, so I suggest the following. If you want, we can meet in Santiago, I would send you an airline ticket, or if you prefer, I could go to your place. Just let me know. Even if the answer is negative, I still would like to hear from you.

Adolfo, I know you must be hurt by what I did, I just hope you can give me the opportunity to meet so we can talk. For now, receive from Patricio, my two sons, Felipe and Roberto, and me, our warmth and best wishes.

I hope to hear from you soon,
Zita Cabello B.

I e-mailed my letter to Victor, who agreed to deliver it to Nicole before she left the hotel. Soon after, I learned that "Señor Figueroa," as Nicole called him, had already spoken with Adolfo by phone and he was expecting their visit. This surprised me. I had felt sure Adolfo would not speak with a lawyer.

The next morning, my kitchen phone rang.

"Do you know whom you are speaking with?" asked a male voice.

"No," I said, afraid to be wrong.

"This is Adolfo Gonzalez."

Trembling, I found a pen and paper and sat down on the kitchen floor.

"Let me speak," Adolfo said. "Don't say anything. I'm calling you from a pay phone."

As Adolfo spoke, I took the following notes:

"I received your letter. Your Chilean lawyer gave me the letter. I did not want to speak with your lawyer from the United States. I firmly told him that I did not want to meet your lawyer from the States, though I repeatedly told him that I would speak with you. I insisted that he should give you my phone number. But I couldn't wait, that's why I'm calling you.

"Zita, I was very moved by your letter. I want to thank you for it. I have to tell you that I almost lost my job, my reputation as a military officer, and my marriage after my name appeared in the book *Los Zarpazos del Puma*. Thank you for explaining it to me. I lived hard times. I have read your letter at least 40 times. I showed it to my wife. You told me in your letter that your children are thankful for what I did. My wife read that, too, she understands now that what I did was right, that I had to do it.

"Zita, today I had planned to go to Santiago to see my mother, it's her birthday, but after I received your letter, I couldn't go. It seems to me that the painful memories of 1973 are here with me today. That's why I couldn't go to Santiago. And that's why I'm calling you.

"I felt so moved by your letter. I think this letter is more meaningful to me than to you. We were on opposite sides, but here we are, talking to each other. We understand each other, many things happened, but nothing justified the crimes.

"Zita, I can't help you with your lawsuit. I had an excellent career in my institution. I retired as a major with honors. I'm very proud of my accomplishments. I can't tarnish my image, especially among those who love me, like my children. I don't want that to change. I will lose their trust if I get involved in anything. I'm sorry.

"How could I trust your lawyer? You understand me, especially after what happened to you with your own testimony at the Vicariate."

"Zita, are you doing this out of revenge? For what other reason, if not revenge, might you be doing this?"

"I can't explain it to you on the phone," I said, once Adolfo had finished speaking. "If you'll allow me, I would like to send you a documentary I produced in December 1997. I'm sure by watching it you will understand my reasons for seeking justice. I would also like to see you. Would it be okay for me to fly down there so we can talk? It's something I've been wanting to do for years."

Adolfo was silent. "Yes," he said, finally. "As I told you at the beginning, and as I told your lawyer, I didn't want to speak with them but I specifically said, 'I would speak with Zita. If she wants to call me, please give her my phone number.' Do you have my phone number?"

"No, I don't."

Adolfo gave me his number and home address. "I'm glad to know you searched for me. I left Copiapó in 1982, and I have never returned. Ever. Thank you again for the letter. It touched me deeply."

After Adolfo hung up, I sat on my kitchen floor for a while, trying to process what had just happened. Suddenly, my kitchen phone rang again.

"I have bad news, Zita," I heard Adam say. "I just spoke with Nicole. Adolfo refused to speak with her. He was very moved by your letter, but he told Señor Figueroa that he doesn't know anything about Fernandez."

I waited for Adam to tell me that Adolfo wanted to speak with me and had repeatedly asked Nicole and Figueroa to give me his number. Instead, he briefly updated me on Nicole's trip to Chile.

"That's all?" I asked when he had finished.

"Yes."

"I think you forgot something."

"What?"

"Adolfo just called me," I said, angrily. "You forgot to tell me that despite the fact that he didn't want to speak with Nicole, he would speak with me. Not only that, he specifically asked you to give me his phone number."

"What did he say?" Adam asked, laughing nervously.

I related our basic conversation, and then said, "I don't know what is happening. First you decide to go to see Adolfo, violating our agreement. Then you hide information. You didn't tell me that he wants to speak with me. Is it because it would show that I was right when I asked you to let me speak with him first? Why would that matter? Don't we all want to win the case? Don't you think we can still convince him to testify if you let me try? If not, he might provide valuable information to us. Why this lack of transparency? Not only that—Nicole just went over to Veronica's house and interrogated her. I spoke with Veronica right after Nicole left. She was crying and upset by Nicole's visit."

"But Veronica was very nice with Nicole," Adam interrupted. "She even agreed to testify."

"What do you expect from her? Of course she had to be nice. She agreed to meet Nicole. But we never talked about interrogation. Veronica now thinks I misled her."

Shortly after that conversation, Adam pulled out of the case. We never spoke again.

I felt awful after hanging up with Adam and called Shawn to tell her what I had done. "These things happen," Shawn said. "This is not the end of the world. We have to find a way to keep working with Adam and Nicole. Remember, they are your lawyers. You are entitled to tell them when you are not happy."

I had not thought it necessary to accompany Nicole to Chile, but now, knowing the results of her visit, I was determined to go on my own.

"I've decided to go to Chile," I told Shawn.

"Great," she said. "If you want, I can go with you."

Adolfo's notion that revenge motivated my search for justice deeply troubled me. That night, I asked Victor Canales to mail Adolfo a copy of my documentary, believing it would help explain my reasons for pursuing a lawsuit. Victor mailed it immediately with a powerful letter of his own:

September 15, 1999

Dear Adolfo:

I am an old friend of Aldo Cabello and I am writing at Zita's request. She has asked me to send you a copy of a documentary she authored, and I believe it is dated early 1998.

When I saw this video, I was left ruminating over what I had seen for a couple of weeks. First, I felt miserable because, in spite of my old and warm relationship with Aldo (we were classmates throughout our university life), I had no clear idea of the circumstances of Winston's death, nor did I know of the dark sufferings in his family, nor about the circumstances under which his body was found in 1990—except from newspaper accounts. Also, because in spite of seeing each other a couple of times a year at social events with other old friends, Aldo never mentioned one word on the subject. It is possible that my ignorance about all of this was due, at least in part, to the fact that for the last 30 years my work as an international consultant forces me to travel a lot and I am rarely in the country. But, I thought, it is also possible that I did not know because it is neither comfortable nor fun to know all of this. That is why—as I am trying to tell you—this video and Zita's serene narrative touched me tremendously.

Zita, Aldo, and all the family are now involved in a judicial process in the USA. In my modest understanding, it is an exemplary effort to know and divulge the truth about what happened to their brother, and it seems to me it is destined to deeply move the conscience of many who have not thought, or who have avoided thinking, on the subject of mutual respect that we owe each other as human beings regardless of the circumstances. I think that that public trial is an urgent call to heal ourselves, confronting for once our personal and collective histories, so we can weigh and balance our miseries and our generosities to be better men, better parents, reasonable grandparents. From my own point of view, the Cabellos' initiative, which without a doubt causes them a tremendous personal pain, is an effort that deserves to be supported by every person of dignity who loves his family, his motherland, and humanity. It is maybe a small task in the middle of so many pains that the human race inflicts upon itself, but it is inspirational and full of nobility, and seeks nothing else but to give us an opportunity to be better within our own and innumerable limitations.

Zita has asked me to say that she would like for you to watch the video with your wife. I imagine that she thinks, I believe quite correctly, that this is a subject that deserves to be shared with those we are close to. Frankly, I myself would not have been able to see the light that this video has shown me without my own wife's opinion and perception. It seems that feminine sensitivity has ways to illuminate corners in our minds and hearts that otherwise would have remained in darkness. I transmit to you this assignment in the best of spirits and with great hope.

Maybe life will allow us to meet and talk sometime. For now, receive my regards.

Victor Canales

TWENTY THREE

In October 1999, I took a week off from teaching and flew to Chile to search for witnesses. Veronica met me at the Santiago airport, and we spent the day catching up at her house. The next morning, Shawn and I flew to the city where Adolfo lived.

Our lawsuit's discovery phase had been extended by six months, so our lawyers planned to formally request assistance from the Chilean judicial authorities in interrogating witnesses. They wanted me to ask Adolfo if he would be willing to testify by letter rogatory, a process through which a US court would formally request that the Chilean judicial system interrogate a number of witnesses for us, using questions that we prepared in advance. (Fernandez's lawyer would review our questionnaire and add any questions of his own before it went to Chile.)

Shawn and I spent the day in our hotel room, waiting for Adolfo to call. At 3:50 p.m., the phone rang. "I'll be there in ten minutes," Adolfo said.

I had waited more than twenty-five years for this meeting. Hoping I looked more confident than I felt, I stood alone in front of the hotel, holding a box of chocolates. A few minutes later a car parked across the street. The driver, a brown-haired man with sunglasses, waved and called, "I hope you didn't wait too long!"

Adolfo and I embraced warmly, and I handed him the gift, saying, "I brought some chocolate for you and your family." It seemed such a small thing to say. At a nearby mall, we ordered two Cokes and found an empty table in the noisy food court.

"I know you want to talk about 1973," Adolfo said. "Not yet."

We talked so steadily that five hours later, we still had not finished our Cokes. I had known very little about Adolfo in 1973. Now his face brightened as he spoke of his childhood, his love for his mother, and his family. Eventually, Adolfo said, "I watched your documentary. It touched me deeply. I understand now why you are pursuing justice for Winston's death. I know it's not revenge that motivates you to do this. I respect you enormously for that. I wish you success."

I asked if he would be willing to testify by letter rogatory. Adolfo hesitated, and then said, "The armed forces, an apolitical institution until 1973, were asked to intervene in politics to solve the problems created by the politicians. Problems created by the same people who are in power today, by the same people who talk today about reconciliation. The armed forces are in no way responsible for what happened. Their involvement in the overthrow of Allende's government had to do with the irresponsibility of those who destroyed the country. They only stepped in to solve problems."

"Let's assume you are right," I replied, "that the country was in chaos, and the armed forces stepped in to fix the problems. Was it necessary to destroy the soul of our country by killing, torturing, and disappearing defenseless citizens? I hope you are not suggesting that."

"Zita, imagine this was a boxing match," Adolfo said. "The boxer who gives the first punch usually wins. You don't have time to think about your opponent—you want to destroy him as soon as possible, and that was exactly what was done. It was necessary. Think also that this was a war, and that in a war there is no other choice—you have to kill people. In addition, if we had not done it, we would be the ones dead now."

I had heard that argument before. Listening to Adolfo, I recalled a conversation many years earlier with a UC Berkeley professor, Dr. William Kornhauser. "People who commit crimes on a large scale, like Pinochet, for example, believe they are doing the right thing," Dr. Kornhauser had said. "They feel justified. Otherwise, they couldn't sleep at night. I'm sure Pinochet has no problem sleeping."

"Would it be possible to disturb his sleep?" I had asked. "What could cause him to ask himself the question 'Is it morally right what I'm doing?'"

"Yes, but you must be aware that one of the hardest things to do is to question what we take for granted, to challenge our strongly held beliefs. Because that is what you are asking." Dr. Kornhauser had paused, and then he smiled. "Don't feel discouraged. It can happen."

A few years later, I asked the Chilean philosopher Professor Humberto Maturana a similar question: "What compels us to question our lives, challenge our beliefs?"

"A conflict in our emotions," Professor Maturana replied. "Let us assume that the son of Manuel Contreras, the head of DINA, is being tortured. That could be the catalyst for Contreras to ask himself, 'What am I doing? What am I doing if my own son is being tortured? What am I doing?' But if the son is of no importance to him, there is no question. There is nothing for him to reflect on. There is no conflict. Everything is fine."

As I sat with Adolfo in the crowded food court, listening to his reasons for not testifying for our case, I wondered how he felt about what he was saying. Perhaps I could create some emotional conflict.

"But Adolfo," I said, when he had finished speaking, "if you felt that what happened was justified, why did you help us in 1973? Because you did."

"No, Zita, I didn't help you. Don't ever say that. I didn't."

"Yes, you did."

"No, Zita. I don't want you to think that I helped you. That's not what I did. I don't want you to repeat that to anyone."

"What do you want me to do, change my memories? Everyone I love knows about you."

"I would never betray my institution," Adolfo said. "If I disclose what I know happened in 1973, I would be betraying not only my institution, but my entire life: my family, my friends, the people who trained me, and the people whom I helped train."

I began to see a challenge. "Loyalty requires you to ignore crimes?" I asked. "To ignore injustices? Is that what you are saying? Don't you think that the people who committed the crimes betrayed your institution, and that you are protecting them? Don't you think it's your responsibility to defend the honor of the institution you love and make public the names of those who dishonored it?"

"The responsibility to speak out lies in those who committed the crimes," said Adolfo, avoiding my eyes. "They should say, 'Yes, I did this; yes, I gave the order to do such and such.' It is not my responsibility to do it."

"How does speaking the truth make you disloyal to your institution? Don't you feel any responsibility toward the truth? If we hide the truth, how could our children, humanity at large, make better moral choices in the future?"

"You will never understand that kind of commitment. That kind of loyalty."

"I want to understand."

"Loyalty goes two ways," Adolfo said. "When it doesn't work one way, it doesn't mean the others have to be disloyal. For example, if I know you committed a crime, you've been disloyal, not me. You should be the one talking."

Adolfo seemed unlikely to change his mind. I was ready to let it go, until he said he was a devoted Catholic and that God played a larger role in his life than his family and military institution. Having been raised as a Catholic, I understood.

"Don't you think God would expect you to do something when you witness a crime or an injustice being committed, no matter who commits the crime?"

"Zita, please, don't go there," Adolfo said. "I see the contradictions. I have plenty of conflicts within myself."

"I will honor that." We changed the subject. "In 1973, when you came to my house, I told you that on October 17 I looked for you everywhere," I said. "I couldn't find you. You explained that you were guarding the bodies. Did somebody assign you to it?"

"Of course somebody assigned me. Mayor Enriotti ordered me to do it."

"Were you alone?"

"No, Enriotti and Morales were with me all day long." Adolfo described guarding the bodies at the *predio*, a vacant military facility in Copiapó.

"Were they killed there?"

"No, of course not. They were killed at *Cuesta Cardones*. They loaded the bodies on the truck after they killed them and brought the truck to the *predio*."

"So the bodies were in the truck all day on October 17?"

"Yes."

"Did you see the bodies?"

"Why are you asking?" Adolfo asked, narrowing his eyes.

I hesitated. "Can you tell me about the condition of the bodies, how they were killed?"

"That's morbid," Adolfo said.

I changed the subject. An hour later, I asked Adolfo if he knew Victor Bravo, whom I considered a key witness.

"Yes," he said. "He worked at the civil registry in Copiapó."

"I read that he took the fingerprints of the victims before the military buried them," I said, tentatively. "Do you know exactly when they were buried?"

"That same night of the seventeenth."

"After you left?"

"I don't think I told you this before," Adolfo said, "but I drove the truck to the cemetery. Captain Patricio Diaz ordered Morales to do it. I was getting ready to go home, but Morales was in such a state of shock that he couldn't do it. He couldn't drive a truck loaded with thirteen bodies. Just to get the truck out of the *predio*, we had to cross a narrow bridge. Morales was afraid to miss the bridge, so I got into the truck and asked him to move over. I drove the truck and followed the military jeep driven by Captain Diaz to the cemetery. We entered the cemetery through the back gate. I got out of the truck, gave the keys to Morales, and left. I wanted nothing to do with what was happening."

At the time of the Caravan of Death killings, the military and government had carefully created a paper trail to support the false report they were publishing about the massacre in Copiapó. The military held all the power in 1973; their actions would have been legal under Pinochet's rule, but they seemed to make a real effort to document events in a way that would support their claims. I believe they did this to protect themselves from any possible future legal action. With this in mind, I asked Adolfo about the cryptogram that Mayor Enriotti had written to the commander of La Serena's garrison, informing him of a prisoner transfer from Copiapó. I had found the cryptogram in the documents from the Vicariate that my cousin Irene had sent me.

"Enriotti is a sinister man," Adolfo replied. "After the truck left the garrison with the prisoners, Enriotti asked me to send the cryptogram to La Serena. I was ready to comply when he said, 'Don't do it yet.' Minutes later, we heard the sound of the gunshots being fired from *Cuesta Cardones*. At that moment, Enriotti said, 'Don't bother—don't send it.' It was then that I drank a bottle of *pisco* and walked toward Winston's house to tell Veronica that Winston had been killed. I know she didn't believe me because I was drunk. It was about 1:30 a.m. Already October 17."

Adolfo and I talked in the food court until nearly 10:00 p.m. Shortly before leaving, he said, "Zita, you should stop doing what you are doing. Don't you realize that since the moment you set foot in this country, you have been followed? If you don't worry about your own safety, do it for your sons. This is their country, too. You are placing them at risk. Don't you want them to visit Chile and be safe? Stop doing this, for *them*."

I looked into Adolfo's blue eyes and then thought of my father who, more than anything, had wanted a better world for his children. I wanted that for my children, too, and I knew that remaining silent after human rights atrocities would make that an impossibility.

"But Adolfo," I said, "I am doing this for them. I'm doing this for my sons."

Back at the hotel Shawn asked hopefully, "Did Adolfo agree to meet me?"

"No."

Shawn looked disappointed. I felt somewhat guilty for discussing unrelated issues with Adolfo instead of talking directly about the lawsuit, but I was grateful to have been able to ask my own questions. I lay awake that night thinking about everything Adolfo had said. During our conversation, I had told Adolfo that when Captain Patricio Diaz testified in response to Judge Guzmán's summons in October 1998, all he had said was, "I don't remember anything from that time."

"He should use this opportunity to clean up his conscience," Adolfo had replied. "I believe that the only way to know the truth of any events that took place during those years is for those who participated in them to feel the need to speak. If they feel the need to do it, they should do it. If Diaz speaks up, it would help him. It would help him unload his conscience. Because it's one thing to receive an order to execute prisoners. It's quite another to do it the way they chose to do it, to massacre them."

I had stared at Adolfo then. Never before had I heard him use the word "massacre" in connection with my brother's killing.

What do you know? I thought.

TWENTY FOUR

The next evening, Shawn and I met my *new* Chilean lawyers—Gonzalo Figueroa and son—at a fancy restaurant in downtown Santiago. When the waiter came to our table, I ordered *reineta*, an inexpensive fish that is delicious cooked with butter in a skillet.

"Why are you ordering *reineta*?" demanded Figueroa Senior, frowning.

"I like it."

"Waiter," he commanded, "bring her *corvina*."

Figueroa's patronizing manner annoyed me, but we were in such an elegant restaurant that I felt uncomfortable speaking up. As we discussed the lawsuit and events surrounding Wito's death, Shawn and I quickly realized that the Figueroas did not know the specifics of our case.

"According to our sources, it is quite possible that your brother was killed at the garrison at midday," Figueroa told me. "You should be open to considering this new information."

"I know they were not," I said.

"Don't be stubborn, Zita," chided Figueroa Junior, who looked to be in his early thirties.

The conversation wore on through dinner. Finally the plates were cleared and a waitress approached our table with a tray of beautiful desserts.

"Take them away!" Figueroa commanded.

Over coffee, the Figueroas repeated General Arellano's well-worn argument: that Arellano had had nothing to do with the Caravan of

Death killings, and the officers who accompanied him in the helicopter—Marcelo Moren, Sergio Arredondo, and Armando Fernandez—had acted behind his back, killing prisoners while Arellano was holding private meetings with local commanders.

I had heard this many times before. Now, coming from the lawyers who were supposed to be interested in helping our case, it infuriated me.

"General Arellano, the highest-ranking officer in his group, a general from a disciplined hierarchical institution like the army, wants us to believe that he *never* learned that every time his helicopter landed in a city, a number of prisoners were killed?" I asked. "That lower-ranking officers overstepped his authority, killing prisoners at random how many times? In how many cities? How many victims? And the poor guy never learned that his subordinates were killing people behind his back?"

Figueroa and his son glared at me across the table, and suddenly I knew: through the Figueroas, Arellano's lies had wormed their way back to Nicole. The Figueroas had arranged for Nicole to meet with Arellano's lawyers while she was in Chile, and upon her return she had written in a memorandum to our legal team:

"Arellano's pleading to the Chilean court suggests that Manuel Contreras may have put his own people into the *Caravana* to do the dirty work and smear Arellano…Arellano Stark, who had been an extremely popular general, was put into his position as the leader of the *Caravana* by Pinochet in order to make him dirty…Given Pinochet's penchant for removing his competition, killing Generals Rene Schneider, Carlos Prats Gonzalez, and nearly assassinating Bernardo Leighton this is not an unreasonable conclusion."

Figueroa Senior began describing the actions he and his son had taken to locate witnesses for our lawsuit. "We *found* Veronica," he bragged. "Winston's wife."

"You *found* her?" I asked, suppressing a smile. "That's nice."

"Have you spoken with her?" he persisted. "You should."

"I will. Thank you!"

I was, of course, already in contact with my sister-in-law and had been the one to arrange the Figueroas' meeting with Veronica in the first place. Shawn shot me a questioning look. Unaware, Figueroa boasted that he had recently phoned Commander Haag: "I called him 'General' instead of calling him 'Commander.' This way I make him feel more important. *These* people like that."

Figueroa and son promised to arrange meetings in the coming week so we could talk with Oscar Haag; Haag's former assistant, Enrique Vidal: and investigative journalist Patricia Verdugo. They also said they knew a private detective who could help locate a few other witnesses from my list, and we agreed to pay for his services.

Finally, our evening with the Figueroas ended. Shawn and I caught a taxi outside the restaurant and shut the car door with a sigh of relief. As we rode back to the hotel, Shawn teased, "How was your fish, Zita?"

TWENTY FIVE

The next morning, Shawn and I flew to Copiapó and met with two former political prisoners: Eddie Fúnez and Julio Hernández. Julio had seen Wito at Haag's office the day he was taken prisoner, and now he had arranged for Shawn and me to meet with Victor Bravo, the civil registry official who had fingerprinted the thirteen victims in Copiapó. Julio, Eddie, Shawn, and I ordered drinks and chatted in the hotel lobby as we waited for Victor to arrive.

At 5:00 p.m., we were still waiting. We called Victor's house but there was no answer, and as we sat in the hotel lobby wondering what to do next, Julio mentioned that Victor Bravo never spoke to anyone about the night of October 17, 1973. Although Victor had been summoned to testify several times, he had never shown up until the judge issued an order for his arrest. Only then had he appeared in court to give a very brief testimony.

We were having no luck reaching Victor, so I asked Julio and Eddie to drive us out to the house of Juan Morales, the soldier Adolfo had told me about who had been emotionally unable to drive the truck to the cemetery after the thirteen prisoners were killed. In Morales's brief testimony, he had told the judge, "I saw Fernandez Larios at the garrison in Copiapó reviewing the files of the political prisoners the night the helicopter arrived, although I didn't know why he was reviewing them."

We drove to the outskirts of Copiapó, getting lost a few times before finally finding Morales's house at the top of a steep hill in a poor, isolated neighborhood. I knocked on the front door and asked to see Mr. Morales, but the young woman who answered said no one by that name lived in the house.

I insisted.

Morales's wife came to the door, and I told her I was from the United States and wanted to speak with Mr. Morales about his testimony to Judge Guzmán. I explained about our lawsuit against Armando Fernandez.

Mrs. Morales looked frightened. "He is not here," she said; she then changed her mind. "He is sleeping. He has been drinking. He is in no condition to see you."

"If you don't mind, I can come back later. At what time do you think he will be awake?"

"I'm not sure. Afterward he will go out to work."

"I know he drives a taxi. Where can I find him later?"

"I don't know."

"When does he get back home?"

"Around 10:30 p.m."

"Would you please tell him that I really want to speak with him, so I'll be back between 10:30 and 11:00?"

"Why don't you come back tomorrow?"

"Unfortunately, I'm leaving tomorrow. I'll see you later tonight." I shook Mrs. Morales's hand and hurried back to the car.

At 6:00 p.m., we got Victor Bravo on the phone. He apologized for being unable to meet in Copiapó and agreed to meet us at 7:15 p.m. at a restaurant in downtown Caldera. Julio, Shawn, and I arrived early and ordered tea while we waited.

At 7:30 p.m., we started calling Victor Bravo's house. Shawn and Julio looked tired.

"Let's wait until 8:30," I told them. I called Victor's house every five minutes until finally at 8:15 p.m. he answered.

"Let's meet at my office in fifteen minutes," he said.

Shawn, Julio, and I took a taxi to the address he gave us, and at 8:30 p.m. a white truck pulled up in front of the building. A small man with a creased face and long gray mustache got out, and as we shook hands, I was surprised by the gentleness in his eyes. I had heard that his wife supported Pinochet and had just assumed that Victor Bravo was a *Pinochista* as well. I had even worried that he had been toying with us by making appointments and not showing up. But something in his demeanor told me that Victor Bravo was a man to be trusted.

As we followed Victor through the dark, empty building to his office, I asked Shawn if she wanted to question him.

"No, Zita, you do it," she said.

Victor snapped on a light and pulled a chair over to the coffee table in the center of his office. I sat on the floor facing him and pulled a notebook and folder from my purse. Victor told me that he already knew about our lawsuit.

"I read your testimony to Judge Guzmán," I said. "In fact, I have a copy of it here with me."

Victor nodded.

"Would you want to tell me about your experience of the night of October 17, 1973?"

"I knew Winston," he said quietly. "A fine young man. I don't give testimonies to anyone. I don't like the abuse many people make of these tragedies. I want to protect the dignity of the victims. But I'm familiar with your work. I saw your documentary. I read about your lawsuit. I'm willing to speak with you. I hope my testimony will help.

"On Wednesday, October 17, a military jeep came to my house around 7:00 p.m. The soldiers in charge of the operation ordered me to get into the jeep. I asked where they were taking me. They ignored my question. They drove me to the garrison, leaving me there, seated in a corner in a large room for at least four hours. No one ever came to tell me why I was there.

"Close to midnight, an officer came to fetch me and ordered me to follow him. Once again, I was instructed to get into a military jeep. When they started driving away, I thought they were taking me outside the city to kill me. A few days earlier, somebody had broken into my office and stolen some passports. I reported the incident to the military authorities. I thought they were going to kill me as reprisal for losing the passports. When the jeep turned in the direction of the cemetery, I calmed down.

"They opened the back gate of the cemetery and drove the jeep inside," Victor continued, his voice shaking. "They parked the jeep beside a truck. I saw a few people walking around. It was dark. I couldn't distinguish their faces. Many of them knew me because they greeted me by my name. Once inside, I summoned enough courage to ask, 'Why did you bring me here?' At that moment they turned the lights of the truck on and, pointing to the ground, said, 'For this.'"

Victor's eyes filled with tears, and as he wiped them away his hand trembled. "A night that seems like yesterday," he said.

Occasionally, I interrupted with a question. We both avoided talking about my brother. "When I finished, I was instructed never to speak to anyone about what I saw," Victor said quietly. "'If you don't want to be number fourteen,' they said."

We talked until after 10:00 p.m., and then we all walked outside and stood together in silence. Unable to express the immensity of my gratitude, I embraced Victor Bravo.

"You are great at asking questions," Shawn said in the taxi. "Adam would have had a tantrum hearing you."

All the way back to Copiapó, I felt nauseous. Even so, I asked Julio to give our taxi driver directions to Juan Morales's house.

"You're not planning to go to Morales?" asked Shawn and Julio.

"Yes, I am."

"Are you sure, Zita?" Shawn asked. "It will be almost midnight when we get there."

"I'm sure."

"You know Zita, we don't have to go."

"I know we don't have to," I said. "But *I* have to."

Morales's house was dark when we arrived. Two large men stood outside guarding the property. As I was getting out of the taxi, Shawn asked if I wanted company.

"Yes, please," I said. I wanted a *gringa* as my bodyguard. We walked toward the house.

"What do you want?" a guard demanded.

"This is Shawn Roberts, a lawyer from the United States, and I'm Zita. We came to see Mr. Juan Morales."

"He can't see you."

"He is expecting us," I said, struggling to keep my voice from shaking. "I spoke earlier with his wife and she told me it would be okay to come back."

"He is in no condition to see you."

"Is he home?"

"He is home, but unable to see you."

"Why?"

"He is inebriated," the guard said. "He has been drinking."

"Let her in," called a woman from inside the house. The guards moved aside, and when Shawn and I walked into the living room, a young man in a suit introduced himself as Mr. Morales's lawyer.

"This is *my* lawyer," I said. "Shawn Roberts from the United States, and I'm Zita."

"No, my client can't speak with you," the lawyer said, after I told him what we wanted. "He has already testified to a Chilean judge and you are interfering with Chilean law."

Shawn was explaining that we were not violating any law, just asking for voluntary testimonies, when suddenly Juan Morales walked into the room looking like someone had just roused him out of bed. He squinted at us through bloodshot eyes and then slumped into a chair, his head hanging down.

Instinctively, I felt it was too threatening to give my full name, so I introduced Shawn and myself in the same way as before: I was just "Zita." Somehow I felt that if I said my name was Cabello, people might be afraid to talk to me because of all that had happened. Instead of opening doors, my name might close them.

Morales said that with Judge Guzmán's investigation still open, he was not legally allowed to testify in any other case. I explained that nothing prevented him from giving a voluntary testimony. "The only thing we want is for you to tell us exactly what you said to the judge," I said. "That you 'saw Fernandez the evening of October 16 reviewing the prisoners' folders at the garrison.' That's all we need from you."

Morales's attitude changed slightly. Unfortunately his lawyer noticed it, too, and quickly said, "As your lawyer, and your friend, I advise you not to testify." The lawyer turned to me. "You have no idea what you are doing. You do not know how much we have suffered in this country. Why don't you stop bothering people with your questions and your thirst for revenge and go back to where you came from? Don't you realize how much pain you bring to people by reviving the past? Don't you think it's time for you to forget and forgive? As a country we want to focus on the future. Get over it. Leave."

We left.

It was past midnight when Shawn and I got back to my friends' house where we were staying. Steaks, rice, and raw mushrooms were set out on the kitchen counter for our dinner. Discouraged by our lack of success with Morales, I sat on the kitchen table and watched Shawn cook the mushrooms. She began kidding around. "I'm Zita," she mimicked.

I had to laugh. I could see how weird it must have seemed for me to keep saying, "This is my lawyer. I'm Zita." Shawn started laughing, and then we could not stop. We ended up under the kitchen table, covering our mouths with our hands, and trying not to disturb our hosts with our uncontrollable laughter.

The next morning, Shawn and I held a press conference about our case at the Copiapó cemetery. Then we flew to Santiago, where we tried calling the Figueroas from our hotel room to see if they had arranged the meetings they had promised with Haag and Vidal. After two hours we gave up and went out, instead, to meet with some Chilean human rights lawyers I knew: Eduardo Contreras, Carmen Hertz, and Hiram Villagra. Later that night, we went to an elegant restaurant in bohemian Barrio Bellavista to meet with human rights lawyers Hugo Gutierrez and Adil Brokvoic. When the waiter came to our table, I ordered *reineta*.

"Good choice," Hugo said.

Each lawyer asked the same question that night: "Zita, why did you choose Gonzalo Figueroa as your lawyer? You knew all along that we were willing to help you."

The next morning, Shawn reached Figueroa Junior by phone.

"Haag seemingly changed his mind and Vidal is out of town," she told me, after hanging up with him, "though the private investigator will call me later to confirm."

Something was not adding up. I did not believe anything the Figueroas were telling us, but Shawn seemed so hopeful about meeting Haag and Vidal that I kept my suspicions to myself.

Secretly I was worried. We only had one day left in Chile to find the information we needed.

TWENTY SIX

The next morning a journalist from *El Mercurio* interviewed Shawn and me about our case, and then invited us to stay and use her office phone and computer. As Shawn waited for a call from the private detective, I flipped through my phone book, searching for someone useful to call. I saw a number and hesitantly dialed.

"I'm not sure if I have the right number," I told the man who answered the phone, "but I would like to speak with Commander Oscar Haag."

"You have the wrong number."

"I'm sorry," I said, somewhat relieved.

"My neighbor across the hall is Mr. Haag's daughter," the man continued. "She lives in apartment B with her husband and son. I live in apartment A."

"Did you say that across from your apartment supposedly lives Mr. Haag's daughter?"

"I didn't say supposedly. I said she *lives* across the hall."

"I'm so sorry. Would it be possible for you to give me the address?"

Hardly believing my luck, I rushed to the lobby to buy a thank-you card and wrote Haag a quick note requesting a meeting before 6:00 p.m. the following day. When I got back to the journalist's office, Shawn was still waiting for the private detective to call.

"Let's go drop off this card at Haag's daughter's house," I said.

Soon Shawn and I were standing in front of apartment B. "Sorry to bother you, sir, but I have this letter for Mr. Oscar Haag," I told the man who answered the door. "Would it be possible to ask you to deliver it to him? It's very important that he gets it tonight."

"Why the hurry?" asked the man, inviting us in. I introduced Shawn as my friend and said we lived in the United States and were going home the next day, but that I wanted to thank Mr. Haag personally for a favor he had granted me many years earlier.

"That's the hurry," I said, smiling.

"Why don't you deliver it yourself?" The man surprised me by writing Haag's address on a piece of paper and handing it to me. As Shawn and I were leaving, the man asked, "When and where did you meet him?"

"It was in Copiapó, in 1973."

The man blanched.

"He really did help me," I said quickly, trying to put him at ease.

Thirty minutes later, Shawn and I stepped out of a taxi into a quiet, wealthy neighborhood and stood in front of the fence surrounding Oscar Haag's house. Bright flowers crowded Haag's beautiful garden. Fragrant roses, all in bloom, climbed the locked gate. We stood for a minute, taking it all in, and then I rang the bell.

"What is this all about?" shouted an older man, rushing out of the house.

Shawn and I exchanged glances. Haag's son-in-law had obviously called.

"Mr. Haag?" I said loudly as he walked toward us.

Oscar Haag did not answer. He opened his gate and ushered us quickly into the bright garden, staggering slightly as he led us into the house.

I had not seen Oscar Haag since 1973, when I had asked him to spare Pato from Chacabuco. Now, in ordinary clothing instead of his military uniform, standing in his living room near a table beautifully set for tea, he seemed somehow smaller.

Haag invited us to sit on the sofa, then jumped up from his chair and rushed to the kitchen, bringing us Cokes, then glasses, then ice, then napkins. Everything about Oscar Haag was moving very fast. He seemed unable to sit still. Finally, he sank into a large chair near the sofa, breathing heavily as sweat ran down his forehead.

"I'm the sister of Winston Cabello and the wife of Patricio Barrueto," I said, introducing myself as I had in 1973.

"This is the first time a family member from Copiapó has come to speak with me," said Haag, wiping his brow.

"I understand from what Mr. Gonzalo Figueroa told us that you agreed to meet us, but later changed your mind…"

"I don't know what you are talking about," Haag interrupted.

"Didn't you speak with a lawyer named Gonzalo Figueroa a few days ago?"

"No."

"How about the first week of September?" I faltered. "Didn't you speak with Mr. Figueroa regarding a meeting with a lawyer from the United States named Nicole, in connection to a lawsuit my family has against Armando Fernandez in Miami for Winston's death?"

"I haven't spoken with any lawyer whatsoever," Haag said, "let alone agreed to meet anyone."

I did not know what to say. Wanting to put Haag at ease, I thanked him for the kindness he had shown Pato and me nearly thirty years earlier. Haag had not forgotten. He even remembered Pato's black-framed glasses and dark curly hair. I was amazed.

Haag gestured passionately as he spoke, trying to convince me that the military coup had saved Chile and blaming political leaders for breaking the Chilean tradition of military nonintervention. "The same people who run the country today beseeched us to topple President Allende," he said, his face flushing deep red. "And those same people today feel they have the moral authority to prosecute us."

I listened respectfully. That did not mean I agreed with him.

As Shawn and I sat in Oscar Haag's living room, drinking Cokes and listening to his explanations, I felt keenly aware that the man in front of me had personally detained my brother and organized thirteen prisoners' deaths in Copiapó. But Haag had also spared Pato's life by sending him into internal exile rather than Chacabuco and had moved us again at my request to be near my ailing father.

How can I sit here with a man who bears so much responsibility for my brother's brutal murder? I wondered. Yet there I was, politely saying, "I'm here to learn the truth, not to judge you."

These words seemed to shock Oscar Haag; a family member of one of Copiapó's victims was approaching him in a nonaccusatory way. Disarmed, he spoke a truth that he had concealed from everyone, even from Judge Guzmán: "General Arellano wantonly selected his thirteen victims. Armed with a red-ink pen, General Arellano and Pedro Espinoza went over the names of people who were detained in Copiapó, approximately seventy people, making a red mark beside certain names. I didn't know at the moment that the red mark meant a death sentence but in less than three hours, General Arellano decided who was fit to live or die."

Oscar Haag shook violently as he spoke. Whatever truth was buried in his body seemed to be forcing its way out. "Arellano kept passing notes to his henchmen, Arredondo, Moren, and Fernandez, who burst into the room where we were meeting from time to time. I don't know what was written in those notes. The meeting ended around 10:00 p.m. It was then that General Arellano ordered me to organize the logistics for the killings. Without explanation, Arellano handed me a handwritten list with the names of the thirteen prisoners selected for execution, shouting, 'All these people must be eliminated at once.'" Haag added that as the thirteen prisoners were being removed from the garrison, General Arellano had invited him for a late supper at the Diego Rivera Hotel.

"General Arellano has said repeatedly he had nothing to do with the killings. Is that his alibi?" I asked.

"He is a coward," Haag said. "Shame on him for blaming others for the cowardice of his actions. Shame on him for not taking responsibility for the wrongdoings he caused. And shame on him for expecting others to pay for his crimes."

I explained to Haag that I had read his testimony to the judge, and then asked, "Would you be willing to go to Miami to testify in our case against Fernandez?"

Haag was silent.

"I gave the order to bury the bodies in a mass grave," he said, finally. "It was my decision. I take responsibility for that. I followed wartime's modus operandi. In times of war, bodies can be buried in mass graves."

Could it be that you were afraid that if we saw the bodies, we would uncover the lies you told us? I thought. *That instead of dying in an escape attempt, the prisoners were viciously killed? That we would discover the massacre committed that night?*

I repeated my request.

"What happens if I say the wrong thing?" Haag asked, visibly upset. "This is the United States where you are asking me to testify." He said that only muddled details of those events now existed in his mind. I knew he was not telling the entire truth.

Haag refused to testify.

If I can't convince him to testify, I'll settle for answers to some of my questions, I thought. I said, "I found it hard to believe that you didn't know Arellano's reason for reviewing the prisoners' folders. How could you have not known that prisoners under your custody were going to be killed?"

"I had an inkling."

"But you did nothing."

"Arellano showed me a document, signed by Pinochet, that rendered me powerless," Haag said.

"A document that nobody seems to have a copy of."

"You must understand, this was 1973," he said. "We didn't have photocopy machines in our offices as we have today. Arellano showed me the document. I read it, then he put it back in his briefcase."

"He ordered you to murder people. You knew it was an illegal order, wasn't it?"

Haag was silent.

"You could have refused."

"I had no choice."

I stopped then. Haag was a man shackled by guilt. Yet he seemed to want to redeem himself and hinted at more truths. He said that Arellano had brought a list from Santiago with names of people he wanted to eliminate. "'Where is Hagel? Why is his name not included in the list of prisoners?' Arellano demanded, reading from a piece of paper he had in his hand. That saved Hagel," Haag said. Dr. Leonardo Hagel, a socialist and well-known congressman for the Atacama-Coquimbo region, was traveling outside the country at the time of the coup, so Haag could not detain him. Since Arellano was unaware that Hagel was outside the country, his name was included on the list of people he specifically planned to kill.

"What other names did Arellano bring?"

Haag shrugged his shoulders. "I don't know."

"Were there other names?"

"Yes. I know it because Arellano and Espinoza kept going back and forth, checking this piece of paper they had in their hands with the names of prisoners I provided him." From Adolfo we had learned that Arellano came to Copiapó with five names of people already selected to be killed. We always wondered if my brother's name was included on that list.

I could tell that Haag was making an effort to answer my questions as truthfully as he thought he could. He would not discuss Diaz, Ojeda, and Marambio, the officers in Copiapó who had participated in the killings, but he did mention his former assistant, Enrique Vidal. He said, "I spoke with Vidal a couple of days ago. He wanted me to know that he testified to the judge, and that he spoke the truth."

"Did he say anything about Mr. Figueroa contacting him?"

"I don't think they had called him. He would have told me."

Suddenly I realized who Enrique Vidal, Haag's former assistant, must be: the tall blond officer who had helped me speak with Commander Haag in 1973. "Can you give me Vidal's contact information?"

"No, I can't."

Haag and I talked for a long time, with Shawn looking on. At one point, I gave him a letter I had once written but never sent to him, expressing my gratitude for agreeing not to send Pato to Chacabuco. Haag sat reading each sentence to himself, then looking up and responding rapidly to what he had just read, then looking back down and reading the next sentence silently to himself. Haag wanted to keep talking, but finally I ended the conversation. As we walked out of the house and through his bright garden, Oscar Haag stopped at a rosebush near the fence. He cut an exquisite rose, the color of deep sunset, and offered it to me. I accepted the rose.

Then he got his car out of the garage and drove us to the Metro station, talking mostly about the driving conditions and scenery we passed. When Shawn and I got back to our hotel room around 6:00 p.m., I collapsed on my bed, exhausted.

A few minutes later the phone rang. The Figueroas' private detective was on the line, saying that he had been waiting all day for news of a possible meeting with Vidal, Haag, or other potential witnesses. Shawn bluntly replied that we had just met with Haag. The line went dead. The private detective never called back.

The next day, Shawn and I flew back to San Francisco. I arrived home so exhausted that I went straight to bed, and I had barely enough energy the next day for teaching.

TWENTY SEVEN

In October 1999, Shawn and Nicole came to San Mateo to meet my mother. As I waited for them at my house, I reread Nicole's memo detailing her findings in Chile. A few statements disturbed me, particularly regarding Nicole's interview with a former political prisoner, whom I understood she had met through Señor Figueroa. This former prisoner had given a bizarre account of the events in Copiapó, which Nicole summarized for our team:

>About midday on that day (October 16th or 17th), the prisoners began to be removed from the cells. Winston Cabello was taken out, maybe between noon and 2 o'clock. They never saw any of the prisoners return. Sometime much later that evening, at midnight or maybe very early in the morning, soldiers that they had never seen before, who he described as wearing battle dress, being fully armed (probably with grenades and side-arms), and wearing black berets came in and said that everybody had to get out. They gave him a hard time because he had a mattress on his bunk. Everyone who was ordered out was required to wear whatever they were wearing to sleep in. So, if they slept in no clothes they went outside naked.

Pato, who had seen the officers take the thirteen prisoners from the garrison sleeping quarters, could not make sense of the man's testimony. I contacted our lawyer friend Hugo Gutierrez to ask what he knew about this former prisoner.

"This particular person has *problems* that make him an unreliable source," Hugo said politely. "You are not considering him as a witness?"

"No, of course not," I said. "I just wanted to know who he was and how in the *hell* Nicole got to speak with him."

"It has to be from your new Chilean lawyers. They have shown keen ability to contact *trustworthy* sources like Arellano," Hugo said, sarcastically.

My frustration increased when Nicole dismissed several testimonies—including Pato's—that I considered important. When I expressed concern about questionable testimonies like that of the former prisoner in her memo, she replied, "You don't know what happened in 1973. That's what we are doing, we are finding out the truth."

I was speechless. Nicole's words felt like an assault on our memories. It is one thing to piece together the truth; it is quite another to replace memories with an entirely different story.

TWENTY EIGHT

Months passed. Our lawsuit's momentum began to slow.

Shawn and I rarely spoke. Lito stopped calling for weekly updates, and when he did call, I had nothing new to report.

Our case was stagnating.

In October 2000, a year after Shawn and Nicole met my mother, I asked Shawn to call a meeting with our entire legal team to discuss the lack of new investigation for our lawsuit. Unfortunately for my family, CJA was busy. Their case against the Salvadoran generals had gone to trial that summer, and Shawn found it difficult to stay current on Wito's case, as well. During our phone conversation, Shawn mentioned a lawyer in Florida who had been working with CJA on the Salvadoran case and had expressed some interest in joining our lawsuit.

"You should meet him," Shawn said. "His name is Bob Kerrigan. I think you will like him."

I told her I would like to meet him, but that we needed to immediately call a meeting with our legal team. "We have problems. We can't pretend that everything is fine anymore."

Without giving details, Shawn confided that there were some problems at CJA, and she had been asked to leave by the beginning of 2001. "Beth will be temporarily in charge of CJA until they hire a new lawyer to replace me," Shawn said.

My world began to fall apart.

In Search of Spring

In mid-November, I asked Beth to arrange a meeting with our lawyers at CJA and WSGR so my family could discuss the problems we were having with the way Wito's case was being handled. Then I asked if she knew Bob Kerrigan and what she thought of him.

"He cracks me up," Beth said. "He wears cowboy boots."

"He has shown some interest in joining our case."

"He *has*?"

"Yes," I said. "Shawn has been in touch with him. He would like to come down to meet me."

Two months later, on January 18, 2001, Karin, Lito, and I took our seats at a conference table at WSGR, with our entire legal team. At the center of the room, the words "Cabello v. Fernandez Larios" stood starkly against the bright background of a projection screen.

Nicole rose from the table.

"This is what we will be covering in today's meeting," she said, striding to the center of the room. "One of our topics will be, 'Factual Overview of the Case.' Another, 'Investigation to Date.'"

I looked around the table, confused. This was not the meeting I had requested. *Shouldn't Beth and Shawn be the ones leading this discussion?* I thought. Across the conference table, Beth and Shawn seemed to be asking the same question.

"Factual Overview of the Case: Significant Events in Copiapó" flashed onto the screen, then:

General Arellano, and possibly other members of his team, met with Colonel Oscar Haag—we have no admissible evidence.

Members of General Arellano's team reviewed prisoners' files—we have no admissible evidence.

After killing the prisoners, the officers loaded their bodies onto a truck and drove them back to the regiment—we have no admissible evidence.

After midnight on the 17th, a group of soldiers directed Leonardo Meza to open the cemetery; they dug a mass grave and buried the 13 prisoners—we have no admissible evidence.

The soldiers directed civil registry official Victor Bravo to issue death certificates stating that the prisoners died from 'military execution'; Bravo fingerprinted the deceased prisoners by the light of the vehicles' headlamps and filled out the forms—we have no admissible evidence.

"Many witnesses have refused to be interviewed," Nicole said briskly. "Adolfo Gonzalez, Commander Oscar Haag, Enrique Vidal, Harry Shlauderman."

Who the hell is Harry Shlauderman? I thought.

"Adolfo's statement to Veronica indicates that he did not observe Fernandez's actions the night the prisoners were killed," Nicole continued.

Adolfo was drunk that night. What is wrong with her?

As Nicole reported what she had done, what she had discovered, and what she had concluded during her trip to Chile, her words piled up in my brain until I could no longer listen. I sank down in my chair, staring miserably at the table as I tried to summon the courage to make her stop. Seeking truth and justice for Wito's murder was a chance at hope for my family, a chance to honor Wito's memory and prove that he had spent his final moments in defiance and courage—not running away in an escape attempt as the military had reported.

As Nicole continued, I began to feel that our lawyers' *unwillingness* to review and incorporate the information I had provided had crossed the line of normality. My lawyers did not seem to want to know or understand Wito's story. Most of all, they did not seem to believe in it.

"We sent the tapes of the exhumations to Dr. Robert Kirshner, a well-known expert witness," Nicole said. "He examined the videotapes and issued a preliminary report. He found evidence of death by firing squad, no visible evidence of *corvo* wounds on Winston's body. No visible evidence that one of the victims was beaten to death."

I glanced at Lito and Karin and saw in their faces the same outrage and sorrow I felt. Wito's body, his pain, our memories—all treated with such disregard.

I sat up in my chair.

"I don't doubt Dr. Kirshner's expertise in his field, whatever that is," I said. "I'm not questioning his qualifications, but can anyone here please explain to me how somebody just by looking at images taken during an exhumation of bodies, buried for seventeen years in a mass grave, can arrive at those conclusions? Can anyone please explain to me here right now, how did he know which ones were Winston's remains just by looking at bones being exhumed?"

The lawyers looked startled. A proud, fleeting smile crossed Lito's face.

"Actually, those were my words," said Nicole, "not those of Dr. Kirshner."

Why is she misrepresenting Dr. Kirshner's conclusions? I thought, angrily. Then there was no stopping me.

"Have you read *any* of the thirteen forensic reports I provided you?" I demanded. "If you had taken the time to read them, you could have easily found out that *no one* was killed by firing squad—that under 'cause of death' my brother's forensic report reads: 'A thoracic trauma produced by a sharp object. No sign of gunshot wounds found on his body.'"

Nicole was silent.

"What did Veronica say to you?" I asked. "That Adolfo didn't see Fernandez the night Winston was killed? Adolfo was drunk that night. Nobody asked him about Fernandez or anybody in particular."

"Actually," Nicole said, "those were also my words."

"What made you conclude that, then?"

Nicole was silent.

Do you respect our loss? I wanted to scream. *Do you care to know about my brother? Do you care to know what happened to him the night he was killed? Does anyone here care about him?* Instead, I began, "Nicole, why did you say that Vidal and Haag refused to be interviewed when—"

"I was ready to meet them," Nicole interrupted. "Señor Figueroa made an appointment with them, but at the last minute they changed their mind."

Shawn and I looked at each other.

"The Figueroas never made an appointment with them," I said.

"That's not true."

"Shawn and I met with Haag," I told the legal team, ignoring Nicole. "I'm sure you all know that. I specifically asked Haag why he canceled his meeting with Nicole. Haag acted very surprised. 'I never received any phone call from any lawyer,' he said. I mentioned to him the name Figueroa. 'No,' he repeated. Haag was also sure that Vidal never received a call from the Figueroas either. For some reason, the Figueroas made Nicole believe they had called."

Leo Cunningham, the head lawyer at WSGR, looked thoughtful. "Why do you think they did that?"

"I don't know. I don't want to speculate. I only know they deceived Nicole. But we don't need them. We have a good, solid network of human rights lawyers in Chile who have been very supportive of our efforts, especially Hugo Gutierrez and Eduardo Contreras. From my point of view, *they* are our local lawyers, and we should work with them from now on."

"Zita," said Leo, kindly, "I had no idea that there were problems with the case until Beth called me. You should never be afraid to come to us to tell us about mistakes we are making or to discuss your concerns. We are your lawyers, this is your case, and we work for you. We want to make things better. Tell us, how can we do that?"

Instantly, the atmosphere changed. "First, we should be looking into Judge Guzmán's investigation to learn about the case," I said. "That is the best source of information there is so far, to learn what happened in connection to the killings of General Arellano and his death squad. We have squandered twenty-two volumes, more than twenty thousand pages, full of information and details unknown before, for no reason."

"We can't use Judge Guzmán's investigation because he doesn't ask specifically about Fernandez's involvement in the Caravan of Death," Nicole interrupted. "The judge doesn't ask questions like we do here in the United States, so the testimonies you have provided us are of no use to us."

Frustrated, I searched the faces around the conference table. "I'm not a lawyer, but I don't need to be one to understand the value of what we have in our possession. For one, we can identify possible witnesses that could testify for us. I already compiled a list of more than twenty-five potential witnesses who talked about Fernandez in their testimony to the judge. We can go to Chile, find these witnesses, and ask them if they can expand for us what they told the judge. Who knows? Maybe one of them witnessed Fernandez killing or torturing someone. There must be a reason why they mentioned him in their testimonies. A few of them specifically described Fernandez 'like Rambo,' taking prisoners from their detention facilities."

"We can't do that," Nicole said. "Our legal system does not allow us to do that."

"Why not?"

Nicole named some legal constraints, and said that since our case was about Winston, we needed to find witnesses from Copiapó: someone who had seen Fernandez take the prisoners and put them in the truck. "Our biggest challenge was to find reliable witnesses," she said. "We didn't find anyone."

"What do you mean we don't have witnesses?" I asked. "How about Enrique Vidal, Carlos Brito, Juan Morales, Iván Murúa? All of them from Copiapó. You think they are not good witnesses? Have you read their testimonies? You have all of them. Instead of concentrating only on Copiapó's events, why don't we also include the killings that took place in the other towns? If we are claiming that Fernandez is responsible for crimes against humanity, how can we do that with just Copiapó's events?"

"This case is about Winston. We can't use information from other places," Nicole kept repeating.

"If you [the legal team] look hard enough, maybe you will be able to find the legal answer," I insisted. "Why not try?"

Leo held up his hands to stop the bickering. "We need to discuss this further among ourselves."

The meeting was going nowhere. I was glad that Leo ended the discussion. As the meeting adjourned, I reminded Beth about Bob Kerrigan's interest in our case. Beth hesitated, and I knew why: CJA had just assigned a new young lawyer, Joshua, to replace Shawn in our case. Why would we want to bring in another lawyer?

I was determined. I wanted the lawyer with the cowboy boots. I sat up straight in my chair. Beth got the message.

"Bob Kerrigan, a lawyer from Florida, has shown interest in helping with Winston's case," she told the legal team.

"Bring him in," Leo said. "We need as much help as we can get."

After the meeting, Karin, Lito, and I talked for a while in the WSGR parking lot with Beth and Shawn.

"The entire case for Nicole rests on placing Fernandez in the proximity of the truck with the prisoners," Shawn said. "If we don't have a witness that saw Fernandez getting into the truck with the prisoners, Nicole doesn't believe we can prove Winston's case in court. My impression is this is going to be Nicole's way or no way."

Driving home that day, I realized two things. Under Nicole's direction, our legal team had expected to build the case with just one witness: Adolfo. And since Adolfo had refused to meet with Nicole, the lawyers had concluded that he was not even a *good* witness, and we therefore did not have a case.

In truth, I was very worried. The lawyers did not believe they had a case. Was there anything more I could do?

PART TWO

I am only one, but I am one.
I cannot do everything, but I can do something.
And because I cannot do everything, I will not refuse
to do the something that I can do.
—Edward Everett Hale

TWENTY NINE

After a few weeks of reflecting on our January 2001 meeting, I knew I was not ready to give up the case. I understood that Wito's case was difficult, that our lawyers' enthusiasm was waning, and that finding credible eyewitnesses was a tremendous challenge. I also knew that some major differences between the US and Chilean legal systems existed, and that the geographic distance between the two countries made it very difficult to progress. Most of all, the evidences and witnesses we needed belonged to a distant past.

Ironically, I felt encouraged by the fact that we faced tangible problems. With clear, identifiable issues to work through, I could better understand the problems our lawyers were dealing with, and this greatly restored my faith in them.

Our legal team sent the letter rogatory through the US Supreme Court, requesting Chilean judicial assistance in questioning General Arellano and his officers, Captain Diaz and Lieutenants Ojeda and Marambio. This took a great deal of time and effort, as we needed to follow strict international regulations to obtain information through official channels. We also had to ensure that our choice of witnesses made sense, and the legal teams on both sides needed to agree on each question that would be asked of witnesses.

I was surprised to learn that the men who had committed the crimes were on *our* list of proposed witnesses and that we would be asking each witness the exact same questions. I had assumed the interrogations would be tailored to each witness. When I asked about this, Nicole replied, "The letters rogatory are not a big deal. We might go to Chile to convince these witnesses to give voluntary testimony directly to us. In that case, we won't need the letters rogatory."

I realized that deposing witnesses outside the letters rogatory process would create its own set of challenges, so I invited the well-known Chilean human rights lawyer Hugo Gutierrez to come to the United States and answer any questions my lawyers might have. I asked Karin and Lito if they could help with travel expenses, and that afternoon Lito's friend Simon Guendelman offered to pay Hugo's plane ticket in full. Simon's twenty-four-year-old brother, Luis Alberto Guendelman, had been detained by the Chilean military on September 2, 1974. To this day, Luis remains disappeared.

A few weeks later, I met Hugo at the San Francisco airport. As soon as he was settled in our home, I gave him a copy of a document that I had sent to my lawyers the week before: a list of twenty people who had mentioned Fernandez in their testimonies to Judge Guzmán, along with a brief summary of each testimony. Hugo, a leading human rights lawyer in Chile, had worked extensively with Judge Guzmán, so I had assumed he would be familiar with each name I had collected. But as I sat with Hugo at the kitchen table, drinking coffee as he read through the document, I realized there were names on my list that even Hugo had never heard of.

"Do you think local commanders like the ones you have here—Castillo, Lapostol, Mena—would give voluntary testimony to your lawyers?" Hugo asked.

"I don't know. Somebody has to approach these witnesses. Only then will we know the answer."

"Who is going to do it?"

"Well, I thought you might know somebody," I said. "A lawyer? Maybe you?"

"Remember that even to this day, an important segment of the Chilean population disapproves of our quest for justice," Hugo said, frowning. "The armed forces in particular are uneasy with any investigations of human rights violations. We are unpopular with many people—so unpopular that some human rights lawyers are under police protection—especially Judge Guzmán, due to his ongoing investigation against Pinochet."

Hugo read the rest of the document and then said, "With the exception of a couple of former political prisoners you have here like Dr. Murúa and Mrs. Sánchez, the rest are military men. Those people won't talk to us. Even if they were not involved in any crime, their distrust is huge. Besides, we can't ignore their fear."

I asked about Haag's former assistant, Lieutenant Enrique Vidal.

"Vidal disappeared," Hugo said. "Vanished. Judge Guzmán's private detective has been unable to locate him. I can't think of anyone who can help. It's a huge undertaking."

We finished our coffee in silence.

"But you can do it, Zita," Hugo said, his face brightening. "I'll bet these people would talk to you."

"Do you think they would be open to talk to me?"

"More open with you than with us," he said, smiling. "Seriously, Zita, I can't think of a better person to do it."

My entire family visited with Hugo at dinner that night, and the next day he came to UC Santa Cruz, where he spoke to my class about Pinochet's legal proceedings in Chile. The next morning as we prepared for our meeting at WSGR, Hugo said he felt anxious about my lawyers' expectations and asked me to define "discovery phase" and "depositions," since Chilean civil lawsuits follow different legal procedures than those in the United States.

"'Discovery' is a period of time when the lawyers gather all kinds of evidence, including witnesses, to prove their cases," I explained. "I don't know the rules. But don't worry, I will ask the lawyers to brief you on these issues today."

At WSGR, I introduced Hugo to everyone at the conference table. Nicole and another lawyer, Ariana, were there from WSGR since Leo could not attend, and Jerry Gray was there with Shawn, who had come for her last meeting with CJA. Nicole announced that Fernandez's lawyer,

Steve Davis, had just agreed to a six-month extension on discovery and all pretrial dates, and she spoke excitedly about finding legal ways to deport Fernandez from the United States. "We can send him to Mexico and from there the Chilean government could ask for extradition."

Why is she doing this? I thought. *Here we have Hugo sitting in the meeting, an expert from Chile who has come specifically to talk about my brother's case, and Nicole is off on this deportation tangent, which has nothing to do with the case.*

"Can you do that?" Hugo asked.

"We don't know yet, but we should explore that possibility. Argentina could be a country that might be interested in Fernandez," Nicole said, referring to Fernandez's ties to the DINA's 1974 car-bombing assassination of former Chilean General Carlos Prats in Buenos Aires.

For the next two hours, the entire legal team talked excitedly about deportation. Hugo glanced at me several times, confused, and at that moment I knew nothing had changed. After all that time and effort, our legal team still did not think they could put together a winning case. They were giving up.

"Please," I whispered to Shawn, "let's talk about the case. That's why Hugo is here."

Shawn was silent.

Frustrated, I stood up and went to get a glass of water. Jerry Gray, who rarely attended our meetings, followed. "You should say something, Zita," he said. "Don't let her do this to you."

I had only myself to rely on. As the lawyers talked animatedly around me, I took my seat at the conference table, staring down in silence.

Finally, Shawn interrupted. "Zita wants to talk about the case."

"I'm sorry," Nicole said. "Deportation is my thing."

The lawyers began discussing the possibility of taking depositions in Chile, outside the letter rogatory. "From the point of view of Chilean law," Hugo said, "there is nothing that would preclude you from gathering voluntary testimonies through depositions. And in no way would that have any effect on the pending letter rogatory."

Our lawyers replied that since depositions were voluntary and would be taken outside the United States, they had no legal recourse to force anyone to testify: "Even if a witness decides to give us a sworn statement, we have no way to compel them to tell the entire truth. And if they lie, it carries no legal consequences for the witnesses."

"Do the testimonies gathered by letters rogatory carry the same problems?" Hugo asked.

"They carry the same problems," our lawyers said. "If Steve Davis agrees to depositions in Chile, we can go ahead with them. Obviously, we need his agreement. He needs to have the opportunity to go down to Chile to interrogate the witnesses, as well."

"I think pursuing witnesses outside the pending letters rogatory is a very good idea," Hugo said. "You can get better witnesses through that venue than, like, the one we have here. There is only one big problem: how to convince *these* people to agree to voluntary depositions." Hugo held up the list of twenty witnesses I had given him a few days earlier.

Our lawyers looked blank. No one had taken time to review the document I had sent the week before.

"If you get Commander Castillo Whyte, Rebolledo, even Jaña," said Hugo, reading a few names from the list, "you can nail Fernandez."

"Who is Castillo Whyte?" Nicole interrupted.

"He was the commander in Cauquenes. He testified to Judge Guzmán that Arellano ordered Armando Fernandez and Marcelo Moren to go to the jail to interrogate the four witnesses killed that day." Hugo read my summary of Castillo's testimony aloud, along with some other names from the list. Then he discussed what was bothering him most: the intense fear and distrust felt by everyone in Chile, particularly members of the armed forces, and the extreme difficulties that human rights lawyers faced in that country.

"This is a huge undertaking," Hugo said. Then he smiled. "Zita can do it."

The lawyers stared at me. A few frowned. "A plaintiff should never talk with witnesses," they said. "The defendant's lawyer might argue that you manipulated witnesses' testimonies, that you told them what to say. That could hurt us badly."

"What matters to me is the truth. I can't jeopardize that. So I assure you, that if I undertake this mission, I would never, *ever*, suggest to anyone to lie. I will defend the truth to the end," I said, looking around the table. "Do we have any other alternative?"

The lawyers were silent.

"If we want to keep moving forward with my brother's case, we have to take chances," I said. "Why not take this one?"

No one answered.

"In order to minimize the defendant's misrepresentation of my involvement, why don't you teach me what *not* to say?" I asked. "You can give me some guidelines as to how I should approach a witness."

The lawyers said I was not the right person for the job. But the more they argued, the more I knew I was. The thought of tracking down witnesses in Chile terrified me. I knew how difficult it would be and I was afraid to fail. But I also knew that giving up would be more devastating than failing. If I stopped trying, if I stopped imagining a way to find the truth, I would never forgive myself.

Finding credible witnesses was our only obstacle to moving forward with the lawsuit. Someone had to do it. Now I knew it was up to me.

Two weeks later, Bob Kerrigan flew his plane out from Florida to meet me. "I'm pretty sure the two of you will hit it off quite well," Shawn said. "No pressure. You need to meet him first. Then *you* decide if you want him on the case or not."

All I really knew about Bob was that he liked to wear cowboy boots and had won the first and largest civil judgment in US history against the tobacco industry. At the train station, he was easy to spot: a tall, pale, white-haired man with sharp green eyes and a genuine smile. Bob wore a sports jacket and carried a briefcase, but he moved with the natural ease of a cowboy. I forgot to check for boots.

Pato and I spent the afternoon talking with Bob at our house. I had gotten so used to lawyers' questions that Bob's third question did not surprise me. "No," I replied. "Winston did not belong to the Communist Party."

"Even so, I would have requested a change of location of the trial," Bob said. "Miami is not the best place to try this case. You are going to end up with Cuban jurors. That poses a potential problem. Winston worked for President Allende, a justifiable reason for them to acquit Fernandez, even if you prove he is a criminal."

I could see Bob's point. President Allende had not been a communist, but the coalition of political parties (ranging from center to extreme left) that had supported him included the Communist Party. To this day, people talk about the "Communist government of President Allende," which seems somehow to make it easier for them to justify the coup.

We discussed what Ximena had told me in 1974. "I don't doubt the truthfulness of Ximena's story," I told Bob. "I know it's true. I knew my brother well. I have no difficulty picturing him confronting Fernandez, defying him, saying, 'You have to kill me here; I won't run.' That was my brother. That was his uncompromising nature. He wouldn't want anyone to think or believe that he was killed because he tried to escape. I understand the difficulties in proving that Fernandez was the one who killed Winston. But there must be a way to prove that allegation. Two people know exactly what happened: my brother and Fernandez. My brother can no longer speak for himself. I don't expect Fernandez to do it, either. Do you think we can use testimonies from witnesses who saw the condition of the bodies to prove our allegation?"

I told Bob about my conversations with Victor Bravo and Adolfo Gonzalez; about the Copiapó cemetery administrator, Leonardo Meza, who had witnessed the mass burial; about Haag's former assistant, Enrique Vidal, who had already testified about seeing Fernandez carrying several weapons, including a *corvo*. We talked about so many things: the *tomos* from Judge Guzmán's criminal investigation against Pinochet, the possibility of conducting depositions in Chile, the idea of traveling to South America to persuade witnesses to testify.

"You as a client have basic rights," Bob said, as he patiently answered all my questions. "Your lawyers work for you. Many times, clients demand that we do certain things that we believe could hurt their cases. When that happens, lawyers must educate their clients. If the client insists, we have to do it. Pro bono cases such as yours follow the same rules. You are the client. Your lawyers *have* to listen to you. They have the obligation to tell you what they are doing. You have the right to ask basic questions.

If at the end you are still unhappy, you fire them. It's your case." Bob leaned forward. "I can win this case for you, Zita."

"I would love for you to do it."

"This is a great case," Bob said. "A case against a man who not only killed your brother but who was also involved in the first terrorist attack that took place on US soil," he said, referring to Fernandez Larios's involvement in the car-bombing assassination of Orlando Letelier and Ronni Moffitt in Washington, DC. "I can win this case. You should go down to Chile to convince witnesses to testify."

Bob offered to pay my travel expenses. He said, "You go first on your own. Then you and I will go back later to take depositions. I don't need another lawyer with me. I don't like young lawyers passing me notes during depositions with questions to ask. You and I will work together just fine."

Bob suggested that Pato travel with me. "Safety should be our number one priority," he said. "We will work together as a team from now on. We will always meet with you. You will be kept informed of any major decisions. No more meetings without you."

Bob knew exactly what I wanted to hear. I could not help smiling.

Unfortunately, Bob's meeting with Nicole and Beth did not go as well. Bob had flown out to discuss his role in our case, but as Beth told me later, "That discussion hardly took place." Bob flew back to Florida without an agreement for involvement in the case or even a clear understanding of whether our lawyers wanted him on the team. When I heard this, I was afraid we had lost him. I immediately e-mailed Bob, repeating my family's hope that he would work on Wito's case and saying I wished he would go to Chile with me to take depositions. From his reply, I gathered that no decision had been reached regarding who would be lead counsel.

I wanted it to be Bob. When I e-mailed to tell him this, he replied, "You are the client. You have certain basic rights. I would write to them and ask them which specific lawyers are going to actually try the case. Those (or that) lawyer(s) should take all depositions."

"We all want you on the case," I wrote back. "The only thing missing is some specific proposal for your involvement. I want you to be the one taking depositions in Chile. I want you to be the counsel. What is the right way to discuss this?"

Finally Bob and Leo reached an agreement. On April 30, Bob e-mailed, "We are a team now."

We decided I would go to Chile in June, and if I found witnesses to testify, Bob would travel down to depose them. This was a new step in our process. In traveling to Chile, we now faced the possibility of real danger. The military was no longer in power, but we still often heard of people being threatened. Chileans had lived for so long under a brutal dictatorship that they continued to fear reprisal, even though Pinochet had been out of power for eleven years. Most Chileans wanted to forget the past. But I was willing to gamble. I saw a chance to bring the truth to light.

To prepare for my trip, I compiled a list of thirty-one potential witnesses based on their testimonies to Judge Guzmán: pre-Copiapó (five), Copiapó (thirteen), and post-Copiapó (nine). I also included four witnesses who had testified about Fernandez's involvement in other crimes: the killing of Manuel Sanhueza in Iquique and the disappearance of David Silberman in Santiago. I mailed Bob their full testimonies in Spanish, along with short summaries that I wrote in English.

Bob identified Victor Bravo, Juan Morales, Carlos Brito, and Adolfo Gonzalez as critical witnesses to our case. "They can provide very valuable information," he said. "The idea is to get bits and pieces from these witnesses. Not full confessions or accusations against Fernandez Larios. Approach them very gently for a minor role."

The legal team asked me to submit a budget and proposed itinerary for my time in Chile. But most of our proposed witnesses were military men who did not want to be found. They had testified only because the judge forced them to, and no contact information appeared in their testimonies. How could I create an itinerary when I had no idea where to find most of the witnesses?

On May 30, about an hour before a scheduled conference call with Nicole, Joshua, and Bob, I received two e-mails from my lawyers. The first said, "Each evening or each morning we would like a brief summary of what has been done that day and the agenda for the next day. Also we would like to have a weekly conference call. We must have a clear goal for each witness we identify before you leave. We will address that today."

The second e-mail said, "The following is a list of witnesses that the legal team has agreed are higher priority than others... These witnesses with top priority were not on your proposed list of witnesses. I don't know if this was an oversight, or because you believe for whatever reason it would not be worth trying to contact them. We should discuss all of these witnesses in particular during our call." This new list included people I had purposely left out, such as General Arellano and his officers, Captain Diaz, and Lieutenants Marambio and Ojeda, as well as some others I had never heard of. Arellano and his men had already testified several times to Judge Guzmán that the killings in Copiapó had taken place before they arrived; I could not understand why my lawyers were giving top priority to the men who had committed the crimes and still denied any wrongdoing. "Why do you want to include these people on our list?" I had already asked my lawyers. "Do you think they will contradict the testimony they have already given to a judge in a criminal investigation?"

My lawyers' e-mails infuriated me. But as I waited to join their conference call, my anger turned into a real ache. I felt so humiliated by their insistence on daily reports, and they obviously considered the witnesses I planned to pursue a low priority. As I waited for the conference call to begin, I seriously considered rescinding my offer to go to Chile.

Several times during the call, Bob asked how I felt about the request for daily e-mails. "If you are not happy, you should let us know," he said.

I already knew I was not going to report to the lawyers every day. I would contact them only if I needed advice. "If I have access to e-mail, I will do it," I said. "But I might not always feel like writing."

The lawyers brought up their new list of witnesses.

"Why would I want a bunch of criminals to be our witnesses?" I asked. "I'm not going to do it. I don't want the man responsible for my brother's murder to be our witness. Let him be Steve Davis's witness. Then *you* cross-examine him if he is so important for you." I grew increasingly stubborn as the call wore on. "I want to win the case with the truth. My brother's case is not a forum to legitimatize the criminals' lies. Arellano will stick to his story. He will repeat unto his death that my brother and the other twelve victims were already dead when he and his team, including Fernandez, arrived in Copiapó."

Bob calmly explained that even if the witnesses lied, the legal team could find a pearl, and that was what they were looking for.

"He is a criminal. He killed my brother. I won't do it."

"I know you are a very intelligent person, Zita, but you are acting like a prosecutor," Bob said. "You are not a prosecutor. You are not a lawyer."

I did not understand why Bob said that. If accusing General Arellano and his henchmen of their crimes made me a prosecutor, I suppose I *was* acting that way. But I was just trying to make my lawyers see that we did not need those witnesses to win our case. Arellano and his men would be excellent witnesses for the defense, not for us.

"I won't approach members of the Caravan of Death, nor the three lieutenants from Copiapó who willingly participated in the crimes," I said. "You have my list…*those* are the people I will approach."

"Nicole, if Zita feels so strongly about this, let's drop them," Bob said.

"We may lose the case," Joshua replied. "We need to include as many witnesses as possible. Zita, do you think we can win the case with only one witness?"

"Why would I believe that and at the same time give you thirty-one names?" I demanded. "But it is not Arellano, Diaz, or Marambio who will help us win the case. You are making the case for the defense. I won't do it. Why did you give Adolfo and Morales such low priority?"

"Well, Zita, since you had so much difficulty convincing them already, we wanted to make things easier for you," Nicole said.

"That is my problem," I told her. "That's why I'm going to Chile, to try to convince witnesses, not to make things easier for myself."

The lawyers asked how I planned to approach witnesses. I said I would introduce myself, tell them I had read their testimony to Judge Guzmán, and explain what I was doing and why I wanted to speak with them.

"No," said Nicole. "We don't want to talk about their testimonies, Zita, because the judge didn't ask about Fernandez."

"I thought we had already discussed that," I said, frustrated, "that these testimonies not only help us identify witnesses, but they open the door to asking our own questions, to ask about Fernandez."

"Well, we can begin with that and then go in our own direction," Bob said finally, to stop the bickering.

"Judge Guzmán gave us this information, but we don't think we can show people that we know it," Nicole said.

You know the judge did not give us the information, I wanted to say. *He cannot do that.* Instead, I replied, "Several testimonies had already been leaked to the press. People would not be surprised that I had read them. Commander Haag and Victor Bravo didn't react at all when they saw me with copies of their own testimonies."

"This conversation needs to end," Bob said. "It's not going anywhere. Nicole, let Zita do what she wants. It's her case. Let her."

I hung up, fuming, and sat on the living room sofa, waiting for Pato to come home. Each new step seemed to have to happen the hard way, and now it felt like the positive connection Bob and I had established during our first meeting had suffered during the call.

Early the next morning, I flew to Chile.

Before our conference call, the thought of searching for witnesses in Chile had filled me with a stimulating combination of fear and excitement. Now I just felt lost. As I walked through the Santiago airport, I tried to focus on my reasons for being there. This was the beginning of a transformative journey, or so I hoped. I was there to find the truth.

I spent my first few days at Hugo Gutierrez's office, making phone calls and searching through documents for witness contact information. I had forgotten how cold the winters are in Santiago, sometimes near freezing, and when I complained, Hugo and his associate Carlos Barreuax jokingly escorted me to a window that got a little morning sun, calling it their heater. "You can stand up here so you won't be cold," they said, smiling.

Victor Canales gave me a cell phone and a list of contact names, including numbers for journalists, lawyers, victims' families, private detectives, and friends. I decided to call Dr. Iván Murúa first, because I felt less threatened by him than the military men on my list. Dr. Murúa, a pediatrician who had been detained immediately after the coup, had been sent to the Copiapó public jail and then transferred to the garrison just hours before General Arellano's helicopter landed. Dr. Murúa had been talking with the military prosecutor, Major Carlos Brito, when Arellano's team entered his office.

Victor suggested I forget Dr. Murúa. "I have called the number you gave me countless times. There is no answer. I have asked around, nobody seems to know anything about him."

I dialed Dr. Murúa's number, not expecting an answer.

"This is your lucky day," said a warm male voice. "Only every other Sunday I spend a couple of hours here. I practically live at the hospital." Dr. Murúa agreed to meet with me at his home, so I took a taxi to *El Cajon del Maipo,* a small town at the foot of the Andes. We sat outside in his tropical garden, bundled up in coats in the fresh, cold air, surrounded by exotic flowers, trees, water, and colorful birds, as he confirmed the testimony I had read. Following his detention, Dr. Murúa had gone into exile in Germany, where in 1986 he had recognized Fernandez in some photographs connected with Orlando Letelier's assassination in Washington, DC. In 1995, while Pinochet was in power, Dr. Murúa returned from exile to live permanently in Chile.

Dr. Murúa gave me his cell number and several others so I could reach him at any time. "I love my work," he said. "I work at different hospitals, clinics, day and night. When I'm not sleeping at the hospital, I go to an apartment my wife and I have in Santiago."

Then he smiled and said, "I'll be more than happy to testify."

The next evening I met with Cecilia Rojas, the widow of a political prisoner named Manuel "Choño" Sanhueza who had been one of Fernandez's casualties outside of the Caravan of Death killings. Cecilia invited her sister's ex-husband, Raúl Poblete, to join us, since he had been detained and tortured by Fernandez in 1974.

We met at the home of Cecilia's friend, Viola, a former philosophy professor and political prisoner who had been detained incommunicado for weeks at the Arica garrison following the coup. "One day, I met Fernandez," Viola said. "It was around the end of October 1973, when I was taken out of my isolation to be interrogated by this young officer. I was surprised by how young he looked, younger than my son. He looked no older than twenty. He seemed polite. But his demeanor spoke of power, the kind that says, 'I'm in charge of your life.'"

"How do you know he was Armando Fernandez?" I asked.

"I saw his picture years later."

Cecilia said she had also been detained in Arica with her husband, Choño, and her father, Orlando Rojas. On July 27, 1974, a guard had led Cecilia from her cell to a small room and ordered her to wait. Soon Fernandez had entered, followed by two guards who supported her husband, Choño, under his arms. Choño could barely walk. He had been physically broken by torture.

"But not his spirit," Cecilia said, proudly. "Choño smiled at me. He forced himself to sit up straight, to show me that he was okay. He told me that he was fine. That was the last time I saw him. I believe Fernandez knew that Choño was going to be killed. He arranged that meeting as a good-bye."

During the 1990 exhumations, Choño's body was discovered in a mass grave in Pisagua—mummified like many victims buried in that area, due to the high concentration of nitrates in the soil. "He was the first body found in Pisagua," Cecilia said. "He was blindfolded. His clothes and his chest had been perforated by bullets."

As Cecilia spoke, I realized that I had opened my documentary with footage of Choño being lifted from the ground during the exhumations. I had not known who he was at the time. It was perhaps the most powerful testimony of Chile's darkest time.

I was having trouble dealing with the flood of emotions that Viola's and Cecilia's testimonies stirred up in me. Soon Raúl arrived and described the day that Fernandez and a group of men had forcibly entered his home in Arica, where he had lived with his wife and two-month-old daughter.

"It was 6:00 a.m.," Raúl recalled. "Loud noises woke us up. We heard people banging on our door and shouting, *"Abran, Ejercito de Chile!"* ["Open, Chilean army!"] My wife and I rushed to the door. A number of men, all dressed in civilian clothes, barged into our house and began searching everywhere, turning everything upside down, talking loudly, and asking questions.

"I noticed a young man who looked different from the rest. I admit that what attracted my attention to him was that he was wearing American jeans, highly esteemed by young people like me at the time. While the search continued, this young man remained behind. He was giving the orders. After finding nothing in the house, he took the men aside and talked to them. I didn't hear what he said except for the last part: 'I'll stay here with the prisoner.'

"Afterward, everyone left except him. I didn't know at the time that the men had been instructed to go to Cecilia's house, where they arrested Cecilia, her husband, Choño, and her father, Orlando.

"Fernandez sat down at our kitchen table and began flipping pages of a book he found in the house, made some comments. He seemed an educated man. He tried to make conversation with me. He proudly told me that he'd participated in the assault on the presidential palace on September 11, 'an operation directed by General Palacios,' he said. Fernandez described how General Palacios's hand got hit during the assault and that he gave him his handkerchief to stop the bleeding. That is how years later I learned his name. The story appeared in a book—the story of a proud young lieutenant, Armando Fernandez, who used his handkerchief to help stop the bleeding of General Palacios's hand on the day of the coup.

"Of course, years later I saw his pictures in newspapers, pictures in connection with the Letelier case," Raúl said. "A haunting face."

Raúl described how Fernandez had taken him into custody that morning. For more than two weeks, Raúl, his father-in-law, Orlando, and Choño were interrogated and tortured. Fernandez interrogated them, playing the role of *nice* guy. Following the coup, Raúl and Choño, both members of the Communist Party, had published an underground newspaper. Fernandez wanted the names of everyone involved in the organization.

"Fernandez interrogated me for days and nights," said Raúl. "He wanted names. I didn't give him any. So after each session of interrogation, a torturer walked in. Fernandez would say, 'It would be good for you to talk. We can end all of this.' After two weeks, I was literally destroyed. I gave him some names—names of people I knew were no longer in the region. Fernandez was happy. 'I'm glad for you,' he said. Then he left the room. Ten minutes later he came back. He discovered I had misled him. 'So you are playing games with me, motherfucker!' he yelled. He began hitting me, hitting me with all his might. He looked like an injured animal, out of control. He wouldn't stop. I passed out."

Two days later, on July 27, 1974, a conscript had gone to the homes of Raúl and Orlando to get some clothes for them. "Why not clothes for Choño?" Cecilia's mother had asked, anxiously. Then Fernandez, the only officer in the group, had driven Raúl, Orlando, Choño, and several conscripts in a truck to Pisagua.

"We all three sat in the front seat," Raúl said. "We put Choño in the middle to hold him up. While Fernandez drove, he talked to us. He even told us jokes. Choño could barely speak, yet he managed to tell us a joke, too. We arrived in Pisagua at night. Fernandez took us to a police station. We were put into separate cells. I threw myself to the ground. I heard my father-in-law screaming, 'Why are you placing shackles on Choño's ankles? Don't you see he is ill!' He demanded that they remove the shackles.

"'Okay,' I heard somebody saying. That's all I remember. An officer woke me up the next morning to take me to another detention facility. He took me to a patio where I saw Orlando. We asked for Choño. My father-in-law demanded to see Choño. At our insistence, the officer went back in to ask for him. He came back, his demeanor totally transformed. He said harshly, 'I was only given two names—that's all.'

"We never saw Choño again," Raúl said, choking back tears. "We asked for Fernandez, but no one seemed to remember him, either."

Raúl agreed to testify.

THIRTY

On Wednesday morning, I dressed as well as the contents of my suitcase allowed and went downtown to the ministry of defense, hoping to arrange a meeting with General Emilio Cheyre, commander-in-chief of the Chilean army. My lawyers had e-mailed to say that they needed some documents from 1973, and I thought if the records still existed, they must be in the army's possession.

The ministry of defense was the most intimidating place I had ever seen: a modern fortress of a building, with armed guards everywhere and a steady stream of men in suits and uniforms flowing through the doors.

In my blue dress, red jacket, and high heels, I stood nervously across the street, clutching my purse to keep my hands from trembling. I took a deep breath and stepped out into the street, walking as confidently as I could toward the ministry of defense. At the front gate, a guard blocked my path. "May I help you?" he asked.

"Yes," I said, smiling. "I would like to see if I could speak with General Cheyre."

"You can go in and ask the guard inside," the guard said, managing to keep a straight face.

The next guard asked for my *carnet de identidad*, or Chilean identification card.

"I don't have one," I told him. "I have my passport."

The guard examined it and told me to submit my request through official channels. "It takes about a month to get a response," he added.

"I don't have much time. I'm returning to the United States next week."

Slowly the guard repeated that there was an official procedure to follow.

"I understand," I said, smiling. "I just want to know if you can give him my business card. On the back I wrote some phone numbers, the hotel and the cellular, in case he wants to call me."

The guard smiled back. "You can leave it on the fourth floor." He summoned another guard to escort me upstairs to a small window, where I handed my University of California business card to a man in uniform and explained that I needed to speak with General Cheyre.

"I'll do my best," the man replied.

Later I told Victor Canales about my experience at the ministry of defense. "You're crazy," Victor said, laughing. "But don't do that again."

That afternoon, I searched for Enrique Vidal. I went to the address listed in his testimony to the judge, but Vidal did not live there, and no one in the neighborhood seemed to know who he was.

"These people are experts in covering up their tracks," said the private detective Victor had recommended. "I don't think we are going to find him."

"I *want* him," I said.

"I have reached the end of my rope," the detective said. "I'm sorry."

By Wednesday evening, I was physically and emotionally drained. I decided to take a break and asked Veronica to dinner. As I waited for her at Hugo's office, I glanced through some testimonies, and on the back of one page noticed a short paragraph: a notarized statement signed by Enrique Vidal testifying to the authenticity of certain documents. Next to his name was an address.

When Veronica arrived, I asked her to go to the address with me. Twenty minutes later, we stepped off a bus into a pleasant, isolated neighborhood and walked toward the guard post of a gated condominium complex.

"I came to see Mr. Vidal," I told the guard.

The guard picked up his phone and said, "Mrs. Beatriz, there is a lady here that came to see Mr. Vidal." He looked at me. "Is he expecting you?"

"No, he is not."

The guard blanched. He scrambled to his feet.

"I'm visiting from the United States," I said, trying to calm him. "I met Mr. Vidal many years ago. I just stopped by to say hi."

The guard repeated my words into the phone, then handed me the receiver.

"How did you get our address?" a woman asked.

"I don't exactly remember," I faltered. "I believe it was from a common friend…It could have been someone who lives in the States…I'm not sure."

"Why do you want to speak with him?" she asked.

"I'd rather not say that on the phone."

"Oh!" said the woman, with a hint of complicity. She seemed to take my reluctance to answer as an indication that I was a friend who did not want to reveal private information about her family in front of the guard. "He is not here right now. Why don't you call him later, around 10:00 p.m.?"

"I don't have his phone number."

Mrs. Vidal gave me the number, which I repeated for the guard to write down. His face had returned to its normal color.

At 10:00 p.m., I called Vidal's number. He was not home. For the next hour, I called every fifteen minutes, reaching his wife each time.

"He is not home yet," she kept saying.

I imagined Vidal probably was home but did not want to talk with me, so I gave Mrs. Vidal my cell number and said I would be out of town for the next week. Then I went to bed. Pato would be flying to Chile the next morning, and I had to pick him up at seven before we caught our flight to Iquique. It was past midnight, and I was just drifting off when the phone rang.

"Mrs. Barrueto?"

"Yes."

"Enrique Vidal."

I jumped out of bed. "Thank you for returning my call," I said, nervously pacing the floor. "Probably you don't remember me. In 1973 we met in Copiapó, a difficult period in my family's life, and you helped me."

"I'm glad to know that," Vidal said.

"My husband was imprisoned at the garrison. His name is Patricio Barrueto. He was going to be sent to Chacabuco. With your help I met Commander Haag, who changed his mind and sent him instead to Huasco."

"I'm glad to know that," Vidal repeated.

"I'm also the sister of Winston Cabello."

"Oh, Winston! I knew him well."

"Did you?"

"Yes. We had lunch together several times. I even remember the vehicle from his office. It had black seats." Vidal paused, and then said gently, "I'm really sorry."

I explained that my family was pursuing a lawsuit against Armando Fernandez related to Winston's death.

"Ah, Armando," said Vidal. "We were classmates in the military academy. Where are you now?"

I said I was staying in downtown Santiago but would be out of town for a week. We arranged to meet the following Thursday in front of the Theater of the University of Chile.

"How am I going to recognize you?" I asked.

"I will recognize you."

THIRTY ONE

The next afternoon, Pato and I searched the city of Iquique for former Lieutenant Patricio Lapostol, who had been stationed in Calama when the Caravan of Death killed twenty-six political prisoners in the desert. Those victims' bodies are still missing.

In his brief testimony, Lapostol had told the judge that on October 18, 1973, he was instructed to organize a guard to watch over the twenty-six bodies. Lapostol had not witnessed the executions nor did he know where the victims had been buried, and he had not mentioned Fernandez in his testimony.

I felt sure that these prisoners had been brutally murdered, and I believed that Lapostol was a key potential witness to help prove our allegation of torture. If our lawyers could question him about the condition of the bodies he had guarded, they could establish a pattern of torture in each city the Caravan of Death had visited.

Pato and I gave our taxi driver the address from Lapostol's testimony, but it turned out to be an empty lot. We knocked on doors in the neighborhood. Few people answered. No one seemed to know Lapostol.

As Pato and I searched, we became convinced that a number of military people had given false contact information, because in many cases the house numbers did not exist or the street names did not make sense. We speculated that if witnesses were deliberately giving wrong information under oath, they were probably using clever tricks to avoid perjuring themselves. If the error was discovered, it would be easier to justify a wrong number than a street or city name. Witnesses could blame the court reporter.

Based on this theory, Pato and I decided that we must be on the right street, in the right city, but with the wrong house number. We tried every combination our mathematics training allowed. We knocked on many doors. We ran from many dogs.

No Lapostol.

By evening, we were exhausted. We struck up a conversation with a friendly woman on the street, and when I said that Lapostol was a former military officer, she replied, "Three houses down lives a couple with a teenage son. I believe he was in the army some years ago."

We had already tried that house, and no one was home. Discouraged, Pato and I went back to the hotel. We did not talk much at dinner. Although we had to be at the airport at five the next morning, I asked, "Can we go back to the house again?"

The house was dark when we arrived. I felt like crying.

"You tried," said Pato, putting his arms around me. "That's all you can do. Look at how much you have already accomplished, and in less than two weeks. Don't worry."

We stood on the sidewalk, facing away from the house as we held each other. We did not see a car pull into the driveway. When I looked back toward the house, a man in his early fifties was walking toward us.

"I'm not sure if I'm at the right house," I said when he reached us. "I'm looking for Mr. Patricio Lapostol."

"That's me."

I introduced Pato and myself and asked Lapostol if he had time to talk. He was about to answer, when his wife came up and embraced us. "Come in," she said, smiling warmly as she ushered us into the house.

Pato and I looked at each other, and then followed Mrs. Lapostol into the living room, where we sat down with her on the sofa. I began to explain that we lived in San Francisco, but Mrs. Lapostol enthusiastically interrupted with a story about the time she had visited her brother in New York. Mr. Lapostol sat in a chair a little apart from the three of us, arms crossed, smiling, taking it all in. I turned to him several times trying to encourage his help, and then finally I said to Mrs. Lapostol, "I think your husband wants to know who I am and why I'm here."

"You don't know each other?" Mrs. Lapostol asked.

"No."

"Oh!" she laughed. "When I saw you outside talking with him, I assumed you were friends."

Mr. and Mrs. Lapostol listened silently as I talked about Wito and our need to find witnesses for the lawsuit against Armando Fernandez. I shared the little I knew about depositions and explained why we needed them to build our case. "I read your testimony to the judge," I told Lapostol. "I would like to ask you if you would be willing to give a voluntary deposition to my lawyers."

"If you think my testimony would help you," he said, "yes, I'm willing to testify."

I sighed loudly. Everyone laughed.

Lapostol struck me as a kind, straightforward man. I asked how he felt about the army's actions during Pinochet's rule and explained that a few military officers had refused to testify on the grounds that doing so would betray their institution.

Lapostol's smile faded. "Those who committed the crimes are the ones who betrayed the institution."

I asked if he could describe the day that Arellano and his men had arrived in Calama. Lapostol said that Major Moren had recognized him as the son of Ariosto Lapostol, the commander in La Serena, where Arellano's squad had killed fifteen political prisoners just two days earlier. "I hope you will behave like a man, not like a motherfucking *coward* like your father did," Moren had sneered.

Lapostol's father had repudiated the killings ordered in La Serena and told General Arellano he would have nothing to do with them. "That explains Moren's animosity toward me," Lapostol said. "In the case of Calama, the local commander, Colonel Eugenio Rivera, learned of the killings a few minutes before a dinner he was holding in honor of Arellano's *special* visit. Rivera was a devoted Christian man, and he was devastated to hear that twenty-six of his prisoners had been killed."

Lapostol remembered Fernandez and said that he had been covered with weapons, including a *corvo*, when he had seen him in Calama. "In the early afternoon, we heard rumors of the killings, but it wasn't until 5:30 p.m. when a local officer, Lieutenant Mandiola, confirmed the news to me. He requested that I go with him to install a guard at the location where the executions had taken place, an area outside the city called *Topater*, about twenty minutes into the desert. When we arrived, we saw many bodies on the ground, crowded together, one on top of the other."

"I noticed you keep using the words *fusilamientos* and *fusilados* [killed by firing squad]," I said. "From what you saw that evening, are those the right words to describe the killings that took place in Calama?"

Lapostol smiled sadly.

"After seeing the bodies, would you say they were killed by firing squad?" I persisted.

Lapostol did not answer.

"Can you think of a better word to describe what happened?"

"Yes." Lapostol seemed to want to say more.

"Were the victims massacred?"

"I don't like that word," Lapostol said. "Let's say they were dead."

"I don't like the word 'massacred,' either," I replied. "But if you are asked to describe the condition of the bodies, what word would you use?"

Lapostol hesitated.

"They were destroyed."

Lapostol gave me his phone numbers so I could call in August to arrange his deposition. As Pato and I were leaving, I asked, "Do you think your father would agree to speak with me?"

"I think so," Lapostol said, "though I can't say he would agree to testify."

THIRTY TWO

Early the next morning, Pato and I flew to Copiapó. It was Pato's first time back in Copiapó in twenty-seven years. Pato has never been good at expressing his feelings, but after so many years together I could tell that he wanted to reexperience the freedom we had all felt before the coup. Searching for witnesses, we spent our first few days walking up and down the streets of the city that had taken so much from us.

Juan Morales was my top priority. He had already testified to Judge Guzmán that he had seen Fernandez reviewing the prisoners' folders at the garrison, and I imagined Morales had more information about Fernandez's activities in Copiapó that could be helpful to our case. I wanted my lawyers to be able to ask him their own questions.

I knew it was unlikely that Morales would consent to testify, but it was not impossible. Perhaps I could persuade him if I could speak with him alone. Based on my last visit, I felt sure that Morales's lawyer would not allow him to add any new information to the testimony he had already given the judge in Chile.

Pato and I took a taxi to Morales's house, but he had moved since my last trip to Chile, and no one in the neighborhood seemed to have a single memory of him or his wife—not even the children who played all day in the streets. Discouraged, we went to see Julio Hernández and Eddie Fúnez, two former political prisoners from Copiapó, who immediately agreed to testify about their experiences regarding the night the thirteen political prisoners were taken from the garrison and the jail to be later killed in the Atacama Desert, just outside Copiapó. Then we went to talk with Victor Bravo.

Victor seemed comfortable with the idea of testifying. He even offered to travel to Santiago if that would make it easier for our lawyers. As we talked, I asked Victor if he thought the Caravan of Death had intended to frighten the soldiers in Copiapó and other towns.

"Terrorizing the local military was clearly one of the expedition's goals," Victor said, "to plunge them into a state of uncertainty and fear. So they could be forced to obey any and every order. It was a tiny group that operated alongside the regular army, kind of like the Gestapo. Everyone was afraid of them, which was exactly what they wanted. Fernandez Larios was part of that tiny group. Local military officials tried to keep him out of things, but he operated outside the usual hierarchies, so he didn't have to obey anybody."

Pato and I took a taxi back to Copiapó. As we walked through the town that had once been our home, we were also unconsciously searching for reminders of good memories. It felt like the town had hidden them all.

Nothing seemed the same. We could not find our little house.

And Wito's home had burned to the ground. Nothing was left but an empty lot.

On Wednesday morning, Pato and I visited the regional planning office in Copiapó where Wito had worked, to talk with his former coworker Pablo Torres. "I have always dreamt of organizing an event to commemorate Winston's life and to honor his work," Pablo said. "One day I will do it. I want this conference room to have Winston's name."

Pablo's warm remembrance touched us deeply. As we were sitting in his office, my cell phone rang.

"May I speak with Mrs. Cabello-Barrueto?" asked a pleasant male voice.

"This is she."

"This is General Juan Fuente-Alba. I'm the general secretary of the army. I'm calling you per order of my commander, General Emilio Cheyre."

I literally almost fell out of my chair. My voice failed. After an embarrassing silence, I finally managed to say, "Sorry, I can't hear you very well."

General Fuente-Alba repeated what he had said, adding that General Cheyre would be out of the country for a couple of weeks and had instructed him to place himself under my orders. I am sure that is what he said. General Fuente-Alba asked if there was anything he could help with, and before hanging up he repeated that General Cheyre had asked him to help me. (Once I returned to Santiago I met with General Fuente-Alba to request his help in gathering documents from the garrison and the jail, pertaining to the detention and killing of the thirteen political prisoners. He said he could not help me with that, and that I had to go through legal channels.)

"How did all of this happen?" I asked Pato as I put my phone back in my purse.

"You asked for it," Pato said, grinning.

A few hours later we left Copiapó, happier than we had been in a long time.

On Thursday at 5:00 p.m., I went alone to the University of Chile to meet Haag's former assistant, Enrique Vidal. I was extremely nervous about meeting Vidal, because I knew that if I failed in this conversation or made any mistake while talking to him, he might not agree to testify. Without him, it would be more difficult to prove our case in court.

Vidal arrived all wrapped up in a coat and scarf. "I came just the same," he said, and explained that he had a bad cold. "If I had canceled our meeting, I don't think you would have believed me that I was sick."

We walked to a coffee shop around the corner and found an empty table. Vidal did most of the talking. With his piercing blue eyes fixed on mine, he vividly described the moment that the truck carrying Wito and the twelve other prisoners had left the garrison. As he spoke, I could hardly breathe.

Throughout our conversation, Vidal grew increasingly uneasy, watching every movement around us. When he finished speaking, I asked if he would be willing to testify.

"Look around," Vidal said, leaning toward me. "Do you notice anything in particular about *anyone* in this room?"

"No," I said, although I *had* noticed Vidal's vigilant behavior from the moment we had entered the coffee shop.

"Do you know that you are being followed? You should be careful. You already know what happened. Leave it at that."

"I just want to make sense out of it all," I said, suddenly thinking of my father whose spirit had died with Wito. "I want to understand *why* my brother was killed. How was that possible?"

"There is no need to intellectualize it," Vidal said. "It is possible. That's all you need to know."

Vidal's fear was very real, just as Adolfo's had been. As former military men they knew what their own people were capable of.

"You are a very dangerous person to be with," Vidal said gravely. "Everybody in this country knows who you are and what you are doing. You'd better be careful."

"Justice will not change what happened to our family," I said, "but it will help prevent other parents, brothers, sisters, sons, and spouses from suffering the magnitude of pain that many like us have had to endure."

Vidal studied me in silence. Finally he promised to think it over, and we agreed to meet again in August.

"My wife doesn't want me to get involved in anything," Vidal said. "She is scared. She is also sick. If I convince her, I will do it."

THIRTY THREE

The next day, I went to see Commander Ariosto Lapostol at his office in Santiago. The visit began badly. Pulling a copy of his testimony from my purse, I introduced myself and explained why I wanted to speak with him.

"You can use that testimony if you want," he said, showing me the door. "I have nothing to add."

Ignoring Commander Lapostol's "invitation" to leave, I explained about Wito. "I understand you didn't witness the killings. But can you tell me how Arellano and his men selected the names of their victims?"

Commander Lapostol hesitated. Then he offered me a seat. "You want to know what happened?" he asked, clearing his desk. "Imagine this was my desk in 1973. Arellano and Pedro Espinoza were standing at this end and I was standing at the other end. The rest of his team was outside my office. Arellano asked me for the list of political prisoners. He and Espinoza reviewed the list. They talked to each other. I didn't listen to what they said. After consulting with Espinoza, Arellano placed marks beside certain names, using a red pen he took from my desk."

Commander Lapostol had met with Arellano for an hour before storming out of his office, telling his assistant, Lieutenant Emilio Cheyre, on the way out that none of his men were to obey any order from Arellano. "You know who Cheyre is?" Lapostol asked.

I nodded and followed him over to a photograph of the garrison in La Serena. Lapostol pointed to where his office had been and to the patio where he had waited for Arellano to finish meeting with Espinoza. Later, Arellano had joined him on that patio, saying, "Don't be like that, Ariosto." Just then, they had heard gunshots.

"I didn't see Fernandez shooting," Lapostol said, "but I can *assure* you that none of my men participated in the killings."

Commander Lapostol agreed to testify.

Pato was waiting for me outside with Jean-Christophe Klotz, a French producer who had come to Chile to film a documentary about our case. Jean-Christophe had heard about my family a year earlier while filming a documentary in San Francisco about Amnesty International. With CJA's approval, he decided to make a documentary about our case on the conditions that he would not interfere with our work, that I would tell him when it was or was not acceptable to film, and that he would not release the documentary until after our trial.

When Pato and Jean-Christophe asked how my meeting with Commander Lapostol had gone, I burst into tears.

"What happened?" Pato asked, holding me tightly.

I could not stop crying long enough to answer. The vision of Arellano and Espinoza marking names on a list, coldly deciding who would live and die, suddenly overwhelmed me. Sobbing, I clung to Pato.

Finally, I managed to say that Lapostol had agreed to testify. This made it even harder for Pato and Jean-Christophe to understand why I was crying. "You are making greater strides every time," Pato said, soothingly. "However, this is going too well. You have to be prepared for a few leads that won't work."

It was prophetic advice. With one exception, none of our subsequent contacts agreed to testify.

On Pato's last day in Chile we went to meet Grimilda Sánchez at her apartment. Grimilda, a smiling, rosy woman with soft, strawberry blond curls, embraced us warmly when she opened the door and offered us tea and cookies, making us as comfortable as possible on her living room sofa. Then she shared her story.

A former nurse and political prisoner, Grimilda told us that her husband had been executed after a court-martial and she had been tortured for days in her son's presence. Shortly after, the Caravan of Death had killed her only son, a young man in his late twenties. Years later, Grimilda recognized three officers from photographs she saw in the news: Marcelo Moren, Armando Fernandez, and a lieutenant from Calama whose full name she could not remember.

"They took my son," said Grimilda, her eyes filling with tears. "They took the only thing that belonged to me."

Grimilda Sánchez agreed to testify.

Later that afternoon, Pato and I traveled to the wealthy beach resort of Viña del Mar to search for Ruben Castillo Whyte, the former commander of Cauquenes, where four political prisoners had been killed. In Castillo's brief testimony to the judge, he had directly accused Arellano of the executions, testifying that Arellano had selected the victims' names and given Espinoza the orders to go to the jail with Moren and Fernandez to interrogate prisoners.

We found Castillo's apartment building easily in downtown Viña, and when the manager answered the bell, he gave me Castillo's apartment number and buzzed the door open, no questions asked.

"My husband is not home," said the pleasant older woman who answered Castillo's apartment door. "Why do you want to speak with him?"

"I want to talk with him about his experience with General Arellano in 1973."

"He doesn't give interviews," Castillo's wife said. "He never talks with anyone about that."

"My brother was a victim of Arellano in Copiapó. I know your husband has nothing to do with the killings in Cauquenes. I know it was all Arellano's doing."

Castillo's wife invited me in and asked me to sit on the sofa. "He should be here any minute," she said.

As we waited, I explained about our lawsuit and said I wanted to ask Mr. Castillo to testify against Fernandez.

Soon Castillo arrived. "Please leave," he said, when his wife had explained who I was. "I have nothing to tell you."

"Please," his wife said, "listen to what she has to say."

Castillo listened without interrupting but refused to testify on the grounds that he had not seen Fernandez kill the victims. I could do nothing to change his mind.

As Pato and I were leaving the apartment, Castillo suggested I contact his former assistant, Jorge Acuña. "He witnessed the executions. Find him. He can help you." He also recommended someone already on my list: Efrain Jaña, former commander of Talca.

Pato flew back to San Francisco that night. It was hard to see him go. Before leaving the airport, I e-mailed my lawyers a list of witnesses who had agreed to testify in August.

The next morning, Jean-Christophe and I flew to Concepción to speak with Diego Muñoz, a priest who had witnessed the Caravan of Death's executions of eleven political prisoners in Valdivia on October 3, 1973. In Father Muñoz's testimony to the judge, he had said, "It is important to point out that General Arellano and his delegation, Major Espinoza, Commander Arredondo, Lieutenant Fernandez Larios, Major Moren Brito were all present during the executions carried out in Neltume."

Father Muñoz was critical to our case because Fernandez had always denied participating in the Caravan of Death killings, saying that he had not even witnessed the executions. If a Catholic priest would testify that not only had he personally witnessed the executions, but also had seen Fernandez there, it would be very difficult to doubt his word.

Father Muñoz invited us into his office and described how he had accompanied each of the eleven prisoners to execution. His was one of the most heartbreaking stories I heard. These eleven prisoners had been workers of the *Complejo Maderero Panguipulli*, a Chilean state-owned company that managed forested lands and sawmills. It was very difficult for people to get news in such an isolated area, so on the day of the coup the eleven men had walked to their local police station to ask what was going on. That was all they did. They just went to the police station to ask what was happening. The police detained and incarcerated the eleven men on the spot.

Father Muñoz trembled as he told his story. Tears and sweat ran down his face as he described the executions, the smell of fear on the prisoners' bodies, his last conversation with each prisoner. All eleven men had asked him to give messages to their children and families.

The last prisoner executed that night was José Liendo, a young man accused of every imaginable subversive action. His execution was scheduled for 4:00 p.m., but General Arellano said that he wanted to witness it and ordered his officers to wait until he returned from a nearby town. Father Muñoz stayed with Liendo for more than eight hours as he awaited his death. Liendo shared his dreams and his hopes for a better world. After midnight, Arellano's men killed Liendo. His last words were, 'Father, tell the man who imprisoned me that I forgive him."

"What were their families' reactions?" I asked hoarsely.

"I never talked with their families," Muñoz said. "For years I wanted to do it. I kept well-guarded notes of the conversations I had with all of them. A few years ago, I burned them all."

"How could you do that?" I asked. "How *could* you?"

Father Muñoz closed his eyes. "It was too painful of an experience," he said, trembling. "It is *still* painful. You read my testimony to the judge. I only said that I accompanied prisoners to their executions. I was unable to say anything more. This is the first time I have given details of what I witnessed that day. I just want to forget."

Speechless, I stared at the priest.

"I won't testify in your case," he said, after a long silence. "I can't do it."

"Why not?" I asked in disbelief. Raised as a Catholic, I had come to this meeting with expectations of how a priest should respond to the principles of truth and justice.

"I'm old," Father Muñoz said. "I have my peace. I might get in trouble with the church authorities."

I insisted.

Father Muñoz's reasons kept mounting: "My supervisors won't be too happy about it"…"I might lose my job"…"I want to retire soon; I might jeopardize my safety net"…"I don't want trouble."

"You are a religious man," I said, desperately. "You believe in Jesus's teaching. You follow God's word. Don't you think Jesus would want you to tell the truth? Don't you believe in the value of the truth?"

"Not even Jesus said the truth all the time," Muñoz replied.

"But maybe Jesus didn't have the opportunity to tell the truth as I'm giving it to you."

"I will pray for you to succeed in your efforts to bring justice for your brother's death," the priest said.

"I'll pray for you to change your mind," I said.

Father Muñoz chose not to testify.

My search for witnesses was often painful and frustrating. While everyone readily agreed that truth and justice were of the utmost importance, when it came to actually agreeing to testify, some critical witnesses did not follow through.

Diego Muñoz's refusal felt particularly crushing. Unlike other witnesses I approached, he did not seem to be in a situation where he would be risking his life to testify. If Father Muñoz were unwilling to come forward, how would other key witnesses react since they probably faced greater risk in helping me?

Discouraged and exhausted, Jean-Christophe and I flew back to Santiago. A few days later, he returned to France.

With only two weeks left to find the witnesses I needed, I continued the search alone.

THIRTY FOUR

The next day I met Efrain Jaña, former commander from Talca, at his home.

"I didn't let my men stain the uniform of the homeland with blood," Jaña said proudly.

"All the local commanders said they had no choice but to follow Arellano's orders," I replied. "But you didn't?"

"Arellano's orders were arbitrary orders," Jaña said. "Everyone could and should have questioned those orders. They chose not to. Everyone knows that you can't be forced to follow ethically immoral orders, and everyone should know that it is *necessary* to question those orders. I did it at a great personal cost, but my regiment should feel very proud they didn't stain their uniforms with blood."

"We always hear about 'evil' committed by people, but we don't hear much about goodness," I said. "The world should know stories like yours, that it is possible to stop evil."

"Yes," Jaña said. "It would help us to make better moral choices in the future."

Efrain Jaña agreed to testify.

In the city of Cauquenes the following day, I met Clodomiro Garrido, a detective in charge of guarding political prisoners at the local police station who had seen Armando Fernandez on October 4, 1973. In his brief testimony to the judge, Garrido had described Fernandez as a young officer covered with weapons "like Rambo." I felt Garrido had more to offer.

We agreed to meet in a public place, but when Garrido did not show up, I found his house. Surprised to see me on his doorstep, Garrido did not want to talk, and it was obvious that he was not listening as I explained about the lawsuit.

"If I had known you wanted me to testify, I would have told you not to come." Garrido gave some reasons that were similar to Father Muñoz's: "I don't want to be bothered"…"I want my life in peace"…"The day I had to testify to the judge he made me go to Talca [a city about two hours north of Cauquenes] and I had to wait all day long to give my testimony"…"I'm tired"…"I have my work; that's all I care about."

I talked about the importance of truth and justice for society, for our children, for future generations.

"What is in it for me?" Garrido asked.

As we continued talking, Garrido mentioned that one of the four victims in Cauquenes, Claudio Lavin, had been his dear friend since elementary school.

"Do it for your friend," I said, "for his life cut short. They didn't give him a chance. Tell the world that. The world should know about his senseless killing. Claudio, your friend, should be remembered with the truth and dignity he deserves. You can make that happen. He wasn't a criminal."

Garrido's eyes filled with tears. "I won't testify. I will do it only if I'm forced to. However, I'm prepared to tell *you* everything I witnessed that day."

Garrido told me about a young woman named Fulvia, a close friend of Lavin's, who had been taken as a political prisoner and brutally interrogated by Fernandez. "Fulvia is a nun now. She is probably in a convent in a remote southern area. She will be a better witness than I."

One of the last witnesses I approached was Leonardo Meza, a frail old man who had been administrator of the Copiapó cemetery in 1973. Meza looked sick and exhausted as he described the mass burial of the thirteen victims. I was exhausted, myself, and as Meza spoke I could not seem to emotionally detach myself from the memories he shared.

Meza agreed to testify, but the following morning he called to say that he had changed his mind. "I'm just tired of testifying. Judge Guzmán forced me to go to Copiapó several times to give the same testimony, over and over, to answer the same questions, over and over. I'm just tired. A twelve-hour bus ride to Copiapó is too much for an old man like me. Besides, I didn't ask to be at the cemetery that night. That was my job. It's not my fault that I was there. I wished not to have lived that experience. The military was the one that took me from my house to the cemetery that night. I won't testify again. I just want to be left alone."

I listened silently, my head throbbing. I had been pushing myself to exhaustion for so long that I had come down with a severe flu, with a blinding headache, high fever, and aching body.

"I understand what you said," I told Meza when he had finished speaking. "Nobody deserves to experience what you experienced. But unfortunately, you lived it. You can't change that. It's an experience that doesn't belong to you anymore. It belongs to me. It belongs to my family. It belongs to the world. You have to talk about it."

Wearily, Meza agreed to testify. But the moment I hung up, I regretted my words. I dragged myself out of bed and took a taxi to Meza's home on the outskirts of Santiago, where I asked him to forgive me. "We have Victor Bravo's testimony," I said. "It's very similar to yours. It would be okay if you don't testify."

I dropped Meza from my list.

My flu became so severe that I needed medical attention, and the doctor recommended postponing my flight back to California. But suddenly I needed to be home with my family. Pato, Felipe, and Roberto were waiting for me at the San Francisco airport, and for days they cared for me as I stayed in bed with a high fever. I could not stop coughing. When I was finally able to get out of bed, I e-mailed the lawyers a list of my failures and accomplishments: fourteen witnesses had agreed to testify, three needed to think about it, and four had refused.

Still out there were ten or more witnesses I had not been able to contact. If I could reach them, would they be willing to testify for our case?

THIRTY FIVE

A few days later, Joshua came to my house with news that the legal team was reconsidering taking depositions in August. "We don't exactly know when it's going to happen, but why don't you give us the witnesses' contact information so Nicole and I can make arrangements directly with them?"

"So you want to scare the hell out of my witnesses," I said, picturing two young American lawyers arriving in Chile, mobbed by reporters and photographers as they went to interrogate former military men. These witnesses had only hesitantly agreed to give their voluntary testimony, and I had promised them that we would do everything quietly and that only one lawyer would meet with them prior to depositions. I had also assured them that I would contact them personally to make all arrangements.

"*Normally*," Joshua said, "lawyers expect their plaintiffs to give them all of the witnesses' information so they can arrange depositions."

"*Normally*," I replied. "You said it right. But this is not a normal case. Not anymore. You already squandered that opportunity when I gave you, all of you, every piece of information I had, and you did nothing."

I reminded Joshua that I had traveled to Chile based on an agreement with the legal team: that Bob would go to Chile in August to take depositions and I would accompany him to make all logistical arrangements. "So what you are asking me to do is not going to happen."

Joshua replied that among other things, the legal team needed to find a court reporter, an interpreter, and someone to film the depositions. Most importantly, they needed to confirm that both Bob and Fernandez's lawyer were still available for the last two weeks of August.

"What's the big deal?" I asked. "Why should it be so difficult to find a court reporter or an interpreter? Have you asked Davis if he is still available? How about Bob's availability? Can you ask them? Why do you need witnesses' contact information? How would that information help you to decide whether you can take depositions in August or not?"

Joshua shrugged.

"You have to do better than that," I said. "These are not difficult problems to solve, you know."

A few days later, Joshua called insisting that I provide the witnesses' information so that he and Nicole could plan. "There will be no depositions in August," he said, without explanation.

In late July, with no news from my legal team, I met CJA's new director, Sandra Coliver, for coffee. Sandra listened carefully, and then asked, "How can I help?"

I explained what I had been going through. Immediately, Sandra called Leo to share my concerns and handed me her cell phone. Awkwardly I told Leo that I had just returned from Chile, and several witnesses had agreed to testify in August.

"That's the problem, Zita," Leo said. "We can't use those testimonies. The judge didn't ask questions about Fernandez. We don't know if those are good witnesses."

Suddenly I understood the lawyers' reasons for reconsidering depositions in August. These were *my* witnesses, not theirs. "How can you make that judgment, Leo, if you don't even take this opportunity to ask your own questions? So you mean that everything I've done will be wasted?"

"No, no, Zita," Leo said. "Your work will not be wasted. Don't worry. I'll speak with Bob, and we will let you know."

Sandra advised me to go ahead with a camping trip that Pato and I had been planning in the Pacific Northwest and assured me that things would get better. She promised to keep me informed of any new developments and gave me her cell phone. "We need to make sure we can reach you any time we need to," she said.

Two days later, Joshua e-mailed to say that Bob was prepared to go to Chile for up to three weeks in August, and I was to send a list of witnesses I thought he should depose, a calendar of depositions, and a brief summary of each witness's testimony. Fernandez's lawyer would also need this in advance. I prepared the materials in a few hours, including some *maybes* like Vidal and Haag, and then Pato and I went camping. A few days later in Victoria, Canada, I checked my e-mail and saw a new message from Joshua. Bob had asked that either he or Nicole assist with depositions in Chile, and I was to decide who would go.

I e-mailed Bob directly: "In my conversations with witnesses, I agreed with them that I would come back, sometime during the second week of August, for a private meeting with one of my lawyers, that being you… The agreement was that you and I, and only you and I, would come back for an informal visit…They understand that during depositions other people will be present…In order to maintain the credibility and the trust I was able to build, I can't stress enough the importance of respecting this agreement…Yesterday I received an e-mail from Joshua telling me you have requested him or Nicole to assist you with depositions, and he indicated that I should decide which one. I am in no position to make such a decision because you are the one who knows what you need from them. I can only tell you that as long as they do not interfere with my responsibilities as described above, everything is okay with me."

Bob replied that he wanted to honor my directions where possible and reminded me that he was working with CJA and WSGR. "I want to talk to Leo about the advantage or disadvantage of others going," he said.

The day before I left for Chile, Joshua came to my house. "I'm prepared to go," he said, "but if you say that Nicole or I can't meet witnesses before depositions, why would I want to go? I would have nothing to do."

"Don't ask me," I told him. "Ask Bob. He's the one who requested your assistance."

On August 9, 2001, I left for Chile to prepare for our second round of depositions. At the airport bookstore, Felipe bought me *Blindness* by

José Saramago. "This is a *terrible* book," said my son, smiling. "You are going to like it." He was right; I was riveted all the way to Santiago.

The next morning I flew to the southern city of Temuco, where Fulvia the nun had agreed to meet me. My friend Juan Muñoz had helped me locate Fulvia, and I had called her twice before leaving the United States.

"How do you know about me?" Fulvia had asked.

"We have common friends from Cauquenes."

Fulvia had given several reasons why she would not be able to testify: "My mother is sick; she has gone through too much," "I belong to an institution; my superiors would not let me," and so on. When I had insisted, Fulvia had asked what her personal cost would be if she testified.

"Let's talk about that in person," I had said. We had agreed to meet at the cathedral in downtown Temuco, and then go somewhere quiet for lunch.

Temuco was cold and rainy. I arrived early at the cathedral with no umbrella, just a small hat to shield me from the rain. As I waited, I walked around the plaza looking in some shops. I recalled Clodomoro Garrido's description of Fulvia's experience with Fernandez. "Armando Fernandez came to the police station to interrogate prisoners whose names he had written on a piece of paper," Garrido had said. "He asked me to bring out those prisoners, one by one, to an office where he interrogated them in my presence. The first prisoner Fernandez asked me to bring out was a young woman, Fulvia, who was a good friend of Lavin and of the other three victims. Fernandez politely greeted Fulvia. I said to myself, finally a nice man, a gentleman."

Garrido had described Fulvia as a large woman in her early twenties. "Fulvia walked toward a sofa and sat down without waiting for Fernandez's authorization," Garrido had said. "I tried to make eye contact with her to stop her, but she didn't see me. Fernandez yelled, 'Who gave you authorization to sit, *bitch*!' He went from being a very polite man to becoming a beast, a cruel man. He slapped Fulvia until she fell to the ground, and while she was on the ground he kicked her entire body with his boots. He left her bleeding on the floor. 'I'll come back for you later, bitch,' he told her.

"Fernandez arrived in a jeep at the police station. He came with other officers. Once they finished their interrogations, they asked us for a larger vehicle to take prisoners out. We told them that they needed authorization. We couldn't let them use any of our vehicles without proper authorization. They were in a hurry and since they could only fit four prisoners in the jeep, they *warned* us, 'We'll come back for the others.' Not much later, we learned that the four prisoners had been killed. However, they never came back for the others."

I walked back to the cathedral and waited for Fulvia to arrive. Around 12:15 p.m., I saw an elderly nun at the main entrance. She asked my name and handed me an envelope with an address inside. "Fulvia is waiting for you at the convent," the nun said and walked away.

The rain came down harder. I took a taxi to the convent, and when I rang the front bell, a large woman in a light gray apron, whom I assumed was the housekeeper, answered the door. The woman said nothing, just moved aside to let me in and led me down a silent hallway to a cold, empty room with a wooden crucifix on the wall. I thanked her and waited for Fulvia to arrive.

"I won't testify," said the woman.

Startled by this odd greeting, I said, "So you are Fulvia."

"Yes, but I won't testify."

Not sure what to do, I sat on the sofa. Fulvia sat in a chair a short distance away, avoiding my eyes. "I spoke with other people," she said. "We thought that since your case is from Copiapó and not Cauquenes, I have nothing to do with it. My testimony won't help. Besides, I belong to an institution. My bishop told me not to do it. Moreover, the head of my congregation is in Switzerland. I couldn't ask him for advice."

I explained that events in other cities were relevant to our allegation of crimes against humanity. "Probably you are the only victim that Fernandez left alive. You can speak for all of those who can no longer speak."

"For three years I suffered," Fulvia said. "My mother suffered too much. I have already accepted what happened to me. Most probably you are going to obtain *absolutely* nothing out of your efforts for justice. In reality, nothing can be done…the politicians control everything. What you are doing is a waste of time. No good will ever come out of it."

"It takes time for justice to arrive," I said. "Pinochet's arrest in London opened up new opportunities to pursue justice."

"Don't you see? Pinochet is back. There is no justice." Fulvia spoke bitterly about the involvement of the CIA and US government in the coup. Like most people in Chile today, she was aware that the CIA had paid some $6.8 to $8 million to Chilean right-wing opposition groups to destabilize Allende's government. "Too much power," Fulvia continued. "We can't do anything to change that. I don't feel hatred toward Fernandez, nor toward anyone. I don't see them as my enemies. History will judge them. That's not my role…I think this is what God wants, to leave things the way they are."

"Don't you feel a moral obligation to tell the truth? Aren't you betraying the very virtues your church lays claim to—justice, truth?"

Fulvia reddened. "Truth doesn't serve any purpose. This case has been investigated completely. Did it bring justice? It is very easy for you to come down from the United States and do what you are doing. There are no personal costs involved for you. It is very easy for you to do this. It's not the same for me. I have my personal costs. Not like you."

"I believe you are assuming too much about me," I said, trying to catch her eye. She would not look at me. "But this is not about me. Besides, when you do what you believe is right, you don't think about the personal consequences—your costs. Those become part of the process. You only hope that one day you will achieve your goals, that the world is a better place to live, and that you had something to do with it."

"You don't know what it is to live under a dictatorship. You didn't suffer what we suffered. You left the country. I didn't."

I felt I would have to let Fulvia go, but I had to ask one more question. "With all due respect, I want to ask you a very personal question. I teach college students. Every opportunity I have, I like to invite my students to reflect on our personal responsibilities in the construction of the world we live in. I want to tell them about our conversation. But I need to better understand your reasons for not wanting to participate in the search for truth and justice. Don't you feel any responsibility in the construction of our future?"

Finally, Fulvia looked at me. "I spoke with other people. We decided…"

"I don't want to know what other people think or say. I want to know, if possible, how *you* feel. What are *your* reflections?"

"History is manipulated by the politicians," she said, looking away. "We can't change that. Justice won't happen. Nothing more can be done. I suffered for three years. That's enough. People who pursue justice—that's their business. They do it for personal gain, for the publicity, to get political appointments. They like to appear on television. That's not me."

There was nothing more to say.

I left the convent and slowly walked back to the plaza in the pouring rain. Soaked and shivering, I sat on a bench and began to cry. People stared as they walked past, but I was too disillusioned to care. My meetings with these religious people, first Father Muñoz and now Fulvia, a nun, had shaken me to the core. Their unwillingness to testify was one of my greatest shocks during the process of our lawsuit.

It was 1:30 p.m., and my flight back to Santiago was not until 6:00 p.m., so I had plenty of time to sit and think and get depressed in the rain. I recalled my friend Margarita Carrasco saying that everything happens for a reason. I don't know if that's true, but it did make me think: *What would be a good reason for all of this? Move to a dry place first.*

I found a decent restaurant and ordered some lunch, and then carefully wrote the notes from my meeting with Fulvia. As I looked out the window at the rain falling on the cathedral and all the people running for cover, I suddenly thought of my friend Mauricio who had lived in Temuco. I had tried to locate Mauricio several times since our escape from Chile but had only managed to learn that his wife, Gloria, had passed away.

Mauricio was not in the phone book, but I thought if he was still in Temuco he probably still worked at the planning office. "The building across from the cathedral is the governor's office," said the waiter. "Maybe somebody there can help you."

I walked across the plaza, and as I was reading some flyers on a wall near the governor's office, a *carabinero*, or Chilean civil police officer, asked what I was doing there.

"I'm trying to find somebody who works here."

"But today is Saturday," he said. "Don't you know that?"

I had barely slept in forty-eight hours and had lost track of the days. Smiling, I asked the *carabinero* if he knew my friend or if there was any way to learn whether Mauricio Olivares worked at SERPLAC. The *carabinero* looked at some papers inside his guard office. "He is an old friend of mine," I added. "I haven't seen him in almost thirty years. We went to school together."

"Thirty years! And you expect him to remember you?"

"Why don't you call him and see?"

The *carabinero* dialed the number. "I have a lady here who says she is your friend from school that you haven't seen in almost thirty years. Her name is Zita Cabello." The *carabinero* looked surprised and handed me the phone. "He remembers you," he said, smiling.

"What are you doing here?" Mauricio exclaimed over the phone. "Wait for me in the plaza. I'll be there in fifteen minutes."

I walked back to the bench where I had been crying just a few hours earlier, and soon Mauricio came strolling across the plaza. We embraced warmly, and then, just as he had outside Commander Haag's office in 1973, he picked me up and threw me into the air.

We spent the rest of the afternoon in a coffee shop, talking about Copiapó. Mauricio and Gloria had been engaged around the time of the coup and had asked Wito to be their witness at the wedding. A few weeks after Wito's death, they had asked me to take his place. I recalled Gloria's beautiful, contagious laugh and said, "She also had her temper."

"She sure did," Mauricio said, smiling wistfully.

Back in Santiago, I called my friend Margarita to share my experience. "In the end, it was a great day," I told her. "It would seem that I have a guardian angel."

"No, Zita," she said. "You don't have a guardian angel. You have an army."

THIRTY SIX

While I was in Chile searching for witnesses, Leo and Nicole flew to Miami, Florida, to depose Armando Fernandez. His lawyer, Steve Davis, was also present. For two consecutive days Nicole interrogated Fernandez. Many of her questions concerned his involvement in the 1976 car-bombing assassination of former Chilean Ambassador Orlando Letelier and his American assistant, Ronni Moffitt, in Washington, DC. Later, while reading the deposition transcript, I was surprised to see how many of Nicole's questions were unrelated to Wito's case. I was not surprised, however, by Fernandez's answers to her questions about the Copiapó killings:

"Did you review any of the prisoners' files in fiscal's [military prosecutor's] office?" Nicole asked.

"No," Fernandez said.

"Did you review any of the prisoners' files at any time on this trip?" Nicole asked.

"No, never."

"That evening, did you go into the barracks where the prisoners were being held?"

"No, no."

"You and Marcelo Moren Brito didn't go in and take some prisoners out of the barracks?"

"Totally sure I did not, totally sure, no."

"You don't remember some of the prisoners had a chocolate cake?"

"No, no."

"Do you recall," Nicole asked, after more questions, "a group of prisoners being made to stand in a line in the dark with lights shining on their faces?"

"No."

"Did you interrogate any of the prisoners?"

"No, no."

"Thirteen prisoners were taken out of the regiment that night, by truck, and were later killed outside the regiment," Nicole said, after more questions. "Were you involved in putting them on the truck?"

"No."

"Did you see anyone put them on the truck?"

"No."

And so the interrogation continued, with Fernandez denying any involvement whatsoever in the murder of the thirteen prisoners.

On August 13, 2002, the day that Nicole and Leo deposed Fernandez in Miami, I received an unexpected blow in Chile. Bob e-mailed, then Joshua called, to say that the legal team had decided not to go ahead with the depositions at that time. Bob would still come to Chile, but instead of spending two weeks as planned, he would now only be there from August 19 to 31 "to meet with witnesses, to make sure we get the best testimony possible." Sometime in November, the lawyers would go to Chile to take depositions.

I e-mailed Bob to express my extreme concern that if we did not immediately depose certain witnesses, we would lose our chance. As I waited for his reply, I began to feel overwhelmed by the news that our depositions had been canceled and by our lawyers' constant maneuvering. I called Pato from my hotel room, sobbing into the phone. "It won't happen. This is the end."

"Don't throw away the hero in your soul," Pato said, quoting one of my favorite lines from Nietzsche.

Exhausted, I hung up the phone and closed the heavy window drapes, shutting out every bit of daylight in the room. In darkness, I crawled into bed and lay motionless, my mind flooding with doubts. *What's the point?*

Fulvia must be right. There is no point in searching for truth and justice. It's a waste of time. Why would I want to keep wasting my time?

For days, I lay in bed in the dark hotel room, trying to recall my reasons for filing the lawsuit. I tried to feel hopeful that one day I would find the missing evidence so we could offer Wito's last moments of courage to the world. Wito had always wanted me to look for beauty in sorrow. Now I was even failing at that.

Once, I had found the strength to struggle for a new beginning in my brother's last words to me: words that held pain and suffering, faith and hope. The last time I had seen Wito—and I did not know at the time that it was fated to be my last visit with him—my brother had been so happy. He had received the news that he would be released in a just few days, and he smiled radiantly as he asked me to have faith in what was to come. Wito's unbroken faith in me had inspired me to keep on searching for truth and justice, but now the situation was so far out of my hands that I felt myself surrendering hope and starting to believe that there really was nothing more I could do. Without hope, I felt my dreams start to die. It came to me, then, that I had two choices. I could accept that there was nothing else I could do and go back to my old life, to my family and teaching. Nobody, especially my family, would blame me if I just gave up and went home. Or I could keep trying. A voice inside me—I think I could hear my brother's voice—said that when you reach an end, that's when you can find a new beginning. I wanted to find a new beginning, but I didn't know how. I would have to keep fighting, and I hated to fight. It felt like everything was about fighting now. I felt such a sense of powerlessness, because I had all this information, but if I wanted a lawsuit, I needed the lawyers. There in the darkness, there was a fight within myself, and I could feel myself starting to lose. I felt utterly alone.

At least twice a day, Pato called my hotel room to check on me. "Don't give up your dream," he said, anxiously. "You can make it happen."

Nothing seemed to help. Lost in darkness, even my dreams were falling to pieces. I felt like all hope had died.

My entire family started calling with words of encouragement. My sons, my brother, my sister all sounded worried. When Lito called, I knew something must really be wrong; he never called during my trips to

Chile. "You have done everything in your power to make this happen," Lito said. "There is nothing else you can do. Don't blame yourself. It won't be your fault if we lose the case."

Veronica came to see me. "While I was riding the bus on my way here," she said, "I heard clearly Wito's words: 'Tell Zita she has done everything in her power. There is nothing else she can do.' Those were your brother's words. I heard him. Believe me. You have done so much already for your brother. It's time to let it go. Go back to your teaching, to Pato, the boys. They need you."

Victor and many other friends called with the same message: "You have done everything you can do. There is nothing else."

That just devastated me further.

On August 16, Victor called and said, "I'm going to your hotel right now. I'll be there in fifteen minutes. I'm bringing some Prozac for you."

That got me out of bed. I stood unsteadily, looking around the darkened room. Papers were everywhere. I had been living in a chaotic mess. Twenty minutes later, Victor called again. "I won't bring Prozac. I just found out that it takes about fifteen days to take effect."

The next morning, still feeling utterly defeated, I went down to breakfast with the copy of *Blindness* that my *maldito* son had given me. Then I checked my e-mail. Bob had sent two messages, saying that he would arrive August 21 instead of the 19 and that the legal team had decided "to take the depositions of a few key witnesses" after all.

Those e-mails buoyed me to instant recovery—no waiting period required. Bob asked for my list of witnesses and said he needed me to schedule depositions from August 27 to 30, arrange meetings with witnesses in the five days prior to depositions, and provide notice to the defendant's lawyers, since Steve Davis needed to know all the witnesses' names and what we expected from them. That gave me just four days to squeeze in more than seven key witnesses.

I did not know if Bob would actually be able to depose all the witnesses in four days, but I wanted him to meet most of the people I had lined up. Realizing that some witnesses might cancel, I created an ambitious schedule of two to three depositions a day, including ten key witnesses and some "maybes" such as Haag and Vidal. I also scheduled

Raúl Poblete, even though his connection with the Communist Party might cause problems, depending on the jury.

Several phone calls and two meetings later, Enrique Vidal agreed to testify. "When would it be a good time for you to meet my lawyer?" I asked.

"I don't want to meet with your lawyer," Vidal said. "Tell me the day and time you want me to testify. I'll be there."

I called Commander Haag's daughter and was saddened to learn that her mother had passed away six months earlier, and shortly after, her father had suffered an accident. Oscar Haag had passed away.

I still had no lead on Major Carlos Brito, the military prosecutor from Copiapó who had decided to free my brother and Pato the day Arellano arrived in Copiapó, so I did not include him as a potential witness. But a few hours after sending the witness list and deposition calendar to my lawyers, I found a possible home address for him; so early Saturday morning Veronica and I took a bus to Quillota. The emotional strain of the past few weeks and the long hours spent preparing for Bob's arrival were catching up with me, and I felt so nauseous with headache and fever that I almost threw up a few times on the bus. After the two-hour bus ride, my head was throbbing.

Veronica and I found the street we were looking for in Quillota, but as usual, the house number I had did not exist. Slowly we walked down the street, asking people if they knew Carlos Brito. No one did.

We walked to another address I had, which I thought might be Brito's office. The building was closed. I asked a man walking out the door if he knew Carlos Brito, and he said, "He doesn't work here. His son, who is a lawyer, works here, but I don't know where he lives, either." The man gave us a tentative street name for Brito's son.

Veronica and I wandered several blocks, looking for the street, but I felt so ill that we decided to stop the search. I bought an apple at a small fruit stand, just to fill my stomach, and asked the vendor if she happened to know Carlos Brito.

"Yes," the woman said. "His son lives in that house, but he is never there. Mr. Carlos Brito asked me to keep an eye on his son's house because one day somebody broke into it." The woman flipped through an old notebook. "I have his phone number somewhere and his home address."

Veronica and I found Carlos Brito's home, and we talked with him for a long time. Finally he agreed to meet with Bob on August 21.

Early Tuesday morning I met Bob at the airport and drove him to our hotel, where I had scheduled a 10:00 a.m. meeting with Ariosto Lapostol, the former commander from La Serena. When Lapostol arrived, we found a private corner in the hotel lobby, and I translated between English and Spanish as Bob asked questions. In vivid detail Lapostol described Arellano's visit to La Serena, from the moment the helicopter landed until it lifted off for Copiapó.

That afternoon as Bob and I rode a bus out to Quillota, I briefed him on Brito's testimony and shared my impressions. I felt that Brito knew more than he was willing to tell, but at least his testimony confirmed what Wito had told my family on two separate occasions: "I'll be home in a couple of days. The military prosecutor just told me that he was letting me go free."

Bob and I reached Carlos Brito's house around 4:00 p.m., and he invited us in, saying that he wanted his wife and son to be present for the meeting. As soon as Bob and I were settled, Brito looked into my eyes and said, "I had decided to free Winston. I told your brother just hours before Arellano arrived in Copiapó that there were no charges against him, that there was no reason for him to be detained. You probably don't believe me."

"I do believe you," I said, "because you allowed Winston to call my mom from your office to give her the good news."

Brito did not remember the phone call, but when his wife walked in, he repeated what I had said.

"He always talked about Winston," Brito's wife said, "and how nobody would ever believe that he had decided to let him go home."

Responding to Bob's questions, Brito explained his responsibilities as military prosecutor and his reasons for deciding to release Wito. "The city was pretty peaceful," Brito said of Copiapó. "There were no subversive actions against the military regime. We had about fifty people detained for no reason."

Bob asked about Fernandez, and Brito said he had seen him striking a prisoner with a rifle. "Stop!" Brito had shouted. "What are you doing? That's not a way to treat prisoners." According to Brito, Fernandez had responded, "Tell that to General Arellano. I receive orders from him, not from you."

Finally, to my great relief, Carlos Brito agreed to testify. I scheduled his deposition for 2:00 p.m. on Monday, August 27. Then Brito's son, whom I had instantly disliked, began asking questions about the deposition's legal standing in the United States and whether we had authorization from the Supreme Court or Chilean government to create a court in Chile. Bob explained that we did not have to go through those channels since these were voluntary testimonies.

Brito's son asked if we could offer his father protection if it seemed necessary. "Zita found my father. I don't know how she did it. We thought nobody knew where he lived. We are worried about his safety."

"Let's think about that," Bob said. "We have the witness protection program in the United States."

"It would mean your father would have to change his identity, and you would never see him again," I added. "Do you think it makes sense?"

"I still want to think about it," said Brito's son.

Carlos Brito listened in silence, looking as if he did not understand why his son was asking so many questions. As Bob and I were leaving, Brito's son kissed me on the cheek and said, "I'm so proud of my father for doing this." He turned to his father and repeated how proud he was of him.

On the bus ride back to Santiago, Bob said, "If Brito tells us exactly what he said about Winston, that there were no charges against him, and that he had decided to release him, that's all we need from him. We don't have to ask him any other questions."

Over the next few days, Bob and I met with Dr. Iván Murúa, Grimilda Sánchez, Victor Bravo, Commander Eugenio Rivera from Calama, Patricio Lapostol, Jorge Ortíz, and Raúl Poblete. We spent long days traveling around Santiago on buses, subways, and taxis. Bob complained only once: "You don't even leave time for lunch. Poor Pato, I'm sure you did the same with him."

Grimilda Sánchez's and Raúl Poblete's testimonies touched Bob deeply. "How did you get all these witnesses?" he asked, shaking his head.

On Sunday night Bob and I were dining at an elegant restaurant, waiting for Brito's son to confirm his father's deposition the next day, when my cell phone rang.

"Who are you?" asked a male voice in perfect English when I answered. Hesitantly, I gave my name. "Let me speak with the American lawyer," the voice said.

Bob walked outside to take the call. Soon I heard his voice rising. Then he was shouting. A few minutes later Bob stalked back into the restaurant, his usually pale face an angry red.

"That was Brito's lawyer," Bob said. "That son of a bitch wants money. I should have let *you* take the call. His lawyer said his client wants money to compensate him for the pain and suffering he would go through if he gives us his testimony…that *son of a bitch*."

Bob's face shone with anger. He was so visibly furious in the middle of that fancy restaurant that I could not help smiling. "That's okay," he assured me. "Don't worry. We have plenty of good witnesses."

I nodded. Inside, though, I could not help worrying. What would happen to our case if the other witnesses asked us for money?

THIRTY SEVEN

On the evening of August 26, our team assembled at the Crowne Plaza Hotel in Santiago, Chile, ready to begin depositions the following morning. As agreed to by the parties, the legal team flew an American court reporter, Sharon Vartanian, to Santiago to record the deposition testimony and, as is the job of the reporter, to administer the oath. Also as agreed by the legal team, Bob had hired a local interpreter. Fernandez's lawyer, Steve Davis, was staying at a different hotel. All that was missing was someone to videotape the depositions; as is routine for American law firms, depositions are videotaped. To my surprise, my lawyers had decided against videotaping these depositions for some reason; I no longer had the energy to ask why.

Early the next morning, we gathered in the Victoria Room, a private conference room on the twenty-first floor that we had arranged for to keep our witnesses hidden from prying eyes, especially those of the media. I met Steve Davis for the first time that morning and thought the young lawyer seemed too nice to be representing a criminal like Fernandez.

At 8:50 a.m. I went downstairs to wait in the hotel lobby for our first witness, Colonel Ariosto Lapostol. I had overheard Bob and Steve Davis remarking that it was not unusual for witnesses to change their minds at the last minute, and I agonized as I waited, dreading the possibility that Lapostol might not come. I had mobilized an extraordinary team of people, and a great deal of money had been invested. Now the entire operation's success depended on the witnesses I had personally insisted on.

Those last minutes of waiting were almost unbearable.

Lapostol arrived right on time. As we rode the elevator to the twenty-first floor, I reminded him to expect tricky questions from Steve Davis and explained that a deposition was a formal procedure similar to court proceedings on TV shows, where the lawyers work to destroy witnesses' testimonies. The obvious difference was that we did not have a judge. "Fernandez's lawyer is not going to make things easy for you," I warned him.

At 9:53 a.m., Ariosto Lapostol's deposition began.

On the record, and before the court reporter swore in Mr. Lapostol and the interpreter, Bob explained to him the procedure they were to follow: "I'm going to ask questions and then ask you to respond. The gentleman to my right is named Mr. Davis. He is also from the United States. Mr. Davis represents Fernandez Larios. He is his lawyer. When I complete my questions, Mr. Davis will have some questions for you, as well."

Then Bob said to Steve Davis, "Did you want to state your objection?"

"Sure," Davis replied, "then this will be on the record." That took me by surprise.

"We are about to commence some depositions here in Santiago," Steve Davis said for the record. "On behalf of Fernandez, the defendant in this case, we object to these depositions. We object to these proceedings. We believe that they are not in compliance with federal rules of civil procedure, that they are not going to provide inherently reliable information for the parties, that because of the nature of the proceedings, that there is no official participation with the Chilean judicial authorities in this process, that the witnesses are effectively not under any obligation to tell the truth because there's no sanctions that can ever be imposed on these witnesses. Because of that, we believe the procedure itself is defective. However, the depositions have been noticed and we're here and intend to participate to the fullest extent possible."

Once Davis stated his objection, the interpreter, Carmen Oria, was duly sworn to translate from the English language into the Spanish language and from the Spanish language into the English language.

Then Mr. Lapostol was duly sworn and Bob began his interrogation.

In 1973 Ariosto Lapostol had been commander of the regiment in La Serena. Through a series of questions, Bob took Lapostol back through the events of October 16, 1973—the day that Arellano and his delegation had arrived in La Serena—and asked him to explain how fifteen political prisoners had been summarily executed as a direct result of that visit.

"Before we get to what he did, I would like you to tell me, did you know that General Arellano was going to arrive in La Serena?"

"No. No, I didn't know he was going to come," said Lapostol.

"How did General Arellano arrive in La Serena? What was the means of transportation for him to arrive?"

"In a helicopter."

"When you went to the airport and saw the helicopter, did you see who was in the helicopter?"

"Yes. I saw all of them…General Arellano, Arredondo, Moren, Chiminelli, Pedro Espinoza, Fernandez Larios, and the crew, the helicopter crew, who did not leave the helicopter at any moment."

"What happened at the meeting that General Arellano wanted to have, and who was present at that meeting?" asked Bob, after a few questions.

"The people who accompanied him on this mission were present. All the officers of my regiment were also present. And of course I was present. And the next echelon down from an officer was also present."

"About how many total people were present at this meeting, approximately?"

"About forty to fifty people were present."

"What was the purpose of General Arellano's visit as he explained it to the people that were there? What did he say his purpose was for being there?"

"He said he was representing General Pinochet," Lapostol said. "He was delegated by Pinochet. The aim was to solve the problem regarding people who were under arrest, people who had committed minor offenses. And, therefore, they were going to hold a war council to resolve this problem quickly and to set them free. That was essentially the reason for his being there, for General Arellano being there."

"Did General Arellano say that one of his purposes was to hold court-martials and to execute prisoners?" Bob asked.

"No. He was not there to hold court-martials. What I just explained was the essence of his mission, the nature of his mission."

"When the meeting concluded, he addressed everyone; did the officers then disperse?"

"The officers under my command went to their usual posts," Lapostol said. "The ones who came with General Arellano went up to my office so that the attorney, the prosecutor, could show the list of detainees... so that it could be determined who would be set free and who wouldn't."

"So you went up to your office with the group that came with General Arellano, correct?"

"Yes, of course. I was the owner, the house owner, the host."

"In this group that went up to your office, did it include Fernandez Larios?"

"They all went up to my office, but I was a colonel and he was a lieutenant. So I wasn't going to really notice him."

"Did the group that came with General Arellano go up as a group to your office with you?"

"Yes. All of them went up to my office together."

"What happened when you went to your office?"

"The general requested the list of people who were detained in jail."

"On the list, the detailed list, some cases had been concluded and some cases had not; is that correct?" Bob asked, after a few questions.

"Yes, of course," Lapostol said. "Yes. There were several cases of people who had already been sentenced, and they were carrying out their sentence. I always presided over these hearings for the war council. There was no death sentence handed down."

"When General Arellano was reviewing the records, did you watch him as he went down and looked at the records?"

"General Arellano was sitting here. Here are the records on the table. And I was right next to him."

"What did he do as he went through these records?"

"General Arellano especially looked over the section that explained what offense the person had committed."

"Did you see him make any notes or notations on these records?"

"Yes. He took a pen, a red pen, and he put a check next to the name, on some people's names, on about fifteen people's names…In the case of three people he put a check next to the names where the war council had already resolved that case and handed down a sentence."

"Let me go back," Bob said. "When you said that he was reviewing what the people had done, in the case where there had been no war council, would these be the charges that were made against the person as opposed to a conclusion or a sentence?"

"In those cases where the war council had not—in about twelve cases where the war council had not resolved the case—it was only the offenses that hadn't been proven yet, hadn't been corroborated firmly yet."

"As General Arellano used the red marker, did you ask him, 'What are you doing and why are you doing this?'"

"After he had finished putting a check with a red marker on fifteen cases, I asked him, 'What does this check mean? What does it mean what you just did?'"

"What was General Arellano's response?"

"You mean what Arellano answered me? He said that given the gravity or seriousness of the offenses committed by these people, they had to face a war council. So when he gave me this response, I pointed out that of those fifteen people on whose name he put this check in red, three of them had already been with the war council and their sentences had been handed down."

"Of those three people who had sentences were any of the sentences for death?"

"I repeat: no one was ever, ever sentenced to death."

"What was the maximum sentence in years of any of the three that were already sentenced?"

"Twenty years."

"When General Arellano said that these men must face a war council, the fifteen, what was your response to him?"

"At first, let's say in a friendly way, I told him let's not do that because I found that it was illegal," Lapostol said. "His attitude to what I just told him, he didn't accept this. He said that given the seriousness, the gravity of these offenses, he felt that, yes, they had to face the war council."

"I need to go back," Bob said. "The helicopter arrived at La Serena at what time in the morning on October the sixteenth, approximately?"

"About eleven o'clock in the morning."

"In a war council proceeding, is the accused entitled to have a lawyer present and assisting him?"

"We are in Chile, which is a very organized country," Lapostol said. "Of course, the accused has a lawyer that can defend him. And the prosecutor is the one who brings the charges against him."

"In the three cases in which you had presided in a war council, the three detainees, did they have lawyers to assist them?"

"Yes, of course.

"When General Arellano said that the fifteen should face the war council, when did he say that the war council would consider their cases?"

"No. It was understood that it would be immediate."

"Did you make any statement to General Arellano regarding lawyers for the accused?"

"That was much later, much, much later. First it was an exchange of opinions, during which General Arellano insisted that these fifteen people had to face a war council...So here we were exchanging, arguing back and forth. He said, yes, these people should face the war council. I kept saying no because it's illegal and against the regulations established by the military government."

"The regulations you were talking about related to the three people who had already been before the war council? You were not referring to the other twelve as well, were you?"

"Only to these three cases. I asked him to have a war council for those other twelve people and not the other three."

"Did General Arellano say that he would proceed against all fifteen or against the twelve?"

"No. He was determined to have all fifteen cases face the war council."

"When General Arellano was looking at the records, were the people that came up there with him still with him?"

"Yes."

"Earlier you said that the discussion about lawyers for the people that were accused came later. When did you discuss the need for lawyers with General Arellano, if you discussed it with him?"

"The problem was that when General Arellano kept insisting on making these three people already sentenced face a war council, and after he said yes and I said no about seven times to this point, I asked him for permission to leave the office because I felt that my authority for presiding for the war council had been trampled on, had been disauthorized."

Lapostol testified that he had told his assistant, Lieutenant Emilio Cheyre, to gather all the officers of the regiment and instruct them that no one could carry out "any order given by General Arellano or any members of his mission or task force" if Lapostol, as commander of the regiment, did not ratify the order. Then he had walked to a garden inside the garrison.

"I was there about ten to fifteen minutes," said Lapostol. "And then General Arellano showed up to speak to me, to talk about the same issue, about making these fifteen people face a war council."

"Was anybody present in the garden when you were talking with General Arellano, other than you and General Arellano?"

"At the beginning, no. About half an hour later…Captain Mario Vargas of my regiment showed up…after Captain Vargas had arrived, we felt—we heard some gunshots inside the regiment. I ordered Captain Vargas to go see what had just happened."

"What happened next?"

"I ordered Captain Vargas to go see what had just happened. I asked General Arellano, 'What were those gunshots for?' 'Oh, it must be the result of the war council.' I said, 'How could there have been a war council if the lawyers who are going to defend the accused haven't arrived yet?' And he, General Arellano, answered me, 'They must have come through another entrance.' And I said, 'There's no way they could have gone through any other entrance because upon my orders all the other entrances were closed except where we are right now.'

"Captain Vargas ran as fast as he could and came back, and came back about fifteen minutes later, more or less."

"What did Captain Vargas say that he had seen?" Bob asked.

"Object to the form of the question to the extent it calls for hearsay," Davis said. "You can answer, sir."

"Captain Vargas said there were several people lying dead on the floor, on the ground, and some were still standing," Lapostol said... "There was no reaction from the general. About ten minutes later we heard more gunshots."

Davis objected.

"...After Captain Vargas returned, what happened next?" Bob asked.

"Object to the form to the extent it asks for what anybody said during that time," Davis said. "You may answer, sir."

"Well, I wasn't really expecting that there would be people dead," Lapostol said. "Because had there been a war council, it was just—everything was just happening too quickly for a war council to have taken place. When we heard—felt the second round of gunshots—Arredondo showed up. Arredondo came to where we were standing and he said something like, 'General, here in La Serena everything has been resolved.'"

"Move to strike to the extent it's not responsive to the question and it's also hearsay," Davis said.

"Although you have stated it earlier, I would like you to tell us again who Arredondo is," Bob said.

"Arredondo worked here in Santiago with General Arellano and he was a member of this mission," Lapostol said. "He was part of this task force."

"He arrived in the helicopter with General Arellano?"

"Yes..."

"In the garden we have you, General Arellano, Captain Vargas, and Arredondo, those four."

"Yes. Four people."

"Fernandez Larios was not in the garden when the gunshots were heard, is that correct?"

"No. He was not in the garden with us. Fernandez Larios was never with us in the garden."

"Arredondo comes up and says, 'Our mission is finished,' or something like that, 'here.' What did General Arellano say to Arredondo, if he said anything?"

"Object to the form of the question," Davis said. "You may answer, sir."

"General Arellano then tells me that he needs jeeps. He needs me to send jeeps over so he can take all his men back to the helicopter. To the airport back to the helicopter."

"Did you provide the jeeps?"

"Yes, I did."

"Did the jeeps take General Arellano and his men back to the helicopter?"

"Yes."

"Where was Fernandez Larios?" Bob asked, after a few questions.

"In one of the other two jeeps."

"The gunshots that you heard you indicated were a pistol or a revolver. Did I hear you correctly?"

"Yes."

"What would be the normal method of a military execution after a court-martial?"

"A firing squad of seven or nine people with a special ceremony, which is common in all the armies of the world."

"Do they use rifles or pistols?" Bob asked, after another question.

"Rifles…This is the normal procedure for a military execution, which is not what happened in La Serena."

"After the helicopter departed, did you go back to the regiment?" Bob asked, after more questions.

"Yes."

"What did you discover when you went back?"

"I did what you would have done. I went to see what had happened."

"What did you find?"

"Inside the regiment in a firing range there were fifteen corpses lying on the ground…I sent an official, who was Captain Vargas, to the cemetery to order that the cemetery be opened."

"At this time in La Serena, October 14, 15, 16, what was the state of the community?" Bob asked. "Was it in a riot, was it turmoil, or was it peaceful, or something in between?"

"Object to the form of the question," Davis said. "You may answer, sir."

"Everyone was very calm," Lapostol said. "I'm proud to say that I really had the region very well controlled."

"Based on the war council law and rules, on October 16, 1973," Bob asked, after a few more questions, "were the executions at La Serena illegal?"

"They were illegal because there was no defense for the accused," Lapostol said. "In practical terms, there was no war council."

"Why were the bodies of the victims not given to the families?"

"That is exclusively my responsibility," Lapostol said. "At no moment did we hide the whereabouts of where they were buried…On the same day, the sixteenth of October 1973, the newspaper *El Dia* was told about what had happened, and because of the time, they published it the next day, October 17, and also over the radio."

"Did any of the men under your command at the regiment participate in the executions to your knowledge?"

"Object to the form of the question," Davis said. "You may answer."

"Well, I find the question absurd because I said before I had given strict orders that nobody participate or carry out an order that was issued by General Arellano or anybody who had come out of the helicopter with him without my having approved it."

"It's necessary for me to ask questions in which I might know the answer or you might know the answer," Bob said. "But for people who read this later, they might not know the answer. So I might ask a question that you think is absurd, but it's because others later will be reading this who have not had the benefit of your testimony."

"I use the term absurd to emphasize that my orders were strict, not to offend you," Lapostol said.

"Okay. Were these executions, to your knowledge, carried out by General Arellano's men that came with him in that helicopter?" Bob asked.

Steve Davis objected to the form of the question.

"One hundred percent, yes," Lapostol said.

Bob finished his examination, and Steve Davis began deposing Colonel Lapostol. After some opening questions, Davis asked, "What rank did you have at the time you left the military?"

"Colonel."

"At any time in your approximate thirty-eight years of military service, did you ever receive any type of military discipline?"

"Never."

"Were you ever accused of any wrongdoing at any time during your thirty-eight-year military career?"

Bob objected to the form of the question.

"No, never," Lapostol said.

"About how many members of the military were under your control, under your command?" Davis asked.

"About one thousand people."

"As of October 1973, who did you report to?" Davis asked, after more questions.

"General Herman Brady. He was a commander of the Second Division of the Chilean army to which my regiment belonged."

"As of October of 1973, General Arellano would have been a superior officer to you, correct?"

"Yes, of course. I was a colonel then. He was a general."

"Prior to October 16, 1973, had you ever had any direct contact with General Arellano?" Davis asked.

"Yes."

"Tell us what that contact was."

"When I was a student at the war academy he was my professor during the first year."

"Is that the only contact, that he was a professor of yours sometime in the 1940s?" Davis asked.

"Yeah. We probably met at some social function like a cocktail [party]."

"Now, at any time during any of your interaction with General Arellano, did he mention that he was there on the orders of General Pinochet?" Davis asked, after more questions.

"General Arellano had a document with him that said he was delegated, commissioned by General Pinochet to look at these cases of people who committed minor offenses and to set them free," Lapostol said.

"Did you see that document?"

"During that general meeting, I can't remember whether it was my assistant or one of the members of General Arellano's task force [who] actually read out this document. And in deference to me, so I could corroborate that it was an authentic document, he handed it to me and he allowed me to sit down in spite of the fact that he was standing so that I could read it thoroughly, so that I could not only hear it being read out, but I could actually see it and have it in my hand."

"Did you, in fact read it and did it say what General Arellano said it said?"

"Yes. And the document said what I have already explained, that they had to do a case-by-case analysis and those who had committed minor offenses could be set free. That was essentially the spirit of this document."

"It was signed by General Pinochet?"

"Yes."

"When you discovered that individuals had been executed, did you report to your commanding officer that the prisoners had been illegally executed?" Davis asked, after more questions.

"I called Santiago directly by phone. A colonel who was on shift at that moment answered the phone. I explained the situation to him because General Brady was not in his office."

"Was that it? Did you just have the one conversation with the assistant to General Brady?"

"No. He wasn't General Brady's personal assistant. He was just a colonel on shift at that headquarters."

"Is that the only thing you did? Fifteen people were illegally killed and you made one phone call?"

"Yes...I also notified the press of what had happened..."

"Why didn't you tell the press that the people had been illegally executed?"

"Because I didn't know they were illegal."

"I thought you just told us earlier they were illegal?"

"When I asked General Arellano to give me the minutes of that war council, he said that Chiminelli had them in his briefcase."

"Did you ever receive this document?"

"No. General Arellano told me that Chiminelli had them in his briefcase...This was on our way back to the airport. When we got there, the helicopter was ready to take off, and the general and the members of his task force quickly went into the helicopter because it was already late. The general got into the helicopter and the rest of them as well...I took Chiminelli by the arm and asked him, 'Please give me these documents.' But he threw the briefcase into the helicopter. They said something to him inside the helicopter. He came back to where I was. And he said to me, 'We will send the documents to you from Santiago.' I never got those documents."

"Did you ever follow up and try and get the documents from Chiminelli?"

"No. Well, no, because when I went back to the regiment, I corroborated there hadn't, in fact, been a war council. So therefore there were no documents or minutes of this war council."

"When you found out there had not been a war council, did you then conclude it was an illegal proceeding that had occurred?"

"Of course, it's totally illegal. Because if there's no war council and someone is sentenced to death, he is not even put on trial. So it's definitely illegal."

Davis moved forward in his seat. Pointing his finger accusingly at Lapostol, he said, "Then why didn't you do anything about it, sir?"

As Davis grew nastier with the witness, my anxiety increased. At times, Lapostol seemed uncomfortable with the exchange. His face turned red several times, but he controlled himself.

"I'd like to say something, please," Lapostol interrupted in a calm voice. "I understood at the time that the person who had to explain what had happened to my immediate superior, General Brady, and to General Pinochet was not me, but General Arellano."

"Now, based on your testimony an answer ago, not this last one, then, did General Arellano violate the written order that he presented to you on October 16, 1973?"

"Well, he didn't carry out the order exactly as it was issued."

"But what happened while General Arellano was there bore no resemblance to the order you just described?" asked Davis, after a few more questions.

"That's what's caused me distress to this very day."

"But I'm correct, General Arellano did not carry out the order he was given and showed you?"

"Yes, that's correct."

"In 1973 was there a procedure that you could follow within the Chilean army to report an officer who violated an order?"

"Yes. We have the code of military justice."

"Under the code of military justice, what, in 1973, could you have done?"

"Well, if I had done something, it would have meant that I would be one of those fifteen prisoners executed."

"Meaning that you believe if you would have done something you would have been executed in 1973?"

"Given the circumstances, I think if I had opposed or protested against these illegal executions, I would have been executed person number sixteen. The other option was putting General Arellano and his task force under arrest using personnel from my regiment, which would have caused a huge breakdown, a conflict within the institution. Very serious, very grave."

"So you were afraid to tell the true story in 1973?"

"I don't like the word 'scared.'"

"Well, you just told me that you feared that you might have been executed. What is the other word besides afraid?"

"No. At no moment have I said I was scared of being number sixteen. I said that I'm sure that if I had opposed these executions, I would have been most certainly number sixteen, but not that I felt scared about being number sixteen."

As Davis continued his interrogation, he questioned Lapostol's character, judgment, and responsibility in the killings. "So am I correct in saying that when you learned that there were dead people who were under *your* responsibility, that you did *nothing*?" Davis asked repeatedly.

I expected Lapostol to get up and leave.

It was so difficult to just sit quietly through all this, but the rules prevented me from saying anything. Rarely are plaintiffs invited to sit in on depositions, but they did not have much of a choice in this case. However, Bob had instructed me to avoid speaking with Davis at all cost. "During informal conversation," Bob had said, "is when lawyers fish for new information about the case."

After a confusing exchange of questions and answers, Davis said to Lapostol, "So I don't know if you're deliberately avoiding answering my question or you don't understand it, but I will try one more time. Did you protest to General Arellano the fact that people under your responsibility were killed?"

"I couldn't—I didn't protest because I had no valid reason to do so," Lapostol said. "I wasn't absolutely sure of what had happened. All I hear was from this Captain Vargas who came to where we were. What could I have told General Arellano?"

"I wasn't there, sir," Davis said. "I'm only asking what you did."

"I asked the general again what was all this about and what was happening. From the very minute General Arellano arrived, I was told repeatedly that there would be a war council with all the proper proceedings, with lawyers, et cetera. And that didn't happen. It wasn't happening."

"So am I correct in saying that when you learned that there were dead people who were under your responsibility, then you did nothing?"

"I didn't do anything because immediately after that we heard another round of gunfire about 250 meters away from where we were.

And about five minutes later Arredondo showed up and said that everything in La Serena had been resolved."

"What contact have you had before with Zita Cabello?" Davis asked, after more questions.

"I didn't know her. I had no idea she existed." Lapostol explained that we had first met on the day I asked him to testify.

"Are you being paid any compensation for your time that you're spending here today discussing this case?" Davis asked.

"I think it is a stupid question. I take it as an affront. I'm a colonel of the Chilean army. I don't know if you use that system in the United States, but not here in Chile."

"You still didn't answer my question," said Davis. "I would like an answer to my question, please."

"It's a gross insult to me what you just asked me."

"You still have not answered my question, sir. Are you receiving any money for the time you're spending here talking to us?"

"If you call the coffee that I have just served myself money."

"Sir, I call *money* money. And I ask the question a third time. Are *you* receiving any money for your time here today?"

"No. No, not at all."

The exchange grew so heated that I feared the deposition would end. I felt terribly uncomfortable at Davis's rudeness and got up from my seat, pretending to get a cup of coffee. I walked away from everyone and sat alone, near a window, hoping the deposition would end soon. Lapostol seemed furiously insulted by Davis's suggestion that he had accepted money for his testimony.

Both sides asked more questions, and then the deposition ended at 2:57 p.m. I accompanied Lapostol down to the first floor, ready to apologize for Davis's questions. "Did you see me getting upset?" Lapostol asked. "I did not like Fernandez's lawyer."

We already knew that Carlos Brito had decided not to testify unless he was paid, but during the morning break, Bob had instructed me to call Brito and ask if he was coming for the 4:00 p.m. deposition.

"No," Brito had replied over the phone. "I'm not going."

"What?" I asked. "You promised me you would be here."

Brito was silent. "My lawyers advised me not to," he said finally, "because what you are doing is illegal. You have no authorization from the Chilean Supreme Court to take testimonies here in Chile."

"But Bob already explained to you and also to your son that's not the case."

"I can't go."

Overwhelmed by emotion, I began to cry. "You are the only one who can testify to the fact that my brother had no charges against him," I sobbed, "that he was not a criminal who deserved to be killed, and that you had decided to let him go home free."

"Calm down," Brito said. "Calm down. I will talk to my lawyers, and if they say I can go, I'll be there at 4:00 p.m."

We waited until 4:30 p.m. Brito never came.

Exhausted, I walked out of the Victoria Room and Bob came over and put his arm around my shoulder. "What great witnesses you have, Zita," he said. "We need to *immediately* find somebody to videotape these depositions."

So that's why they decided not to videotape the depositions. Because they didn't think my witnesses' testimonies would warrant that kind of expense?

With those thoughts running through my mind, I went out alone for a walk.

THIRTY EIGHT

At 10:07 the next morning, Grimilda Sánchez's deposition began. Her testimony and all that followed were videotaped, with excerpts later presented to the jury at trial.

After Grimilda was duly sworn in, Steve Davis said: "Before we begin, I'd have to state the same objection I stated at the beginning of the depositions yesterday. I will not repeat the objection, but for the record, I just note it."

Bob began his interrogation.

Grimilda testified that she had worked as a nurse for a company called Codelco, which had commissioned her to work for the governor of Calama about four months before the coup. On the morning of September 11, 1973, Grimilda was discussing the day's schedule with the governor in his office, when a military jeep pulled up outside and the commander-in-chief of the army at Calama walked in with some officers, all in combat gear. "Everyone had a machine gun in their hands…" Grimilda said. "The commander-in-chief of the army then told off the governor. And he told him, 'I have come here, so you hand over your authority to me as the governor.' Edmundo, the governor, then replied, 'I cannot hand over my authority to you as governor because the president of the republic named me, and therefore, I have more rank. I have more rank than you do.'"

Grimilda went on, "The governor also told the commander that 'When Salvador Allende assumed the presidency you were going to be demoted in military rank and those stripes you have on now on your uniform as colonel were given to you by Salvador Allende and he protected you.' His name was Colonel Rivera…

"The governor then took the keys of his office and placed them on the table. At that moment…I couldn't speak and I saw how brave the governor was speaking in that way, in that tone, to the colonel. Because at that moment they had the force or the power of their weapons with them.

"And at that moment the colonel realized that there was another person in the room," Grimilda continued. "And he asked the governor, 'Who is this woman? What is she doing here?' Edmundo then answered him, 'She is here working with me and she works for Codelco, but she is offering special services here in the governor's office.' He then arrested me right away. He sent me back home and put me under house arrest."

Five days later, according to Grimilda, plainclothes police came to her home and detained her for a day at headquarters before handing her over to the army. She was placed under house arrest. "And the third time a military police officer showed up. They ransacked my home, searching for something. They destroyed everything as much as they could. They took all the food supplies I had in my kitchen and they dumped everything in the middle of the room and they mixed everything up together. It was just to destroy and destroy and destroy. They put me under arrest. They put me in the back of the truck and they went to pick up my son. At that moment, my husband was not at home."

Grimilda testified that she and her son, a computer programming engineer for a copper mine, were taken to a small police station in Dupont. "They put my son in a small room…At that police station they had organized a torture center…it was very roughly done, very simple… The days passed and there is where they tortured my son in front of me. They removed, forcibly removed, the nails from his fingers and his toes. And at one point they pretended they were going to execute him with a firing squad. And they asked him…'What was your last wish because we're about to shoot you?' And my son cried out, 'I want to see my two daughters'…They placed lit cigarettes on his mouth, on his chest. And I had to be a witness to all these things.

"What they wanted me to say was—they kept asking me, 'Where are the arms kept?' They accused me of terrible charges," Grimilda continued. "For example, they said that four hundred tons of explosives had been missing from the Dupont Factory and that we had put them away. Can you imagine, we were so worried about supplying the population with what they needed and here they were saying that we were taking care of doing this other thing.

"They stripped me naked and wrapped me in a military blanket. And they wet this blanket. They wrapped me in it. And they beat me and they applied electricity on my body, on both my breasts. That was torture they applied there. I almost died. They had me there for four days.

"After those four days, they took me over to the prison in Calama," Grimilda testified. "I was there, and other inmates helped me out. They helped me wash and dress. And there were several female prisoners already there. Those are the things I can tell you. But days kept passing. I was worried because [of] what I had seen in Dupont. I didn't know if my son was there or where he was. So I was very, very concerned…"

Steve Davis interrupted, respectfully asking Grimilda to wait for the lawyers' questions rather than giving a narrative description of the events.

Bob resumed his examination. "In regards to the torture, were you tortured in front of your son as well?"

"Yes."

"When did you…next see or hear from your son? And if you could, tell them the date as best you can remember."

"I can't remember the date, exact date," Grimilda testified. "They brought him over one day at five o'clock in the afternoon and they held him in the second floor of the prison. They held these prisoners in individual cells. They couldn't speak to anyone. They brought them over from Dupont so that they could recover from the wounds sustained during the torture sessions. Once they recovered, they brought them down to the common courtyard shared by all the prisoners."

Grimilda testified that she and her son were held continuously in the same prison from October 4 to 19, and she had seen her son in the common courtyard. "We didn't know if we were going to be subjected to a war council," she said. "We didn't know anything. And we didn't even know the charges that were brought against us."

Through a radio bulletin Grimilda learned that her husband, an agricultural engineer, had been executed with two other prisoners on October 6. Then on October 19 at 5:30 p.m., Grimilda watched through a small window in her cell as the male prisoners were brought out to the common courtyard.

"Please tell me what you saw," Bob said.

"At that moment a police officer, a prison guard, had a list and he started calling out names," Grimilda testified. "So…one of my fellow prisoners, a woman, told me, 'Come look, come look, they are going to be taking away these prisoners.' Therefore, we took a table and pushed it against the wall so we could climb up and look through a high window so we could see what was happening…"

Grimilda described standing on the table with two other women, looking out through the cell window. "Right away we saw that there were military people and military police. The military personnel were dressed in combat gear. Of these people, or these military personnel, I remember two of them…"

"Do you know today the identity of the two military people that were there that were armed?" Bob asked.

"One was Moren Brito and the other one was Fernandez Larios," Grimilda testified. "At the moment this was happening I didn't know the names of these people. Then as time went by, the years passed, and I started reading about what had happened…we all saw pictures in the papers, not just in Chile, but all over the world. I realized that those two military men were Moren Brito and Fernandez Larios."

"How far away were you from Fernandez Larios on October the 19 when you looked out the window, how far in meters?" Bob asked.

"Probably not more than three meters. Because the only thing that separated us from these men was a wall. Plus, I especially noticed that he had long sideburns. He didn't have that typical crew cut that the military personnel always use."

"When you saw Fernandez Larios's picture in the newspaper, did you have any doubt that that was the same man that you saw in the courtyard that day with the other prisoners?" Bob asked, after more questions.

Steve Davis objected to the form of the question.

"No," Grimilda testified. "Beyond the shadow of a doubt. Can you imagine the impact this scene had on me? The way they were carrying the prisoners away and they put a kind of bag over their head. And one of these could have been my son."

Bob asked Grimilda to describe what she saw in the courtyard, particularly Fernandez Larios's actions regarding the prisoners.

"He was standing and watching this work being done," Grimilda testified. "The two of them were watching this. They didn't have lists in their hands. They were just giving orders to the other prison guards to make sure the procedure was being done correctly to take the prisoners away. And they took them away in two groups. One group was taken away through the service entrance, which is the group that we saw. And the other group was taken away through the main entrance, which we didn't see that group. We didn't see in what kind of transportation the group through the main entrance was taken away in, but we did see how they carried away the prisoners who went through the service entrance…

"A prison guard called each name out and the prisoner would come forward. They would put a kind of bag over his head to cover his face and he would be put into this police van."

"How were they put into the van?" Bob asked. "How physically were they put into the van?"

"They put these prisoners very inhumanly [*sic*] into the van, as if they were noodles," Grimilda said. "They stacked them up as if they were noodles. And they would stick them in that way in this vehicle."

"Was this done with Fernandez Larios present? Was he there while this was being done?" Bob asked.

Steve Davis objected to the form of the question, but said Grimilda could answer.

"Yes," she said. "The whole time to the very end, to the very end."

"Did they have all of the bags for their heads, were all the prisoners treated the same way?" Bob asked.

"No," Grimilda said. "There was one who was not treated that way… What happened, they didn't have enough of these bags. They needed one more, which they didn't have. And at that moment there were two female prison guards. They were also there watching this procedure. One of them had a scarf around her neck, a long scarf, very long. And it was pinkish or violet. It was made of nylon and transparent.

"Therefore, they called out the name of Haroldo Cabreres. He was the finance manager of Chuquicamata. And they used this scarf. With this long scarf they wrapped it around four times around his eyes and they tied it back. Besides this, Haroldo had a watch, a beautiful watch. I can't remember the kind of watch. They took it off him."

"What did they do with the prisoners that were stacked in the truck after they got them all in the truck?" Bob asked.

"They closed the doors and they left," Grimilda said. "The police, they closed the doors of this van and the van went off. And they went through…another exit. In this police van, my son wasn't in this police van. He wasn't in this van. My son was taken through the main entrance, and I didn't see him leave the prison."

"Did Fernandez Larios and Moren Brito go with the truck?" Bob asked.

Steve Davis objected to the form of the question.

"No…" Grimilda testified. "Moren Brito and Fernandez Larios went through the main entrance. And in this van were the prisoners, the driver, and a police officer who got into the van and was sitting next to the driver."

Steve Davis was raising so many objections that Bob stopped his interrogation to ask him about it. Then, after a few more questions, Bob said to Grimilda, "The question I'm going to ask you now is going to seem obvious, but I have to ask it this way. Did you ever see any of the men that had been put into that van or your son at any time after they left the prison, any of them?"

"No," Grimilda said. "No. Because my husband was already dead. And my son left in one of those groups of prisoners, and I never saw him again."

"Did you ever see any of the other prisoners that were taken after they were taken in the van?"

"No, never again."

All twenty-six men had been massacred that evening.

Steve Davis's interrogation focused on Grimilda's emotional state, in an attempt to cast doubt on the credibility of her testimony.

"How did you mentally get through day to day after your husband was executed?" Davis asked.

"It was very, very difficult for me because that moment was terrible for me," Grimilda testified. "All I wanted was time to pass very quickly and for them to execute me right away because then it would be all over, especially after the death of my son."

"At the time that you were looking at these events, were you listening for whether your son's name was going to be called?" Davis asked, after more questions.

"Yes," Grimilda said. "What I was concerned about is whether they were going to put my—have my son join this mess that was going on."

"So you were quite scared at that moment about what was going to happen, what might happen to your son?"

"At that moment I no longer knew what it was to feel scared. At that moment anything was possible, but I didn't feel that fear in me. I always had some hope in me," she said.

"Do you know what the word 'surreal' means?" Davis asked.

"Yes, of course."

"Would you describe it as a surreal moment?"

"No," Grimilda said. "I wouldn't ever use that word to describe this moment because it was *tangible*. It was happening right in front of me. I could have *touched* what was going on."

"Well, whatever that time period was, and I know you didn't have a stopwatch with you, did you ever yell or say anything to the military personnel at any time during that period?" Davis asked, after a few more questions.

"No, nothing," Grimilda said. "No. We didn't say anything. I didn't say anything. And we tried to keep as quiet as possible so that they would forget about these women prisoners who were in here."

"Now, would it be fair to say that you hate the military officers who were involved in these executions?" Davis asked, after a few more questions.

"Look, I'm going to tell you something that's very sad for me," Grimilda said. "I have never felt hate. I have never felt hatred toward anyone because I don't know what that feeling is. But, yes, I feel very angry because the damage that they inflicted on the Chilean society is very large."

After Steve Davis finished his examination, Bob asked Grimilda, "Do you understand the seriousness of your testimony identifying Fernandez Larios as the military person that was there that day? Do you understand the seriousness of that testimony?"

Davis objected to the form of the question. "But you can certainly answer," he added.

"Yes," said Grimilda.

"Do you have any doubt in your mind whatsoever that Fernandez Larios was the person that you identified?"

Davis objected.

"No," said Grimilda, "None. Absolutely none whatsoever."

The deposition ended at 1:49 p.m.

A few hours later, Colonel Eugenio Rivera arrived in the hotel lobby. I quickly escorted him up to the Victoria Room, where Bob began his interrogation.

Rivera testified that he was commander of the army in Calama in 1973, and on October 18, General Lagos from Antofagasta had called to say that General Arellano would pay an official visit to Calama the next morning. Rivera asked his second-in-command to make the standard preparations for a VIP visit, including an official reception at the airport, a visit to headquarters and other military facilities in the region, a presentation of plans for the military unit, and a farewell dinner for the authorities. On October 19, around 10:30 a.m., General Arellano's helicopter landed in Calama.

"When General Arellano arrived in the helicopter, did you know then that there were going to be executions taking place within the next day or that day at Calama?" Bob asked.

"No," Rivera testified. "Nor did I know that something had happened in Antofagasta."

Bob asked Rivera to describe what he saw when the helicopter door opened.

"I was very surprised because I saw soldiers equipped for war," Rivera said, "whereas we were just dressed in the usual attire we wear for special military presentations. General Arellano was in combat uniform and carried a regulation pistol and submachine gun."

"Did you think it unusual that General Arellano would be armed like that for a visit?" Bob asked.

"Yes."

"You, of course, knew that he was coming because General Lagos had told you that General Arellano was coming for a special mission?" Bob asked.

"No. I was told he was coming on an official visit."

Rivera testified that Arellano carried an official document signed by Augusto Pinochet, designating him as delegated on a special mission. "Based on that order, General Arellano had superior authority in all the regiments visited," Rivera said. "General Arellano assumed the role of governor of that particular area, the role of a military judge and commander of the regiment. Arellano personally reviewed thirty prisoners' files in Calama and ordered that a war council be convened at 2:30 p.m. that day."

For the rest of the day, Rivera and Arellano toured around Calama and visited nearby Chuquicamata, the largest open-pit copper mine in the world. Around 8:00 p.m., they returned to the garrison and asked the officer on duty how the war council was proceeding.

"He notified us that the war council had finished very early and that the task force or the accompanying officers with General Arellano and the officers from my regiment were waiting for us for the farewell dinner that we had prepared for the general and his men at the officers' club..." Rivera testified. "We had the dinner with the usual camaraderie. I didn't perceive any attitude or situation out of the ordinary during the dinner. We had a cocktail drink, a speech, and a farewell. According to our program, we went to the airport to say good-bye to the general...

And I was quite moved and impressed by the service or attention we had given to them during the visit. I went to congratulate my officers for the good work they had done. And my second lieutenant almost fainted in my arms. He said, 'We have had a huge problem.' All the officers started talking at the same time…"

"Colonel, what did your men tell you had happened that you had not seen?" Bob asked, after further questions.

"I was told that twenty-six people had been massacred," Rivera said.

"Just a minute, Colonel," Bob said. "Colonel, twenty-six people had been massacred? Did you ask the question who did it?"

Steve Davis objected to the form of the question.

"No, I didn't," Rivera testified. "I didn't because of what I said before, because I couldn't investigate the actions or deeds or resolutions taken by a general."

"Is it illegal under Chilean military law to execute somebody or to kill somebody that is already under a sentence that is not a sentence of death?" Bob asked, after further questions.

"Yes, it's illegal."

"Did you tell the families…that there had been a massacre of their loved one?"

"I couldn't do that because I had to keep the morale high in my unit and with the people," Rivera said. "I had to protect the military junta and General Arellano and the honor of the Chilean army…How was I to justify this assassination or this massacre? I ordered the second-in-command, the one in charge of intelligence, that they should help me formulate this *bando*. So they suggested to me that why don't we apply the famous law of flight, fleeing."

"In other words, Colonel, they suggested or you ended up telling the public that these people had been killed trying to escape?" asked Bob.

"Yes," Rivera testified. "That's what they suggested."

"That's what you did?"

"That's what I did…"

"The statement that the prisoners had tried to escape was not true?"

"No," Rivera said, "it wasn't true."

Bob finished questioning Colonel Rivera, and Steve Davis began his interrogation. "Before October 19, 1973, prior to that date, were there any prisoners that were executed in Calama?"

"Yes," Rivera said. "Three."

"Were those executions that you had to order?"

"Yes. I had to order them."

"Prior to October 19, 1973, was there torture of prisoners in the jail in Calama?"

"No."

"So if someone were to testify that their body was wrapped in cloth and their body was soaked with water and electrical shocks were attached to their body, would that be something that happened in Calama between September 11 and October 18 in the jail that was under your supervision?"

"No," Rivera said. He seemed so sure in his answer.

I had so many questions after the deposition that I asked Colonel Rivera if he would like to join me for lunch the following day. I wanted a chance to talk with him alone, to ask how he felt about giving the order to execute the three prisoners—including Grimilda's husband—and why he had decided to hide the victims' bodies. The next day, Rivera and I had a long conversation over lunch at the Cap Ducal Hotel. Rivera is a gentleman, a well-bred family man who is, above all, a Christian. What I found most troubling was his decision to execute Grimilda's husband and two other men. I asked about the circumstances that prompted him to sign their execution order.

Rivera said that the three men had been implicated in a sabotage attempt in the Dupont explosive factory. "In their possession the military found some explosives. Given the severity of the charges, a war council was convened, and the war council recommended death sentences for the three prisoners."

"Were you present during the proceedings?" I asked.

"No. I reviewed the whole process and determined that it was the right resolution. So I gave the go-ahead to the sentence."

"Would you do it again? Would you send these three men to their deaths?"

"No," Rivera said. "With the information I have today, I know that the amount of explosives they found in their possession, just a small box, would not have even put a nick in the Dupont plant whatsoever. They would have needed a *huge* amount of explosives to do any damage. But you have to understand, those were different times. You didn't have all the information you needed, so you followed established procedures and did the best you could."

As Rivera spoke, I recalled Ariosto Lapostol's response when I had asked if he'd ordered any executions in La Serena. "No," Lapostol had said. "To give such an order requires for you to be *absolutely* sure it's the right decision. Once you pull the trigger, it would be too late for you to change your mind, there is no way back. It's done."

"Why didn't you give the bodies to their families for burial?" I asked Rivera.

"After my men informed me that twenty-six prisoners had been massacred, I had the responsibility as the top authority of the region to inform the population of this terrible incident," Rivera said. "But I couldn't tell them that they had been massacred. I had to protect and take care of the honor of the army and that of General Arellano, the honor of the military junta and the commander-in-chief of the armed forces. So I made the decision to tell the public that these people had been killed trying to escape."

"So you didn't give the bodies to the families because they would have discovered the lie that instead they had been massacred?"

"Yes," Rivera said.

After the massacre, the twenty-six bodies were buried in a secret location in the desert. A few years later, on Pinochet's order, they were removed from the desert and thrown from helicopters into the sea.

To this day, the twenty-six victims from Calama remain missing.

THIRTY NINE

At 9:43 the next morning, Dr. Iván Murúa's deposition began.

"For the record," Davis said, "we object on behalf of the defendant to this deposition and to this proceeding on the basis of the grounds asserted at the deposition of Colonel Lapostol on Monday."

"Counsel, would it obviate the objection or resolve it if we had a Chilean notary administer the oath?" Bob asked. "Is that the issue? Or is it the lack of sanctions in the United States that we discussed? You don't have to tell me all the reasons."

"I believe there are several reasons, one of which is that reason, that there is no sanction imposed upon the witnesses, but also the inability of my client to obtain discovery regarding the veracity of the witnesses who are testifying," Davis said. "There's no way that I can really follow up with the names of the witnesses to see whatever testimony this particular witness would say. So it's just all part of the reasons why we believe that these depositions would be improper under federal rules of civil procedure. There's not a level playing field for my client to come to this country."

"We would not solve the problem by administering a different oath?" Bob asked.

"I don't believe so," Davis said.

Bob began his examination.

Responding to Bob's questions, Dr. Murúa described his interrogation by the military prosecutor Major Carlos Brito at the Copiapó garrison, which occurred around 8:30 p.m. on October 16, 1973.

"He started asking me about the post I had, my job responsibilities," Murúa testified. "And he started showing me some cans or tins with holes in them. He was saying they were used as arms, like as explosives. He asked where in the mine I had this clandestine or underground hospital. So I answered him, 'What hospital are you talking to me about? The only one I know is the El Salvador, and it's not clandestine because everybody knows it.' He kept pressing me about these issues.

"And really I didn't realize—I was just laughing. It made me laugh because I didn't realize how serious the situation was that I was in. I thought he was either crazy or trying to implicate me in something that I was not implicated in. And then he started reviewing, looking over my file, the file on me, which was quite thick...

"At that moment we had already been at this for half an hour. Three military men came, showed up. And they stood up and greeted each other military fashion...They came in rather with a harsh attitude. They didn't come in greeting people in a friendly way...They told Brito off for something, I can't remember it, and told him to give over the files...And I noticed he became very nervous...

"They asked him for the files and...the files were given to the officer who was apparently in command of this...a rather big, heavily built man...And that was General Arellano Stark. He opened up the files and started looking through them with a pencil that on one side was blue and on the other side was red."

Armando Fernandez was one of the officers who walked into the room with Arellano, carrying a briefcase, Murúa testified. The three strangers looked at the files and talked to one another.

"What did you see General Arellano do with the red pen and the files?" Bob asked.

"He put a red circle on each file. Because as I realized the situation was not very calm, I kind of looked at this from the corner of my eye."

"In other words, you tried to not be noticed?"

"Yes, as much as possible," Murúa said. "Because my file was among those files…And he said rather vulgarly, 'We have to just eliminate. These are—eliminate them. These are the orders.' At that moment he said something to Brito, who was there. I could see that the situation wasn't very simple…

"Brito then told me, 'You can go.' Every time we came into this room, we were accompanied by a soldier. They took me back downstairs to these tents. I was there for about one hour more."

"Doctor, can you describe Fernandez Larios the way he looked that day you saw him in the office with General Arellano?" Bob asked, after a few more questions.

"He was in combat fatigues, military combat fatigues, not the usual uniform with the stripes," Murúa said. "I couldn't tell the military rank because they weren't in the normal uniform. You could only tell by the attitudes people had who was in command and who was a subordinate and who had to obey. He had a white complexion, dark hair, black hair, more or less tall, slightly thin. Thinner than I am. Years later, I was able to recognize him because I saw a photograph. There I realized what his name was because—and I said, 'Well, that's the one who was in the room there with me and he is the one who killed Vincentti.' I find this out through a civilian who was there called Dr. Juan Mendoza."

"You found out what?" Bob asked.

"Move to strike any testimony that's not based on his personal knowledge," Davis said. "He hasn't gotten to the description of the death, so I don't know if he is going to say he witnessed anything. But I move to strike it to the extent that he is relying on what somebody else told him."

"You had earlier stated that Fernandez Larios was the one who had killed Vincentti," Bob said. "How did you get that knowledge?"

"From two sources," Murúa said. "First I found out through Dr. Juan Mendoza, who was the attending physician of the military junta at that time, but he was also my friend. We had known each other before. And he helped us a lot, independent of what the situation was. And also through Lieutenant Vidal. And he even told me how he had been beaten, with what he had been beaten. Fernandez Larios had like a mace which used to be used like in the Middle Ages. And he had it hanging from here"—Lapostol gestured as if something was hanging over his shoulder—"with spikes. And that's what he used to kill him. Vidal corroborated this and confirmed this with me."

Bob asked again what Arellano had said about the people whose names he marked with red ink.

"'All these people with red circles on their files have to be liquidated,'" quoted Murúa. "I was very surprised because I had no idea that this situation was going to become so brutal."

"What was the response of Mr. Brito when Arellano said these people have to be eliminated?"

"He didn't say anything. He just remained motionless."

A few questions later, Bob asked Murúa which picture of Fernandez Larios had allowed him to make the identification and when he had seen that photograph. Murúa replied that he had seen the photo after his exile in Germany. "I came back to Chile in 1986, more or less. It must have been in 1990. There was a publication and on TV something about this person. And that's where I recognized him. That's where I found out that he took asylum in the States. And I couldn't understand how there could be people like this living in the United States. That was information I got, not that anybody gave me information. Because when you're in exile for so many years and you come back to your country, it's like coming to know another country all over again."

Bob finished questioning Dr. Murúa, and Steve Davis began his interrogation. "Immediately before the general walked in, you were in this room with two other individuals?"

"There was Brito and there was a military man behind him looking for some papers, and no one else," Murúa said.

"And you. How were you dressed at that time?"

"I had a black leather jacket on with a sheepskin or suede inside, which we were given when we were in the field working, and just ordinary trousers."

"Well, was it regular-looking clothes as opposed to something that someone might describe as like the clothes a prisoner might wear?"

"No. Chile is not a rich country like the States. Prisoners don't have special clothes."

"Did Mr. Brito indicate to General Arellano, you know, 'Sir, let us take this prisoner'? Did he identify you as a prisoner?"

"No, nothing…It was a surprising situation for everyone because these people suddenly walked in. So I could tell that he was trying to get me out of there. Brito was trying to get me out of there as soon as possible because he probably had to take orders from these people…

"At that moment they were talking and looking at the files…" Murúa continued. "Many minutes had passed. At a certain time there was a pause, but it was a long period in which I was there. I didn't ask what time could I leave because detained people don't say that. I tried to be as inconspicuous as possible. I was worried that my file was one of those files. In one of those pauses, Brito says, 'Yeah, you can go.'"

Three days later, Murúa testified, Lieutenant Vidal had told him Armando Fernandez's name.

Davis then showed Murúa a photograph, asking if he thought Fernandez was pictured there. Murúa studied the rows of uniformed men and said he could not tell which was Fernandez, "because all of these individuals here look very much alike. All of these people have military clothing on, the same dark hair."

Following Davis's examination, Bob asked Murúa, "Have you ever seen the photograph that's been shown to you before today?"

"No."

"I'd like you to take a pen on this copy," said Bob. "I'm going to hand this to you. And of the people that you see in that photograph, are you able to say with some certainty *who* it is not? In other words, are you able to look at this picture and say this person is not Fernandez Larios?"

Murúa marked an X on certain faces, saying, "This is not, this not, this is not…" until there were only two men without an X. "He could be any of those two."

The marked picture was labeled "Exhibit 2."

"Do you have any doubt in your mind whatsoever that man that was in the room with General Arellano with the briefcase was Fernandez Larios?" Bob asked.

"No doubt at all," Murúa said. "It was him."

The deposition ended at 11:58 a.m.

As we waited for the next deposition to begin, I asked Bob about his offer to bring in a public notary.

"We nailed it. By refusing the offer to bring a Chilean notary to administer the oath, we are now in greater shape that our depositions will be accepted in court," Bob explained.

Later, at trial, Davis introduced the same objection, asking the judge to dismiss our depositions in court. The judge accepted all of our depositions, except for the first three. The testimonies of Ariosto Lapostol, Grimilda Sánchez, and Eugenio Rivera were thrown out because Davis had not yet received Bob's offer to administer a different oath.

Patricio Lapostol's deposition began at 1:05 p.m.

Bob asked him about October 19, 1973, the day that General Arellano and his men arrived in Calama. Lapostol, who had been a second lieutenant in the artillery division at the time, said that Colonel Rivera was commander of the regiment.

"We were surprised that the men who were with General Arellano were carrying more arms than would be normal," Lapostol testified. "They were equipped with handguns, *corvos*, and rifles."

"What is a *corvo*?" Bob asked.

"It's a knife created by the Chilean army whose blade is curved. And it has a sharp edge on either side and a tip. This arm was used for special presentations or parades, but not as a weapon to be used for combat."

"Is there any unusual characteristic of a *corvo* as compared to a simple knife?"

"The *corvo* is a weapon or an arm that inflicts great damage because of the shape it has. Because of its curved shape, when it is used in a human body, it inflicts much more damage to the tissue and tearing away than a normal knife does," Lapostol said. "You can easily slit someone's throat by using the inner curve of this knife."

"Is the knife designed in a fashion that when someone is stabbed with it that it is likely to cause death?"

"Of course."

"And is it likely to cause immediate death or slow death?"

"It causes a slow death," said Lapostol, "because the person bleeds to death slowly."

I stood abruptly and left the room. For a few minutes I sat alone in the hallway, eyes closed, and saw Wito's gentle smile in my mind. I had once told my parents that Wito died without knowing he was leaving us, and without feeling any pain. My story had not helped my father but it had given my mother some comfort. Now, listening to witnesses describe how Arellano's victims had actually been killed, I felt very aware of how much I wished my story had been true.

When I returned to the conference table, Lapostol was saying, "At around 17:30 or 18:00 hours, the lieutenant Mandiola, Jorge Mandiola, asked me to accompany him to organize a guard in the spot where the prisoners had been shot…We ordered the soldiers to protect, safeguard the zone, the area, and to not allow people who were not associated with the division or the unit, specifically civilians."

"Did you personally see the bodies?" Bob asked.

"Yes."

"Would you describe in as much detail as you can, give us the conditions of the bodies?"

"Absolutely destroyed."

"When you went there, did you expect to see bodies that had resulted from a military execution?" asked Bob, after a few more questions.

"Yes," said Lapostol. "But…that's not what I saw."

"Have you ever seen bodies that resulted from a military execution?"

"Yes."

"What was the difference between bodies that result from a military execution and what you observed on October the nineteenth, 1973?"

"In a military execution there is a formal procedure during which the person to be executed, you know, is in a specific place and carries a circle placed over his heart," Lapostol said. "There's a firing squad. There's an officer in command of this firing squad. There is a priest who belongs to the religion professed by the person to be executed. And that constitutes an enormous difference when I compare this with the bodies that I saw on the nineteenth of October. The military executions which took place from September 11 and prior to the nineteenth of October were the result of a formal procedure. The executions that took place on the nineteenth of October were summary executions."

"What was your emotional reaction when you first saw the bodies?" Bob asked.

"I think it was [a] feeling of great distress at seeing the barbarity with which these men were treated."

Bob finished his examination.

Steve Davis leaned forward in his seat. "No questions," he said, unexpectedly.

The deposition ended at 2:06 p.m.

FORTY

The next morning, as Enrique Vidal and I were about to enter the Victoria Room, he turned and asked, "What do you want me to tell them?"

"The truth," I said.

"Fair enough," he replied.

Vidal's deposition, probably the most anticipated testimony of all, began at 9:12 a.m. on Thursday, August 30. Bob questioned Vidal about his military career and responsibilities in September and October 1973, and then asked about the day that Arellano's helicopter had landed at the Copiapó garrison.

Arellano and his men had arrived in green combat uniforms, carrying guns, Vidal testified, and Fernandez also had a *corvo* and a mace. "And then Arellano told the commander of the regiment off because he was wearing the gray uniform that was used for days off," Vidal said, referring to Commander Haag. "He told him, 'In this country we're in a state of war and here you are with clothes that we use when we're off duty.'"

"What did Fernandez say when you asked him, 'What are you doing here? What is your purpose here?'" asked Bob.

"'You will soon find out,'" Vidal quoted.

A chill ran through the room. We all felt it. Bob paused. Steve Davis avoided my eyes. We knew what Fernandez had meant.

"Ask him about the *corvo*," I wrote on a yellow pad, passing it to Bob.

We were having some serious problems with translation, not only today but also in the previous depositions. Unfortunately, the interpreter had no previous experience with court procedures, and there was a lot of back and forth between Davis and the translator. Vidal was also giving longer, more detailed answers than the lawyers needed.

Davis cut Vidal off several times during his interrogation, and then told the translator, "Tell him I will ask the questions. I just would appreciate an answer to my question and not a speech."

"Very well," said Vidal, bristling.

"If he pisses him off," Bob wrote on my yellow pad, "it would be good for us."

Davis asked if the regiment had known in advance that Arellano and his men were coming to Copiapó.

"I just suddenly saw this helicopter land," Vidal said.

"Was there a specific reason that you went to greet it? Was that part of your duties?" Davis asked.

"I don't want to give you another speech," said Vidal, clearly annoyed, "but I have to explain why I went there. Because I [was] in charge of the guard who was on duty in my capacity as assistant to the commander. The chief guard says to me, 'Lieutenant, there's a helicopter coming to land.' I said, 'Well, surround it with the guards on duty.' And all of them were pointing with their arms at the helicopter because they didn't know who it was. And that's when I approached the helicopter…"

"Earlier you testified that [Fernandez] had this chain with a ball and spikes in his hand…" said Davis. "And you'd never seen this object prior to that day…"

"No, never," Vidal replied.

"Was Armando holding it in his hand or was it attached to his uniform somehow?"

"He had it in his hand."

"And then I understood you to also testify that he actually had this in his hand when he got off the helicopter," Davis said.

"No. I believe that when he descended from the helicopter he had it on his waist."

"Was the first time, when Armando got off the helicopter, you noticed that weapon?"

"Yes."

240

"And you'd never seen that weapon before in your life."

"Yes," said Vidal. "I had seen it in movies about the Romans."

"But you'd never seen one in person before."

"No, never."

"And did you ever ask Armando what that weapon was?"

"No."

"And…"

Vidal interrupted Davis. "He told me it was to beat the pigeons with."

"At this first time you saw him?" Davis asked.

"Yes."

"Were any of the other members of the task force holding that new weapon that Armando was holding?" Davis asked, after further questions.

"No."

"And so the last time you saw Armando would have been approximately 11:00 p.m. that night."

"Around 10:30 p.m., 11:00 p.m."

When Davis finished, Bob asked a few more questions to clarify Vidal's statements.

"You said that Fernandez Larios said this device that he had in his hand was for the pigeons," Bob said. "What did you understand that to mean?"

Davis objected to the form of the question.

"Did you mean that to understand that they would kill a pigeon, a bird, or what did that mean?" asked Bob. "Pigeons."

Davis objected to the form of the question.

"No," Vidal said. "He said, 'To caress the little pigeons.'"

"What did that mean to you?" asked Bob.

Davis objected to the form of the question.

"To beat up the prisoners," Vidal said.

"I'm asking you to clarify this, because of the word pigeons and the reason I'm asking that is to make sure you didn't understand it to mean literal pigeons, birds," said Bob.

In Spanish, we use the word *paloma* for both "dove" and "pigeon." Our translator interpreted *paloma* as "pigeon" that day. A different interpreter might have chosen "dove," which I believe would have better conveyed the intended meaning. Listening to Vidal's testimony that morning, I recalled Pato's account of Fernandez and Moren barging into the garrison sleeping quarters: after looking around the barracks, Fernandez had said, "So this is where the little doves sleep."

Following a short break, Vidal testified that Fernandez had worn a *corvo* tied to his right leg.

"Is this a knife that's normally carried by people in the Chilean army in 1973?" Bob asked.

"No. Only the special forces."

"Did other members of the helicopter have this *corvo*?" Bob asked.

"As he had been my classmate, I had particularly noticed him," Vidal testified. "And I particularly noticed that he had a pistol, a *corvo*, and a submachine gun."

"Did any of the other officers that were stationed at Copiapó have *corvos* that they carried on them?" Bob asked.

"No."

"Whether they carried them or not," said Bob, "did other personnel, military personnel, that were stationed at Copiapó have…access to *corvo*?"

"No," said Vidal. "The regiment in Copiapó does not have *corvos*."

Bob handed Vidal the photograph that Dr. Murúa had examined. "I'm going to show you what's been marked in Dr. Murúa's testimony as exhibit number one," Bob said, "and ask you, have you ever seen this photograph before?"

Vidal studied the picture. "Oh, there I am. There I am, and there is Armando Fernandez Larios. Could I have a copy of this picture?" The mood in the conference room lightened.

"Could you show me which one is Fernandez Larios and which one is you?" Bob asked.

"That's Fernandez Larios. He has his arm in a cast. And that's me." Vidal drew a circle on Fernandez's face, and then looked at exhibit two:

the photograph that Dr. Murúa had marked with Xs. The man that Vidal identified as Fernandez was one of the two cadets that Dr. Murúa had left unmarked.

I could not help smiling.

Vidal's deposition ended at 11:38 a.m.

"I didn't like Fernandez's lawyer," Vidal said, as we rode the elevator back down to the lobby. "I just wanted to punch him."

"I know," I said, smiling. "I'm glad you didn't."

When the elevator doors opened I saw our last witness, Victor Bravo, waiting in the lobby. Vidal and Victor were old friends from Copiapó, and they embraced warmly. Then Victor and I rode the elevator up to the twenty-first floor, where our last deposition was about to begin.

FORTY ONE

Inside the Victoria Room, I introduced Victor Bravo to the lawyers, the translator, and the court reporter. After a few minutes of listening to his testimony, I was unable to bear it and had to leave the room, so I did not witness all of the exchange described below.

Bob began by asking Victor to describe his experience on the night of October 17.

"There was a curfew at that time…" Victor said. "Nobody could leave, be on the streets. And it had already gotten dark. At about 8:00 p.m. a jeep showed up at my home. It was commanded by a subofficer from the army and a soldier who had a submachine gun…They asked for Victor Bravo. I came out of the house. 'You have to get into the jeep and come with us.' There was no explanation about where we were going. They just said, 'Get into the jeep.'"

Bob asked if it was unusual that army officers would come and take him from his home without explanation.

"Totally unusual," Victor said. "Because it was—it had to do with an arrest. I didn't know where they were taking me or why. The jeep then took us to the regiment. It stopped near the dining halls and we got out. We went into a large dining room. And they told me to wait in one end of the dining hall…And there I waited for about two hours…"

"Officers came and went. And I knew the majority of these officers because I'm also a diving instructor. I'm also a sailing instructor. So I have given several of them instruction on sailing and diving. Among them were officers I didn't know, I didn't recognize. And they also had other clothes on. And far away from where I was, they talked a lot among themselves. The ones who knew me said hello from far away, but they never approached me close."

"In terms of the officers that…appeared to be dressed differently, how many officers were these and what was the dress?" Bob asked.

"They had combat fatigues on, which is different from what the officers usually wear in everyday life…As they came in and went out…I would calculate about two or three," Bravo said.

"You waited about two hours. Then what happened?"

"And the same subofficer told me, 'Let's go.' He didn't tell me where we were going. We went back inside the jeep. On his lap he had a submachine gun. And the one in the back of him, seated in the back, had a machine gun. The streets in the city were deserted because there was a curfew. We went through the downtown area. We crossed over to get to the northern highway…he crossed the bridge over the river that leads to the cemetery. And when he went toward the cemetery I said here something is going to happen to me. Because there had been a robbery in my office a few days prior to this. And in my office as the authority for identification, I'm the one who issues passports so that people can travel abroad. Several passports and ID cards, blank passports and ID cards, had gone missing…I told the court and the ministry and all the corresponding authorities. And nothing was done."

"Mr. Bravo, you were concerned about your safety, that something might happen to you, when you were going into the cemetery?" Bob asked. "Is that what you're saying to us?"

"I was scared, yes, because I thought perhaps they had arrested someone and this person had on them these missing passports and IDs and they might incriminate me in this event."

"What happened when you went into the cemetery then?"

"There was a group of military personnel," Victor said. "Everything was dark. As they flashed the flashlight onto my face, I couldn't see whom they were with or with whom they were speaking. I could tell from their breath that these military men had been drinking heavily. They were all very nervous…One of them turned to one of the soldiers and said, 'Oh, my *pisco* is all out. Give me your bottle.' And he said, 'Well, Lieutenant, I have also drank all of it.' So what was all this about? So they directed the flashlight toward the ground and there was a whole row of corpses…"

I stood up abruptly. Victor stopped talking and waited for me to leave the conference room. Back in my hotel room I collapsed on the bed, trying to shut out the hideous vision that Victor's words brought to mind.

After I left the Victoria Room (as I know from finally reading the deposition transcript last year), Victor continued, "And they all had the bag in which sleeping bags are put into, the outside cover, they had—each one had this over, tied around his head. You could tell that they had doused them down with water…I was told we have to identify these corpses so we can issue the death certificates.

"I complained to them that in order to make these identifications I needed my usual instruments. The cards, cards that I use to take fingerprints with, the ink. And he said, 'Here they are.' I was surprised because these had been taken from my office. And they had all the instruments ready there. All these objects were on top of the first corpse.

"So they said, 'Please proceed.' So I took off this bag. I have said this very few times in my life because it's very gruesome. I'm glad Zita left. Because I have never wanted to explain in what condition her brother was. They were not shot to death. They were massacred with *corvos*, gunshot wounds, and you could even tell that they made this gesture," he said, holding his hands up defensively, "because they had gunshot wounds on their hands, on their legs, the whole body."

"Did you know any of these people, Mr. Bravo?" Bob asked.

"…The first one that I identified was Alfonso Gamboa. He was a friend of mine from the club. He was the director of a radio. They had shot off or blown off half his face…I took his documents off his body because he was totally—it wasn't possible to recognize him in that state. I took his fingerprints. I put them aside. And on and on, Jaime Sierra, Leonello Vincentti."

"Mr. Bravo, I'm going to ask you about these people," Bob said. "Now, can you tell me anybody that you knew? Any of these men that were killed, I'd like you to tell me if you knew them personally and what you knew about them."

"I have already explained about Gamboa. I knew his family," Victor said. "Jaime Sierra was a young student leader…He was the stepson of a professor much beloved by me. In the case of Leonello Vincentti, I had been the presiding authority when he was married before the civil registry. He was a professor at the university and he was my son's professor."

"As you tell us about these people, can you tell us what you remember about their body, if you remember specific injuries that you saw to the bodies of these people?" Bob asked.

"I remember that Jaime Sierra had deep green eyes, and one was missing. I could tell that they had removed it with a *corvo*. Plus other wounds," Victor said. "Leonello Vincentti was in a deplorable state. He had open gaping wounds all over his body. I have never told the relatives this, and I will explain to you why later on. There was another young man, Larravide, I believe, small, slightly built.

"I say if they had to kill them, why didn't they just kill them and not do it in that way, the way they did it, so bloody, so much hatred. They didn't even know them personally.

"I knew Palleras. I knew his father. His father had just lost a grandson and they found him drowned in Caldera. It was a terrible tragedy for the family…The mass grave was immediately next to them…"

"Were the bodies that you examined, the thirteen bodies, were they all similarly massacred or were there some of the bodies that were just executed, just by execution?" Bob asked.

"No," said Victor. "Not one was just shot to death by execution. Some were in worse state than others…And you could tell that they had tried to defend themselves where they had gunshots wounds through their hands as well."

"Did you see any vehicle that was used to transport the bodies to the cemetery?" Bob asked.

"It was a Tolva truck like the ones used by the mining company. I have a feeling it was not a truck that belonged to the regiment, but rather a truck that came from the Enami Mining Company. The back part of the truck, it looks like it had just been watered down because it was wet."

"In the United States we have something called a dump truck in which the bed of the truck tips up. Was that what this was, a truck with a bed that could come up?" Bob asked.

"Yes. It was in that position. Probably to wash away all the blood."

"Were you able to identify by name the military men that were at the cemetery with you?"

"No," said Victor. "And why? You can imagine the state I was in. I had no idea this was going to happen to me. And then to observe this massacre. I wasn't in a condition to identify the people…"

"You have mentioned a university professor and a student and one or two others. Did you know all thirteen of these men?"

"Not all thirteen. There was some I didn't know. The guard who was from Caldero, I don't remember him exactly," said Victor. "I knew Jaime Sierra, Jaime Palleras, Leonello Vincentti, Perez, Pepito Perez, Larravide, Winston. When Winston was arrested, that same time they had convened a meeting of all the heads of the public services after the eleventh of September. I saw him there for the last time."

"So you knew six or seven of these men previous to that night?" Bob asked.

"Yes."

"Were all of the bodies, once you identified them, placed in a common grave?"

"Yes. In a common grave."

"Did you inquire of the military people that were there whether the bodies should be given to the families?"

"No."

"Did you hear that discussed among the military people there?"

"They were only talking about what had just happened."

"What was being said about what just happened?"

Steve Davis objected to the form of the question.

"That they were all very shocked by this," said Victor, "very surprised and shocked."

"Did they say, the people there talking, who had actually committed the crime?" Bob asked, after a few more questions.

Steve Davis objected to the form of the question.

"No," Victor said.

"Do you know Armando Fernandez Larios?" asked Bob.

"Now I do because everybody knows him," said Victor. "I know him through this whole process that has been going on."

"Was Armando Fernandez Larios present on the date of October the sixteenth, and did you see him at Copiapó at any time?"

"Object to the form of the question," said Davis. "I think it should be asked: Did you see him—"

"Let me state this," said Bob. "Did you see who you now know as Armando Fernandez Larios, did you see that man on the sixteenth of October?"

Steve Davis objected to the form of the question.

"Among the officers there dressed in combat fatigues, there's a tall man, thin, in combat fatigues with a *corvo* attached to his leg," Victor said. "He had all the characteristics of a typical commando leader, which was different from the rest of the officers I knew."

"Was that man Fernandez Larios?"

Steve Davis objected to the form of the question.

"Yes," said Victor. "Now I recognize him because of all the information I have come to know after this event, because of all the conversations I had afterward with the officers. He and another officer in that force had the reputation of being the most bloody, the most cruel."

"Who are you referring to?" asked Bob.

Steve Davis objected to the form of the question.

"We're talking about Fernandez Larios," said Victor.

"Was this conversation about Mr. Fernandez Larios, did it take place on October 17 or 18 or 19, 1973?"

Steve Davis objected to the form of the question.

"I was in the regiment on the seventeenth, because these things happened in the early morning hours of the seventeenth," said Victor. "On the sixteenth we heard a helicopter overhead, and that night we heard the gunshots. And the next day is when they took me to the regiment. After that, as an aside, I'd like to say there was a meeting after that between the officers and heads of the public services in the old jail where some of these prisoners had been held."

"Were you at that meeting?" Bob asked.

"Yes...I was invited to attend. It was a barbecue in the old jail. There were people from the prison guards, from the police, and some heads of public service like me. And the remarks usually centered on this issue. Everyone agreed that these two—there were these two characters, Moren Brito and Fernandez Larios."

"What did they agree about those two people?" asked Bob.

Steve Davis objected to the form of the question.

"That these two had used *corvos* on these prisoners," said Victor, "that they were the most cruel of all the task force."

"This discussion that you have just told us about was taking place at this meeting of all of the ministers and the army people?" asked Bob.

Steve Davis objected to the form of the question.

"Yes," Victor said.

"Had you ever examined bodies of people who had been killed by military firing squad?" Bob asked.

"The next day, yes, I saw three of them who had been executed," said Victor. "Garcia Posada, Maguindo, and another one whose name I can't recall. And Tapia, I think. They had the gunshot wound on their chest."

"And the people that you have just told us about where you examined their bodies, they didn't have any *corvo* wounds or other disfiguring wounds; is that correct?"

"No. Nothing. They had all their clothes on. I remember Garcia had a ring on with a stone in it. The face was perfectly all right."

"The bodies that you examined, the thirteen bodies that you have told us about, did they have watches and rings and money on their bodies?"

"No, I don't remember. I tried to look for their documents...[in] some cases, I took out the person's wallet, took out their ID card and placed it on the body and wrote the ID card number."

"That evening when you were in the dining hall, is that when you saw the person you have identified as, I believe, as Fernandez Larios? Is that when you saw him, in the dining hall while you were waiting?"

"Yes, for the first time," Victor said.

"Did you see the other military men in combat uniform in that dining hall at some point in time in that two hours?"

"As I said before, while I was waiting in the dining hall, there must have been a group of seven or eight military men. But they kept coming in and out, but I figured about seven or eight military people. And there were three who were dressed differently, and I didn't know them at all."

"Are you today certain that the person that you saw on October 16, 1973, in the combat uniform with the *corvo* was Fernandez Larios?" Bob asked.

Steve Davis objected to the form of the question.

"Yes," said Victor. "Because he was slightly taller than the rest, slightly taller than the other two."

"Very early in your testimony today you said that you would explain later why you didn't tell the families how these men had been killed," Bob said. "Would you tell us now?"

"The reason was this," said Victor. "It was just for humanitarian reasons. Because when they would question me, what did my husband look like or my son or my brother, they would go to my office to implore me to tell them about their loved one, as they knew I was the one who identified them. I explained here are the fingerprints I took from them. And there was one card with a lot of blood on it. In one case, that case with the bloody card, I didn't show it to his widow. Her husband was shot to death. It was the widow of Leonello Vincentti. So I never told them in what condition I had seen them. I certainly didn't tell Zita."

"I have no further questions," Bob said. "Mr. Davis may have some questions for you."

"When you were talking about the men who you thought had drunk the *pisco*, these were not the same men in the military—in the combat fatigues?" Davis asked.

"No," Victor said. "They were soldiers and officers of the regiment and, thus, they knew me."

"Did you see anyone in combat fatigues at the location where you saw the bodies?"

"No. You have to remember that it was dark and at night and we only had a flashlight."

"I understand," Davis said. "The time period that you saw the men in the combat fatigues, as far as you can reconstruct the events, would it have been after these individuals had been killed?"

"After."

"What would have been the distance you had between yourself and where the men in the fatigues were?"

"About six to seven meters."

"But it was in a lit room, you were inside a lit room?"

"Yes."

"Did you look closely at the fatigues?"

"Yes," said Victor. "Because it's clothes that are different from the usual clothes they wear. It's the typical uniform used by the commando units with short boots and kind of wide trousers toward the ankles and lots of arms."

"Other than them wearing arms and wearing combat fatigues, did you notice anything else about the men wearing combat fatigues, anything else about them or their uniforms?" Davis asked, after another question.

"No," said Victor. "Because, for example, they couldn't have their helmets on because they were inside the dining hall."

"Do you recall the men in combat fatigues wearing anything on their heads?"

"No, I can't remember."

"At the time you saw these men, they were never introduced to you in any fashion, the men in the combat fatigues?"

"No."

"And you never spoke to them, the men in the combat fatigues?"

"No."

"The first time you ever heard the name Armando Fernandez was when someone told you the following day; is that correct?"

"The general comment was that, yes, General Arellano had showed up with this man, this man, and this man," said Victor.

"Did anyone tell you or did you hear that General Arellano had ordered the death or the executions of the killing of these thirteen men?" Davis asked.

"The general comment was that people were remarking that General Arellano had said—had taken a bunch of files and said, 'Bring me these prisoners.'"

"Did you gain an understanding that General Arellano had ordered the local military personnel to bring the prisoners to General Arellano?" Davis asked.

"Yeah," said Victor. "To hand them over to him, to his task force."

After a short break, Davis continued his interrogation. "The person you described as Armando Fernandez, you described him as being tall?"

"Not very, very tall," said Victor. "As I described him before, he had nothing on his head. He had dark hair, straight dark hair."

"I'm just asking about height right now," said Davis. "Do you have any estimate of what his height was?"

"Taller than I am, about one meter seventy-five centimeters...I'm one meter seventy-three centimeters. Well, I was. I don't know what I am now."

"Just because the way the process is, I want to make sure I understand your answer," Davis said. "So you're around one meter seventy-three centimeters tall?"

"Yes."

"And the person who you refer to as Armando Fernandez is taller than that?"

"Yes."

"That's all I have," said Davis. "Thank you."

Bob turned to the translator. "Tell him we are complete."

FORTY TWO

Despite the rough beginning convincing my lawyers to go ahead with the depositions, we had made remarkable progress. I flew back to California feeling quite hopeful. Bob and I planned to return to Chile for more depositions the following year, and to prepare, I took two short trips to Chile: one with Felipe in December 2001 and one with Roberto in April 2002. My family insisted that I no longer travel to Chile alone, out of fear that I was being followed.

Corporal Juan Morales, who in 1973 had witnessed Fernandez Larios reviewing prisoners' folders in Copiapó, was still a priority for me, but he seemed to have completely disappeared. Felipe and I decided to search for him in Copiapó, and Jean-Christophe flew out from France to film our efforts. We discovered a possible neighborhood for Morales and walked around the area, asking people on the street if they knew him. Inside a small corner store the owner said she knew Morales. As we were asking if she knew his address, a middle-aged woman walked in.

"I don't know his address," the shop owner said. "Why don't you ask her? She is his wife."

When Morales's wife heard this and saw Jean-Christophe's camera, she ran out of the store. Felipe followed her and wrote down the address of the house she went into. Instead of going to the house I asked Vidal, who had been Morales's superior in the army, if he could talk with him about testifying. Vidal traveled to Copiapó and spoke personally with Morales at his home.

Finally, Juan Morales agreed to testify.

I turned my attention to Clodomiro Garrido, the detective from Cauquenes who had once witnessed Fernandez Larios hitting Fulvia. Hoping for assistance in convincing him to testify, I called General Emilio Cheyre.

"We can't help you with that," General Cheyre said. "If a witness doesn't want to testify, we can't interfere. We can't force him."

I explained that witnesses were afraid to testify.

"If they do testify, there is no reprisal against them," said General Cheyre. "I assure you of that." He wished me luck and hung up.

I went to the Human Rights Program of the Ministry of Interior to ask for help in convincing witnesses to testify and managed to schedule an appointment that afternoon with the executive director, Luciano Fouillioux. While waiting to meet with him, I decided to visit Viviana Diaz, president of the Association of Relatives of Disappeared Political Prisoners, whose father had been kidnapped by the Chilean armed forces in 1976. I mentioned my upcoming meeting with Fouillioux.

"I recommend you speak first with a friend of mine who works in that office," Viviana said. I immediately went to see her friend and told her about the lawsuit, the depositions, and my upcoming appointment with her director. Viviana's friend listened carefully, got up from her desk, and closed the door.

"I shouldn't say what I'm about to say," she told me. "Cancel your appointment with Fouillioux. I know you don't realize the magnitude of all the things you mentioned that you and your lawyers have done. The most incredible aspect of all is that nobody in this country knows about them. You have brought lawyers from the United States to Chile to interrogate witnesses. Even military officers. You have created a court on Chilean soil following US legal requirements. I'm not a lawyer, but Fouillioux is a lawyer, and I'm sure he would find legal problems with what you are doing. I understand Viviana's reason for asking you to speak with me first. My advice to you, cancel your appointment immediately and finish your depositions *quietly*. Don't risk the amazing work you have already accomplished."

I thanked her and gratefully followed her advice.

In April 2002, Roberto and I flew to Santiago, Chile. The day we arrived, I called the office of Dr. Elvira Miranda, a forensic pathologist who had examined Wito's remains after Chile's mass exhumations in 1990. Under "Cause of Death" in the forensic reports I had collected, Wito's report read, "A thoracic trauma produced by a sharp object. No sign of gunshot wounds found on his body. Signed, Dr. Elvira Miranda, Forensic Medical Institute." I knew that Dr. Miranda's report held the final pieces of the story.

After a few rings, Dr. Miranda answered the phone. When I explained what I wanted, she said, "I can see you right now."

Each time I met a prospective witness, I wished I could know his or her thoughts about my visit and request. In Dr. Miranda's case, she and I became good friends and I was actually able to ask. This is how she described her first meeting with me:

"The medical legal institute was on a strike. I hadn't been at the office for over two weeks. I stopped by one day to get some documents when Zita called. That's timing! We agreed to meet that same day. Since no visitors can get into our building without a guard calling us first to meet them at the main entrance, I stayed close to the phone. Zita really surprised me when she showed up at my office unannounced. Then immediately, she explained her reasons for her visit. She told me that she knew I had done the study of her brother's remains in Copiapó based on her reading of the forensic report. She asked me if I could testify. I explained to her that we are required to follow a protocol: to perform an exhumation we need an order from the court, and then once the exhumation is performed we send our laboratory results back to the court, so we would have to ask the court for authorization to get copies. In order for me to give Zita a copy of the forensic report, I would have to go through the court to get it. At that moment, I saw in Zita's hands a copy of her brother's forensic report. Not only *that*, but she had all thirteen copies. After seeing her with the reports, I said to myself, 'I don't know how she got them, but if she has them, that means I can testify.'"

The day we met, Dr. Miranda said, "I do remember your brother very well. I remember him *particularly* well because Winston's remains spoke to us. I didn't know what it was; your brother was different from the rest. Then we noticed that of the thirteen victims, Winston was the only one who showed no signs of gunshot wounds on his body. He died of a trauma to his thorax, produced by a sharp object."

Then Dr. Miranda said, "I'll testify. Let me review my notes. I have them in my house." She paused and then said, "I remember your brother's sweater."

On August 28, 2002, Bob Kerrigan and I began our second and last round of depositions in Chile. This time, the legal team decided to fly to Santiago the same court reporter, Sharon Vartanian. Also, instead of hiring a local interpreter, they decided to fly out from Miami a certified court interpreter, Francis Icaza, from the Florida State Courts System.

Fernandez Larios's lawyer, Steve Davis, agreed to participate in these depositions, but canceled the trip at the last minute due to a family emergency, although he agreed to participate by phone. Bob arranged to have a conference phone line available.

Our first witness was Juan Morales, who in 1973 had been a corporal first class, working in the security section of the Copiapó garrison, with duties including creation and maintenance of prisoner records.

Morales testified that on October 16, 1973, two officers from the helicopter came into his office. "One of the men was Armando Fernandez," Morales said. "I know he was Fernandez because his name was mentioned several times within the office." Morales said that Fernandez asked him for all the prisoners' records, and that he had seen Fernandez sitting at a desk reviewing those records and making notes on some of them.

"Did you have occasion later that day to see Fernandez Larios outside of the office?" Bob asked.

"I saw him outside during the mistreatment of someone," Morales said.

Bob and I looked at each other, surprised.

"Describe what you saw him do," Bob said.

"With his rifle, he hit him in the thorax," Morales said.

"Did he strike him any place else?"

"Yes. At the thorax maybe two or three times, and I heard the bones crack."

"Who did Fernandez Larios strike?"

"Jaime Sierra, and he hit him later on again, not with the rifle, but with his foot. He hit him in the head with his rifle. When he hit him in the head with his rifle, the detainee Sierra fell to the ground with his forehead maybe fifteen centimeters off the concrete pavement. Later on, with his foot, with the boot, he hit him in the back of the head on the nape of the neck. And that slammed his forehead into the concrete and it sounded like a watermelon."

Morales paused.

"I would like to add a small part there," he said. "Detainee Sierra asked to be killed. He begged to be killed because he could no longer stand the beating, the pain."

"Who did he say that to?" Bob asked.

"To him," Morales said, "to Fernandez Larios."

"He was a good, credible witness," Bob told me, after Morales's deposition.

Unable to speak, I sat motionless in the conference room. How was it possible that Armando Fernandez could be freely walking the streets of Miami? *Nothing will change*, I thought. Fulvia's words came to mind: "You are wasting your time in pursuing justice." I recalled something a friend had said: "Zita, with all the money you've spent, you could have hired two large men in Miami to take care of Fernandez…justice for human rights crimes does not exist."

Even Wito's daughter, Susan, had told me, "Instead of pursuing justice, I prefer to do things that would prevent these events from happening again."

"Don't you see the importance of justice in preventing these events from happening all over again?" I had asked her.

"I wouldn't do it myself," Susan had said. "No. Justice, it's not something I would do. No."

As I recalled my conversations with Fulvia and Susan, my certainty began to recede.

FORTY THREE

The next morning we deposed Lieutenant Colonel Efrain Jaña, the former commander of the army base at Talca, where Arellano's helicopter had landed on September 30, 1973. The only local commander who refused to carry out Arellano's orders, Jaña was imprisoned, tortured, and sentenced to execution as a result. After three years in jail, however, Jaña's life was spared and he was sent from Chile to live in exile.

Bob began his examination.

Responding to Bob's questions, Jaña described the city of Talca in the days following the coup: "The civilian population of Talca continued to live in an absolutely normal fashion...The local commerce opened its doors and offered all those things that had been denied to the population prior to this time and was done so in order to create a situation of confusion."

Bob asked Jaña if he had worked with the civilian authorities to meet the community's needs in a peaceful way.

"I held two important meetings," Jaña said, "one at the Talca municipality with the workers, and later a meeting with the peasants...in both of those meetings, I made emphasis on the fact that they could be completely and fully secure in the knowledge that they had no reason to fear neither for their lives nor for their work or jobs...

"I think it is important to [emphasize] the fact that I went to this meeting with the peasantry. I went completely by myself except for the presence of my aide...and with the driver of the jeep, which demonstrated the trust that I had in the population and the fact that I knew that they had understood the text of my communiqué in the sense that we should all come to an agreement."

Bob asked about the day that Arellano's helicopter landed.

"When Arellano arrived in Talca, I was at the intendant's office or at the mayor's office," Jaña said. "I moved immediately over to the commander's office of the regiment, of my regiment, and I met with General Arellano at the officers' club of my unit. Arellano had a glass of whiskey in one hand and a submachine gun in the other…"

"When General Arellano arrived, did you have any discussion with him about the role of the military after the coup?" Bob asked.

"Not precisely a dialogue concerning that," Jaña testified. "But I do clearly recall that when I came before him and advised him that at my garrison there was no news to report, I recall that he asked me whether or not I was holding any prisoners, whether or not any legal procedures were being carried out, or whether there were any people incarcerated.

"I informed him that at Talca there was no news to report and there were no acts of force that had taken place. The general's reaction was semiviolent. And he says to me, 'Don't you know, Commander, that we are at war?'

"My reaction was in accordance to his attitude, and I answered, 'General, of which war are you speaking? It was at the military academy and at the war school that I was introduced to the concept that we could only consider our neighbors as presumed adversaries. And I have not been a witness to seeing any individual who was wearing the military uniform of Bolivia, Peru, or Argentina.'"

Jaña took a deep breath. "And that," he said, grinning, "is how that short dialogue concluded between General Arellano and the commander of Talca."

Arellano had immediately relieved Jaña of his command and accused him of failing to comply with military duties. After three years in jail, the investigative service had driven Jaña to the airport and put him on a plane to Colombia. Jaña had to leave his five children behind in Chile. He managed to obtain a visa allowing him to go to Holland, and years later his family joined him there.

"What you observed in Chile in 1973 through 1978 was terror used by the military against the civilian population of the country, based on what you observed?" Bob asked.

"True," Jaña said.

"Could you give us examples of how terror is used against the civilian population, particularly in Chile?"

"Well, there is a strategic principle that is used in the times of war, the application of which was attempted in Chile," Jaña said. "And it materializes or it is defined as the need to act in such a manner as to achieve the weakening of the will to fight amongst the people…And as examples I can give you the case of the Gestapo in Germany, the Chenska in the Soviet Union, and the other organizations involved in intelligence and security, which are the ones that provide support to dictators."

Jaña said he had written a letter to General Pinochet in 1984. "I told him that any punishment, any sanction, has a beginning and an end. I related to him what had happened to me as of the eleventh of September and that to date I had received no notification from the army, which was the institution that had unjustly punished me, as to when my exile was to end…"

"Did Pinochet ever answer your letter?" Bob asked.

"That's where I'm going," Jaña said. "I received no response."

Bob thanked Jaña for his testimony and asked if he wanted to add anything.

"I leave these statements as an inheritance to my children and to my grandchildren," Jaña said, "as a way of leaving a record of the injustice that was committed against this soldier in the sense of being called a traitor to his country and to his army."

For me, Jaña's testimony was the most revealing and hopeful of all. He gave good insight as to how Arellano operated, and his actions contradicted what other local commanders had said: that they could do nothing to stop Arellano.

Through his refusal to comply, Jaña prevented a massacre.

That afternoon we finished our last round of depositions in Chile, with testimonies from Dr. America Gonzales and Dr. Elvira Miranda, forensic pathologists who had worked in the exhumation of Copiapó's victims.

"On twelve of the bodies we were able to identify evidence of injury by bullet or bullet wounds," Dr. Gonzalez testified. "And in the case pertaining to Mr. Cabello we found no evidence on the skeletal remains of any evidence of projectiles or bullets. But we cannot write off the possible presence of that kind of wound. But as pertains to that special case, there were some characteristics as shown on the garments that are compatible with characteristics that indicate that these wounds were caused by a bladed weapon."

"I'd like to ask you now about any conclusions that you may have reached regarding whether Winston Cabello sustained wounds from what I think has been described as a sharp object or a knife," Bob said.

"Well, I will have to go back a little on the case," Dr. Miranda testified. "I will have to compare it at the same time with the remainder of the cases, because in the case of the others, it was clearly visible to us the multiplicity or the large number of bullet wounds that we could see and interpret. But on the body of Winston, on the contrary, we had no holes that would either explain or suggest any type of bullet-entry wound. And that's where the cause of death became so complicated and difficult to establish. In the absence of soft organs, there is no way of proving such an event. Nevertheless, the jacket that he was wearing showed linear tears, which when compared to the tears that appeared on the other garments leads me to conclude that they are compatible with tears made by a blade instrument. Besides, on Winston's garments there are no signs of bullet entry wounds."

"Did I understand you to say that the twelve other bodies showed multiple evidences of bullets?" Bob asked.

"At least one," Dr. Miranda replied. "Which is to say they were all wounded by at least one bullet that we could find."

"But as I understand your testimony, on Winston Cabello's remains, you found no evidence of bullet damage?"

"Categorically," Dr. Miranda said. "No."

It was a defining moment. On August 30, 2001, Enrique Vidal had testified under oath that he had seen Armando Fernandez with a *corvo* tied to his right leg and that "no other military personnel stationed in Copiapó carried a *corvo* at the time." Exactly one year later, on August 30, 2002, Dr. Miranda completed the story for us.

After the deposition, I asked Dr. Miranda to explain Jaime Sierra's forensic report. She examined it carefully, and then said, "From what we wrote here, it seems like his brain exploded, from the inside out."

Her statement confirmed Morales's testimony.

FORTY FOUR

In the face of his own painful death, my brother had defied Fernandez's order to get off the truck so that no one could say the prisoners had been killed while trying to escape. Now I had the evidence I needed to prove it. I was ready to go to trial and offer the world Wito's last gift in life: his courage, integrity, and moral strength.

"There are few people in the world who can say they are doing in life what they are meant to do," I told Bob. "I'm one of those few fortunate people, and I owe it to you. Thank you for believing in me. Thank you for working on the case."

"You would have done it with a lawyer or without a lawyer," Bob said.

"Do you know that the day you came to my house you gave me something? When you told me, 'You are the client, and your lawyers have to do what you ask them to do'? At that moment you gave me the power to do exactly that, to demand from my lawyers the things I wanted to see happen. Probably today you regret your words," I said, smiling.

Bob smiled back at me.

A year earlier—two weeks after our first round of depositions—the legal team had decided to amend our complaint. Concerned that it would be too difficult to prove that Fernandez had done the actual killing, they had downgraded the charges to "conspiracy."

I had e-mailed Bob immediately: "The core of our claim is based on the allegation that Fernandez Larios used his *corvo* to slash Winston's abdomen. This allegation SHOULD NOT be removed."

My lawyers had said it was sufficient to allege that Fernandez had participated in the plan of executions in Copiapó; we did not need to allege that Fernandez had done the actual killing. I would have understood if this had been a criminal case, because winning is what matters. Winning sends the perpetrator to jail. But ours was a civil case by necessity, so it was not just about winning, or even about closure and healing. For me, Wito's case was ultimately about meaning and truth. In the end, our lawyers had changed the allegation to conspiracy. I had felt crushed. I had worked to present the legal truth of Wito's story as closely as possible to the greater historical truth so that ultimately the two truths could emerge as one. I had felt sure that was where the real meaning of my brother's case was to be found, and on the last day of depositions, I knew it was possible.

The day after our last deposition in Chile, Bob and I went to the General Cemetery in Santiago to visit the memorial to the more than three thousand victims of Pinochet's brutal regime. All the victims' names are listed there, and Wito's is among them.

"My brother's life was cut short," I said as Bob and I sat on a bench near the memorial, "but we can learn many good things from his life. Winston teaches us that even in the most repressive, fearful moments, human beings do not lose their power to make decisions based upon ethical and moral principles. Winston could not prevent his death, but he managed to give meaning to it by defying Fernandez and forcing him to kill him on the truck. Nobody could ever say he and the other twelve victims were killed because they tried to escape. His remains speak of his unusual strength and integrity. Ultimately, he overcame death itself. With our lawsuit, I want to offer the world that part of my brother's story. That's my responsibility in the transcendence of his life."

Finally, Bob looked like he understood my motivation for pursuing justice so passionately. "Let me think how we can get this across at trial," he said.

Bob left Chile that night, and from Atlanta he sent me the following e-mail: "I appreciate your kind words and thanks. It is an honor for me to be involved in the case. I understood exactly what you said about Winston's death. I want to think about how to best get that across."

I felt so encouraged by his words. Even though the legal team had changed the charge to conspiracy, I knew now that Bob would really try to convey the greater meaning of our case.

The next morning, I called General Arellano's house on a whim. His son, a lawyer, answered the phone.

"I just want to know, what are your father's justifications for the killings that took place under his orders?" I asked, after introducing myself.

"You cannot speak with my father, but I can assure you that he had nothing to do with the killings that took place in Copiapó," Arellano's son replied. "When my father arrived in Copiapó, they had already been killed. We have proved that. You should speak with his lawyer, my cousin."

Arellano's son mentioned some evidence, including a 1986 *Analysis* interview with a former political prisoner from Copiapó who said that the thirteen victims had been killed on October 16—a day before it actually happened. Had this been true, Arellano would have had an alibi, since he had been in La Serena that day and therefore could not have been involved in the Copiapó killings.

Arellano's nephew called me later, but I saw no point in talking with him.

In truth, I do not think I would have been able to bear talking directly with General Arellano. It would have been too painful. I had drawn a line, and General Arellano was well beyond that line. I think I just wanted to know if he was still hiding behind the same excuses.

Sometimes I think about his son and wonder how he feels about his father's actions. The good thing about making that call was that at trial, Steve Davis wanted to convince the jurors that since I had selected the witnesses, my selection was biased and I had only spoken with witnesses who would support our claim.

Davis asked if I had spoken with Carlos Brito, the military prosecutor of Copiapó.

"Yes," I said.

Davis looked surprised. He paused. I wished Davis would ask what Brito had said. I understand that lawyers do not ask a question if they do not know the answer in advance, but I would have liked to testify that Carlos Brito had witnessed Fernandez hitting some of the victims in Copiapó, and that Brito had confirmed that he'd decided to free my brother.

Instead Davis asked, "Did you *try* to speak with General Arellano?"

"Yes," I said.

Steve Davis did not know what to say. In the end, he failed to show bias in my selection of witnesses.

FORTY FIVE

Trial date was set for June 16, 2003. Then it was postponed until September 22. About six months before the trial, Leo took on an active role as co-counsel in the case.

"How are you learning about the case?" I asked him.

"I'm reading all the depositions you and Bob took in Chile."

"I don't think that will do it. I don't think they will give you everything you need to know about the case."

"How many hours would I need to spend in order for me to learn everything necessary?" asked Leo. "Twenty?"

"Maybe even less."

"Teach me."

For the last two weeks of June, Leo and I met every day at WSGR. Knowing how difficult it was for anyone in the United States, even Chileans, to truly understand what had happened under Pinochet's rule, I quoted a friend of Lito's. "To teach you about what happened in Chile is like teaching a fish the concept of fire."

"I'm willing and ready to swim in different waters," Leo said.

We agreed that I would give Leo all the facts, whether or not we had evidence to prove them, and Leo soon realized that I had much more information than the depositions provided. He invited Nathalie Bridgeman, a young lawyer at WSGR who had recently joined our case, to help take notes on my "lectures."

"This is the first time that I have a complete story that makes sense," Leo said. "The story is whole. It answers many of my questions."

I was grateful to be able to teach Leo everything I had learned about the case. Our meetings offered another gift, as well: I was able to observe the legal team as they prepared for trial and was in awe of their tremendous efforts. As Nicole and several other lawyers worked diligently on the case addressing countless issues in the weeks leading up to trial, Leo made sure I received a copy of every brief, motion, and major decision before it went to court.

A few weeks before the trial, Bob sat down with me to make sure I understood why the lawyers did not want to hold Fernandez directly responsible for Wito's death. All of our evidence was considered circumstantial. "What do you want me to tell you when you look at my face and ask me, 'Why did we lose?'" Bob asked.

At that moment I saw how deeply committed he was to Wito's case, and while the charge of conspiracy was not all I wanted, I understood why the legal team was pushing for it instead of charging Fernandez with the actual killing. Our lawyers worried that it would be too difficult to prove. The charge of conspiracy would be enough to win the case.

Instead of presenting live witnesses at trial, our lawyers decided to play excerpts of the videotaped depositions taken in Chile. When Leo asked how I felt about this, I said it was fine but I had one request: that Dr. Elvira Miranda, the forensic pathologist who had personally studied Wito's remains, testify at trial. With Dr. Miranda on the stand, I knew we would really be able to make the connection between the forensic evidence and Ximena's account of my brother's final moments. Even if the lawyers did not make this connection, I hoped that my brother's courage would be evident to all.

As our trial date approached, the WSGR legal team worked day and night under Leo's direct leadership to prepare a "winnable case." I heard them talking about Winston, and as they asked many questions about my brother, I felt that they really wanted to know who he was.

Something good is in the making. I had thought that on the day WSGR took our case in 1999 and now, in the weeks leading up to trial, I was filled with the same hopeful feeling. We were preparing to honor Wito's name in justice and truth.

FORTY SIX

On September 22, 2003, the trial began in the US District Court Southern District of Florida, Miami Division. The presiding judge was the Honorable Joan A. Lenard. At the courthouse, all of our family and friends wore my father's *besitos*, which I had brought from my garden at home. The tiny pink roses were everywhere—on clothing, on collars, in buttonholes. It meant so much to my family.

As I sat in the courtroom, Pato, Felipe, Roberto, Karin, and Lito surrounded me with love. My siblings and I had decided not to bring our mother to the trial, due to her advanced age and failing health. Patty Blum, a caring, sensitive lawyer from CJA who had developed written instructions for the jury and given warm support throughout the process of our lawsuit, now sat with us in the courtroom answering all our questions as the trial unfolded. Nathalie from WSGR, who had taken notes during my "classes" with Leo, also sat with us, taking special care throughout the trial to make sure I understood everything that happened.

My son Roberto appointed himself my protector. Determined to spare me from having to even look at Fernandez, he did everything possible to keep me away from him. Before the morning session, during recess, and at the end of the day, my family and friends would gather in the waiting area outside the courtroom to talk. Fernandez had to pass through this area to enter or exit the courtroom, and sometimes Roberto, who was very attuned to Fernandez's whereabouts, would surprise me by suddenly putting his arms around me and physically turning me around so I would not see him.

Despite Roberto's best efforts, however, on one occasion we were not able to avoid Fernandez. My family, friends, and I had just entered the elevator and the door was closing, when a forceful male voice shouted, "Hold the elevator!"

Fernandez walked in, and as the doors closed behind him, we were all dead silent. I could not breathe. Slowly the elevator climbed. We all stood behind Fernandez, staring at his broad back and thinning hair, and Roberto—protecting me, as always—stood between Fernandez and me. When the doors opened, Fernandez was the first to leave. The rest of us waited for a while before walking out.

FORTY SEVEN

Jury selection did not take long. Our lawyers requested to include in the questioning of the potential jurors "if any member of the panel has ever lived abroad, in what country, the dates of residence, and the reason for being there." Additionally, they wanted to know if a potential juror "has family that lives outside the United States and if so, what country." Steve Davis requested to ask if there was any member of the jury panel who had strong feelings one way or the other regarding the fact that Fernandez Larios was a member of the military. The judge agreed to include these questions.

The judge then read a statement she had prepared to inform the potential jurors what the case was about and to make inquiry as to whether or not they had heard, read, or known anything about the case. "The plaintiffs in this case are family members of a Chilean National, Winston Cabello, who died in Chile in 1973. The defendant, Armando Fernandez Larios, was a second lieutenant in the Chilean Military at the time [of] Mr. Cabello's death. This case revolves around [the] plaintiff's allegations concerning the circumstances surrounding the death of Mr. Cabello, and whether or not the defendant should be legally responsible for that death."

"Any objection to that statement?" the judge asked.

"No objection your honor," said Steve Davis.

"No objection," said Leo Cunningham.

The potential jurors were brought in. By noon the lawyers had selected a panel of eight jurors, five women and three men.

Before calling the names of the selected jurors, Davis introduced what my lawyers had feared all along: his objection regarding the legality of the depositions we had taken in Chile.

Leo said, "Your honor, most of our case is going to come in through depositions. If we don't have the depositions, we don't really have a case."

The judge seemed upset. "If the issue has never been raised before me and I haven't ruled on it, obviously I haven't considered it," she said. "Why wasn't this raised before?"

She instructed to bring all the jurors in. Once the jurors had taken their seats, she said, "I will dismiss you for the day. There are a number of issues I need to discuss with the lawyers."

The jurors left the room.

"What rule was violated?" asked the judge.

Steve Davis answered, "They brought a notary from the United States down to Chile…there is no one from Chile who was there to administer an oath. It was not taken to any Chilean procedure." After a long interchange of legal arguments made by both parties, the judge said, "Why don't both sides provide memorandum, the plaintiff by four o'clock today and the defendant by nine o'clock tomorrow morning. And you will have to proceed with calling other witnesses."

Leo jumped to his feet. "I understand we put you in a box here. The opening is entirely dependent on this deposition testimony."

"How would you expect me to proceed if you all knew this was an issue or anticipated this might be an issue? Wouldn't it have been better part of valor to make the Court aware of this potential issue?" said the judge.

Leo apologized. It was an agonizing moment.

The judge was ready to end the session when I heard Bob say, "There is one other thing that might save the Court some time. I recall in the courses of the depositions in Chile with Mr. Davis, we offered at some point to have a Chilean notary if necessary, if that was the issue, the notarizing or the swearing in, and I think Mr. Davis, if I recall, said that was not the problem."

The judge replied, "I suggest in your memorandum this afternoon, if there is such a portion in the deposition, you provide me with that excerpt." Then she ended the session.

We all left the courtroom feeling a heavy burden. Without the depositions, we did not have much of a case. I understood that so well. At least we had a terrific live witness to begin with: Dr. Miranda, who had flown in from Santiago to testify on my brother's behalf.

On September 24, after Dr. Miranda was sworn, Bob began his examination in the courtroom. He asked Dr. Miranda about the exhumation process and the steps she had taken to identify and study the remains of the thirteen victims from Copiapó. Images from the exhumation video and the morgue were introduced at trial, and the jury saw the thirteen bodies laid out on a table with numbers assigned as they were exhumed. They also saw remains of clothing the victims had worn the night they were killed.

As the videos flashed onto the screen, Bob asked Dr. Miranda to describe what the jury was seeing.

"These are holes in clothes that correspond or were caused by projectiles, from a firearm," Dr. Miranda testified. "This corresponds to Winston Cabello's jacket, in which you could see oblique longitudinal tears…These tears correspond, clearly, to tears that appear in the lining of the jacket and the front part of the jacket, you can see this area here… This is the area of the jacket where you could see linear tears surrounded by traces of blood around it. This corresponds to the front of the jacket, as I said earlier."

Bob introduced the thirteen autopsy reports as evidence, asking Dr. Miranda to describe each victim's cause of death. She cited gunshot wounds, cranial trauma, cranial destruction, and bodies with multiple wounds and fractures. Except for Winston, all the victims showed signs of gunshot wounds in their bodies or gunpowder residue in their clothing.

The jury never heard Ximena's story. Like many key pieces of information I had gathered over the years, it was considered circumstantial evidence and therefore could not be included as part of our case. As I listened to Dr. Miranda's testimony, however, I thought about what Ximena had told me in 1974. When Dr. Miranda described Wito's cause of death, I was perhaps the only one at the trial to understand its true meaning: I believe my brother realized that all the prisoners were about to be killed and he understood that lies would be told about what had happened. Knowing this, Wito chose to endure a more painful death than he might otherwise have had, in hopes that someday the evidence from his decision could challenge the lies that he knew we would be told. The hallmark of Winston's life was embodied in his final courageous choice.

As emotionally confusing as the court days were, of one thing I was certain: I could not look Fernandez directly in the eyes. I could not, even for a moment, fix my eyes on his. Just the thought revolted me. I did not want to see the evil that I believe led him to kill my brother. In Fernandez's eyes, I feared I would see that he did not care at all about what he had done to Wito, and that given the chance, he would do it again.

FORTY EIGHT

It took a couple of days for the judge to rule that "the depositions on August 27 and August 28 of Ariosto Lapostol Orrego, Grimilda Sánchez, and Eugenio Rivera did not comply with Rule 28B." In other words, the judge ruled that they were inadmissible because they had been taken before Bob's offer to bring a notary public. On the other hand, the judge ruled that "those depositions thereafter would be admissible."

We all held our breath; our entire case rested on those depositions.

The jury heard Victor Bravo's videotaped description of the night the military had taken him from his home to fingerprint the thirteen bodies with their faces covered. They heard Juan Morales's testimony, including his heart-wrenching description of Fernandez savagely beating one of the victims, Jaime Sierra. They heard Dr. Murúa's testimony, with his description of the moment that General Arellano, accompanied by Fernandez, gave the order to "eliminate" the prisoners.

Immediately after Dr. Murúa's testimony, the lawyers played Enrique Vidal's deposition. If the jurors had any doubt about Fernandez's role in the deaths of my brother and the twelve other victims in Copiapó, I felt sure that once they heard Vidal's testimony all their doubts disappeared. Our legal team then played excerpts of Patricio Lapostol's deposition, and the jury heard about his encounter with members of the Caravan of Death, his description of the *corvo*, and the condition of the twenty-six "destroyed" bodies in Calama.

The final excerpt came from the deposition of Jorge Ortíz, a former prison warden. Ortíz's testimony did not directly relate to Wito's case, but it was critical in connecting Fernandez with the disappearance of political prisoner David Silberman, the former general manager of Chile's largest copper company, Cobre-Chuqui.

Ortíz was the acting warden and highest-ranking officer of the Santiago penitentiary when, on October 4, 1974, a military patrol arrived at the facility. The man in charge of the patrol handed Ortíz a document with an order to turn over the prisoner David Silberman.

"The officer identified himself by the name Alejandro Quinteros," Ortíz testified, "but the true identity of the officer was Fernandez Larios."

"When did you learn that identity?" Bob asked.

Ortíz explained that Judge Guzmán, who was investigating Silberman's case, had subpoenaed him three times. During an identification of photographs, Ortíz recognized the officer who had taken Silberman from the penitentiary. "The name of that officer was Fernandez Larios," Ortíz had testified to the judge.

"Would you describe now what happened to Mr. Silberman as he was released to this officer who identified himself by the name you have previously given us?" Bob asked.

"He seemed very concerned," Ortíz testified. "He made no remarks… As they were leaving the unit, they made him climb into the back of a pickup truck that bore no license plate, which was a characteristic for those vehicles that were used within the state security…organizations… And after that, the vehicle drove away."

Bob asked if Silberman had been placed in restraints or blindfolded as he was taken from the penitentiary.

"At that time, with no physical limitations, led away by members of the patrol," Ortíz said.

Toward the end of Ortíz's deposition, Bob asked, "As you observed Mr. Silberman going to the pickup truck, did you see him placed in the truck?"

Ortíz testified that the military patrol had placed Silberman, lying down, in the back end of the truck bed. "The members of the patrol lifted him in. And I recall no other details because this was by then outside."

"Has Mr. Silberman been seen or found since the day he left the penitentiary with Fernandez Larios?" Bob asked during the examination.

Davis objected to the form of the question.

"No," Ortíz testified. "He has not been found."

FORTY NINE

"We call Mr. Fernandez, Your Honor. Armando Fernandez Larios."

Fernandez Larios, the last witness to testify, rose from the defense table with his broad back to the courtroom, where I sat surrounded by family, friends, and members of the press.

I had read accounts of Fernandez describing him as tall, thin, and handsome. However, the paunchy, balding man with a comb-over who now stood in front of me in no way matched that description.

Fernandez strode arrogantly to the witness stand, raised his right hand, and swore to tell the truth. He seemed untouchable.

Bob stood in front of Fernandez, watching him keenly, ready to begin his interrogation.

"Did you receive instruction and did you understand at the time that the military cannot use force of violence against unarmed civilians and protected prisoners?" Bob asked, after some initial questions. "Did you learn that in your training?"

"I think everybody don't need to be a military to understand that," Fernandez said. He had opted to answer the questions directly in English, rather than speaking his native Spanish, but an interpreter stood by in case he was needed.

"You agree with that principle?" Bob asked.

"Yes," said Fernandez, "of course I am agreeable."

"Generally speaking, do you now acknowledge that people were killed at many cities in Chile when the helicopter arrived in those cities and before the helicopter departed those cities, that many, many people were killed in Chile?"

"Of course I know that."

"And you agree, do you not, that some of the people on this helicopter were responsible for those deaths, some of the people? I understand you say you are not responsible but some of the people on the helicopter were responsible for the deaths, for killing these people?"

"Yes, but it is important to tell you the people I think were responsible, they were very high, high level in the military."

"Do you agree people on the helicopter, some of the people, participated in the brutal killing of innocent unarmed civilians, do you agree with that or not?" Bob asked.

"I don't know if they participated," Fernandez said. "I never knew about that. I never knew if they participated. I never knew if they were signing papers or not signing papers."

"I am not asking you about signing papers. I am asking you about killing unarmed civilians."

"Sir, what I am trying to explain you, I cannot tell you. I am not the person that can tell you, yes, they are responsible. I don't know who was responsible of that…"

"Are you saying you never saw any prisoners any place in any of these cities where all of these people were killed, you never saw any one of these prisoners?" Bob asked, after more questions.

"No," Fernandez said.

"You never interrogated any prisoner?"

"Never."

"You were in the cities when all of these things were happening with the helicopter and you never saw anything, nothing, zero?"

"Not zero," Fernandez said. "When you say I never saw, it is very easy to explain that all the prisoners—when the prisoners were in the regiment they were not walking around the regiment. They were in cells or I don't know, in barracks or in jail."

"How do you know where they were if you didn't see them?"

"I don't know. That is what I am saying."

"They can be in a hotel?"

"Maybe they were."

"How do you know the prisoners were in cells if you never saw them?"

"What other part are they going to be? You are putting words in my list [*sic*]. You are changing my words. They must be there. What other part would they be?"

"You never saw one prisoner?" Bob asked.

"I don't remember seeing any prisoner," Fernandez said.

"You never interrogated a prisoner?"

"Of course I don't see, I don't interrogate. That is another point I want to make very clear…"

"You are not saying today in this trial you did anything as a result of an order that came from a commanding officer that was wrong, that was illegal, you didn't do anything like that?" Bob asked.

"No."

"So your response to my question was, I think, you don't know of anything, you admit to nothing, doing nothing wrong at any of these stops in any way?"

"What I recall, no."

"What do you mean, as you recall?"

"My answer is no."

"When you got off the helicopter at Copiapó, did you see somebody there that you knew?…Enrique Vidal?"

"Yes."

"Enrique Vidal graduated with you from the military school or academy in 1969?"

"Yes."

"He testified by videotape deposition; did you watch that?"

"Yes."

"Do you recall that he said he saw you get off the helicopter first?"

"Yes."

"Was that right or wrong?"

"Really, I don't know. Maybe I can give you an explanation about this. I don't know if I did the first, but I am sure I didn't open the door of the helicopter because I am not allowed to do that. If I get out first, I get out first. I don't recall being the first or the last."

"When you went up to Enrique Vidal, you had a conversation with him, did you not?"

"I imagine, yes. He said I spoke with him. Maybe that is true. I don't recall."

"How were you dressed?"

"In combat, in green fatigues."

"What did you have on your person in terms of weapons?"

"I have the normal weapons that an officer used in that day. In that day all of us were dressed in fatigues. We have a rifle or fusil; a rifle. We have a pistol and we have a *corvo*; but everybody in the army used. Listen to me, I have been in the army; Vidal in that statement said they didn't have it."

"So they didn't have any *corvos* in that regiment?"

"Yes."

"General Arellano said everybody on the helicopter had *corvos*?"

"I don't know."

"Did you ever give your *corvo* to anybody at the regiment to use?"

"No."

"And you didn't see when you went around the regiment, you didn't see anybody else with *corvos* that were stationed there?"

"I don't think so."

"When you talked to Vidal, he also, you said, [*sic*] had some kind of weapon with spikes and a ball, a leather strap?"

"Yes."

"What is that?"

"I have never seen a weapon like that…Then he said in one moment that I put this thing in my back."

"He said in your belt."

"With the rifle, with the pistol and this thing with points, I don't know the name he used in my back where I sit is totally—if you ask anybody in the army, if you go to Chile and ask everybody in the army if they have seen that weapon once, I am sure they will say no," Fernandez said.

"You didn't say to Enrique Vidal, it is to caress the little pigeons; you did not say that, or did you say it?" Bob asked.

"Of course not," Fernandez said. "If I don't have this weapon, how I am going to say, listen this weapon is to…caress the little pigeons. I am denying 1,000 percent I have that weapon. How can I say listen, this is to caress the pigeons."

"You would not have a weapon you were not trained in using? You wouldn't carry some weapon you are not formally trained to use?"

"No, but also—"

"That is exactly what you told us about the *corvo*; you had no training with a *corvo*?"

"No."

"So you had a weapon that you had no training but you didn't have this other weapon?…You are in a state of war, you are dressed in your combat uniform and ready for war?"

"Yes."

"And you have an ornament on?"

"We can put an ornament on parts of the uniform."

"Who else had them?" Bob asked.

"I don't know, I don't remember. It was part of our uniform. Maybe the senior officers didn't use it. I don't remember if senior officers used it or didn't use it."

"Is it possible you are the only one on the helicopter with a *corvo*?"

"Yes, maybe."

"One *corvo* in Copiapó?"

"Yes."

I was stunned to hear Fernandez acknowledge that he was likely to be the only person in possession of a *corvo*. Dr. Miranda had already testified that a sharp instrument had killed my brother, and Vidal had testified, there had been no other *corvos* in Copiapó.

"You stated you were at war?" Bob asked.

"Yes."

"Who were you at war with?"

"When I said we were at war, it is what our superior, our government at that moment said, we are at war," Fernandez said. "We are in war against people that were against the government and that means for us, they were enemies of the government."

"The war you are describing is the government against the people who were opposed to the current government; is that correct; and the government at that time was the dictatorship of Pinochet?" Bob asked, after more questions.

"Yes," said Fernandez.

"What was your role in this helicopter?" Bob asked, after more questions.

"I was commandeered to be the bodyguard of General Arellano, a general I didn't know personally," Fernandez said.

"Did you receive a written order to do this?"

"No, sir...Somebody must have called the infantry school and said send a commander to the helicopter. [General Arellano] must have known I was coming."

"Will you tell us about your prior training to serve as a bodyguard prior to that, if you would?"

"We don't have that kind of training in the military..."

"So you had no prior training to be a bodyguard?"

"Correct."

"And you received no instructions from anybody on the helicopter what your job responsibilities would be or your duties as a bodyguard; correct?"

"Yes, sir."

"Is that correct?"

"Yes."

"You said, I believe, in your testimony earlier to the jury that maybe what General Arellano needed was somebody to carry his case, carry his briefcase; you said that?" asked Bob after more questions.

"Yes."

"In fact, you did that, you carried his case?"

"Maybe. I don't remember. Maybe I do."

"At Copiapó you carried his case because you were seen on the second floor of Copiapó with his case from the witnesses that testified?"

"That's what they testified."

"Is it true or not true?"

"No, I don't remember being on the second floor with General Arellano in an office with his briefcase."

"You don't remember being in a room on the second floor at Copiapó where you were interrogating prisoners?"

"No."

"And you don't remember being present with a briefcase with General Arellano?"

"I don't remember that, no."

"Did you hear Dr. Murúa's testimony?"

"Yes."

"Did you see Dr. Murúa there that day?"

"Of course not. I never see him."

"You have never seen him ever?"

"I don't think so."

"Did you…strike any prisoner with the butt of your rifle at Copiapó?"

"My answer, is, no. I never do it. No."

"As I understand your testimony, you do not agree that, or you do not admit, you were on the second floor in the interrogation area of the garrison near Copiapó?" Bob asked after more questions.

"Maybe I will be more clear," Fernandez said. "I don't remember—I never interrogate any person. I never saw prisoners. Maybe I was on the second floor but not with prisoners. Nobody I ever saw. I was not inside of any meeting and I don't know if I was on the second floor one minute and I go back; I cannot remember what I did thirty years ago."

Bob's questions were designed to connect the testimonies of Murúa, Morales, and Vidal. As Fernandez spoke, I recalled Brito telling us that he had seen Fernandez hitting a prisoner, reviewing prisoners' files, and removing prisoners from the garrison.

Fernandez denied everything.

The interrogation was over.

At the end of three grueling weeks of trial, as Leo was sitting at the counsel table preparing to give the closing argument, I walked up and handed him one of my father's *besitos*. "I wanted to give you this," I told him. "It means hope."

Leo delivered the final arguments, and for me it was the most memorable part of all. Leo skillfully pieced together the entire story, offering the jury a thoughtful and comprehensive understanding of the tragedy's immensity. Leo spoke about how young Wito had been, how his life had been cut short without reason. What touched me most during the closing arguments was the fact that somehow Leo actually managed to bring Winston—the real, living, breathing person that he had been—vividly into the courtroom. At the peak of our team's tremendous effort, right there in court, I saw my brother's spirit in a captivating moment of completion and history. I will cherish that moment for the rest of my life.

FIFTY

On October 15, 2003, after three weeks of trial and a day and a half of deliberation, an eight-person federal jury in Miami found Armando Fernandez Larios liable for the extrajudicial killing, torture, and cruel and degrading treatment of our brother Winston, as well as for crimes against humanity. A unanimous verdict, it marked the first time in US history that a jury had returned a verdict of crimes against humanity in a contested trial. It arrived just two days before the thirtieth anniversary of Wito's death.

The courtroom was packed with friends, family, and journalists from around the world. One by one, the verdicts were delivered for each charge: summary execution, torture, inhumane and degrading treatment, crimes against humanity. As the verdicts were read, the courtroom was silent. Fernandez Larios sat at the defendant table with his lawyers. My family and I sat silently together in the first row of seats, directly behind our lawyers. As soon as the judge left the courtroom, the silence exploded into jubilant laughter, congratulations, and rejoicing, with everyone hugging each other. We walked outside the courtroom into the bright sunlight, and reporters and photographers swarmed around us. Leo and I answered questions for the TV, radio, and newspaper journalists and gave our statements to the world. Suddenly, over the crowd, I saw two of the jurors leaving the building. I broke free of the media and ran to the jurors, giving them a big hug.

The victory did not surprise me. Our witnesses' testimonies had clearly illustrated Fernandez's involvement in the Caravan of Death's brutal crimes throughout northern Chile.

Armando Fernandez Larios had sat in court alone. No friend or family member had accompanied him during the entire trial. Not a single witness had testified on his behalf, except himself.

Fernandez had acknowledged traveling with Arellano's helicopter squad, but had claimed throughout the trial to have had no involvement in, or knowledge of, the killing of civilians in Copiapó or anywhere else. His defense had rested on the argument that as the lowest-ranking officer in the group, he could not have ordered the killings.

We got the verdict we wanted, but I felt saddened by the gap between the narrow "legal truth" presented at trial and the larger "historical truth." By holding Fernandez responsible only as a co-conspirator to kill my brother, we had had no chance to present in court how Fernandez had killed Wito with his *corvo* on the truck. There had been no room to talk about my brother's last moments or to offer his gift of courage and integrity to the world.

Were we honoring Wito properly? Was this the best way to do justice to his memory?

After the trial I wholeheartedly thanked the legal team.

"Why are you thanking us?" Bob asked, quite moved. "You prepared the case for us. You gave us all the evidences."

I apologized to Leo for the hard times I had given them. "You are a very demanding person," he said. Later he told me, "I'd never learned from anyone as much as I learned from you on how to try a case."

Reactions to our victory, not just from close friends and family, but also in media around the world, reminded me that we had achieved a monumental goal. We had made history by showing the world that every life has value, and that those who violate that principle will not go unnoticed. However powerful or untouchable human rights violators may seem, they are not immune to justice.

After the verdict I returned to Chile, where I received profound expressions of gratitude everywhere I went. For many families of the murdered, the disappeared, and the tortured, our case was a ray of hope that some measure of justice and truth was still available, even thirty years after the crimes were committed.

Armando Fernandez appealed the verdict. On March 26, 2004, he filed with the Court of Appeals for the Eleventh Circuit. On March 14, 2005, the court ruled in our favor on all four issues.

In the appeal, our lawyers argued that "a jury could have reasonably concluded from circumstantial evidence that Fernandez was directly liable for Winston's death." When I read that sentence, I realized that our legal team had made a real effort to present the story as a whole, and that spoke to me more than anything.

Thinking back to when Bob had sat down with me and explained why the legal team wanted to use the conspiracy charge, I now understood how legally difficult it had been for them to win our case. Because we had used the conspiracy charge, we had not had the opportunity in court to tell the full story of what happened to Wito. But I realized that the trial was not the time for that. A book was the place to tell the whole story.

FIFTY ONE

On Sunday, October 14, 1973, I saw my brother Wito for the last time.

It was our final visiting day at the garrison. My brother saw instantly that I had been crying, and he squatted down in front of me, took my hands in his, and looked into my eyes. "Don't worry, Zita," Wito said gently. "We are going to be just fine."

Then he added, "Zita, I want to ask you a favor. I want you to always remember that they can cut all the flowers, but they can't prevent the spring from returning."

Wito bent down to kiss me good-bye, and his warm, smooth skin grazed my cheek. My brother was so happy that day, but he looked anxiously into my eyes, wanting to make sure that I was all right. As I walked away, I turned and looked back to see the guard taking Wito away across the garrison patio. Typical of my brother, who was very friendly and liked by all who knew him, Wito and the guard were chatting pleasantly as they walked together toward the detention area.

As Wito had asked, for many years, I searched for the spring. I could not find it until finally I realized that I was looking in all the wrong places. If I wanted to see the flowers bloom, I had to search within myself.

The spring is alive in each of us. And no matter how dark the winter may be or how far beneath the chilly ground the promise of flowers may slumber, it is always within our reach.

AFTERWORD

At trial we proved without a doubt that Armando Fernandez was responsible for extrajudicial killing; torture; cruel, inhuman, or degrading punishment or treatment; and crimes against humanity. Ours was a civil case, so the verdict included a judgment against Fernandez of $4 million in punitive and compensatory damages. We knew we would never be paid.

As I heard the judgment, my misgivings about monetary compensation resurfaced. *Was it worth it?* I thought. *Would you do it again? Fernandez didn't even acknowledge wrongdoing.* I was tempted to say no.

I felt happy for Wito. At trial, my dream of many years had come true: Wito's name was recorded in history, to be remembered always in truth and dignity.

We all knew that Fernandez worked in an auto body shop in Miami and had no assets. That was fine with us. Money had never been the issue. Unfortunately, however, just the news that there had been a $4 million judgment gave rise to some uncaring criticisms: "So *that's* why Zita did all the work. Money. Publicity. What else?"

"Quite predictable remarks," my lawyers told me. "Don't worry. You know why you did it. We know it, too. Just be proud."

Hurtful remarks came from only a relative few, but I could not brush them off, and I almost got to the point of wishing we had lost the case. *Was it worth it?* I kept wondering. I felt myself getting stuck.

Pato and the boys tried to help me. "Don't *ever* forget why you did it," Pato said on the night of our victory. "These are just dogs barking. Don't pay attention to them."

"I'm glad this is over," I said. "I just want to go home."

But Felipe and Roberto had other ideas. "It is not over yet," they said. "You have to finish the story."

"It's already finished."

"No, it's not."

My sons reminded me of Adolfo's promise that after the trial, he would tell me everything he knew. "For your book," Adolfo had said.

"You have to go to Chile right now," Roberto told me.

"No. Absolutely not. I want nothing to do with this anymore."

"Zita," Felipe interrupted. "Roberto and I grew up learning from you to never give up. You taught us to work hard to achieve the things we believe in. So you can't give up now—you have to finish the story. I'll go with you to Chile."

Right then, from the condominium where we were staying in Miami, Felipe dialed Adolfo's number. "Adolfo is on the phone," Felipe said. "Tell him that you are going to Chile to speak with him."

Reluctantly, I took the phone and asked Adolfo if his promise still stood.

"Of course," Adolfo said. "Come down and I'll tell you everything I remember."

A few days later, Felipe and I were talking with Adolfo in a hotel room in Chile.

"You look just like Winston," Adolfo told my son. We hear that everywhere. The resemblance is amazing. Both Winston and Felipe inherited my father's striking features: high cheekbones and honey-colored, almond-shaped eyes that were bright, lively, and very expressive. People can still see that special light in my son's eyes.

We talked for four hours that day, and Adolfo completed the story, answering many of the questions I still had. In painful detail, he described the moment that Fernandez had helped load Wito and the twelve other prisoners into the back of the truck, adding, "Captain Diaz drove the truck away."

"Did you see Fernandez getting into the truck before leaving the garrison?" I asked.

"Fernandez did get onto the back of the truck where the prisoners had been loaded and drove away with them," Adolfo said. "Fifteen minutes later, we heard the shots."

When I got home to California, I entered a period of voluntary isolation. I needed to distance myself from what had consumed my life for too long. Finally, after a confusing, painful time, I emerged with a quiet sense of accomplishment.

Would I do it again? Absolutely. No regrets.

Was it worth it? Every moment. Every accomplishment.

I hesitantly began accepting invitations to speak around the United States. Most of my lectures focus on the historic precedent that Wito's case established in holding human rights violators responsible for crimes against humanity. An example of this is the case against Alvaro Saravia, a California resident found responsible in 2004 for his role in the 1980 assassination of El Salvador's Archbishop Oscar Romero. In his ruling, Judge Oliver Wanger of the Fresno District Court cited Wito's case several times. The ruling included the decision that the "assassination of Archbishop Romero was a crime against humanity."

"Your brother's case once again helped to make history—and bring a little bit of justice and accountability into the world," wrote my friend Terry Karl, who served as an expert witness in the Romero case.

Several other human rights cases have already cited Winston's case. I am sure the number of such cases will keep mounting.

No matter who my audience is, at the end of my talks they always ask the same questions: What happened to Fernandez? Is he still living free in Miami? Why is he free? Why doesn't our government deport him?

Undoubtedly, the world is better because of Wito's case. But the issue of personal accountability lingers in people's minds. Their questions go directly to my heart and each time I wonder, *Did Fernandez's life change because of the trial? Does he feel remorse? Will he ever acknowledge the crimes he committed? Will he ever tell us why he killed my brother?*

Searching for closure, I traveled to Chile with Pato, Roberto, and Felipe in the summer of 2005 to film a documentary about the large-scale meaning of human rights cases such as ours. Roberto filmed the interviews as I spoke with several judges who were investigating human rights violations.

I wanted to explore the possibility of extraditing Fernandez to Chile. I had heard that Chile and Argentina had already filed an extradition petition for Fernandez and that the US Supreme Court had never responded. Unfortunately, those were only rumors.

Evidence connecting Armando Fernandez with the car bombing that killed General Carlos Prats and his wife in Argentina on September 30, 1974, has emerged over the years, but "not enough to warrant extradition petition," according to Judge Maria Servini, who was investigating the case at the time.

Despite the mounting evidence connecting Armando Fernandez with the Caravan of Death killings, in the end Judge Guzmán did not ask for his extradition. Guzmán retired in February 2005, and he dropped Fernandez's name from the list of suspects before turning his investigation over to the newly appointed Judge Victor Montiglio. This surprising move is simply explained: most people in Chile believe to this day that Fernandez is living under the US witness protection program or some other kind of protection that would render any extradition effort pointless.

I got tired of explaining that Fernandez did *not* enter the witness protection program and that he continues to live openly in Miami, Florida. Although he did negotiate an agreement with the US State Department in 1987, that agreement does *not* preclude any country from asking for his extradition. The State Department cannot make an agreement that speaks for another country's actions. Anyone can ask for Fernandez's extradition.

I placed my last hope in Judge Jorge Zepeda, who was in charge of investigating David Silberman's disappearance from the Santiago jail in 1974. I gave the judge the evidence that my lawyers had presented at trial concerning Fernandez's role in Silberman's disappearance. These included all of the motions my lawyers had written and a copy of Jorge Ortíz's deposition, in which he testified that "approximately a year after the coup, Mr. Fernandez used an official password and a false name to extract from the Santiago jail David Silberman, a well-known prisoner, who was never seen again."

I knew the judge had already interrogated Ortíz and several other witnesses who saw Fernandez take Silberman from the penitentiary. When I dropped off the documents at Judge Zepeda's office in August 2005, I said, "Fernandez's involvement in connection to Silberman's disappearance is already recorded in a US court. These documents prove that. They also prove that Fernandez is not immune to legal actions." Less than a month later, Judge Zepeda filed a petition with the Chilean Supreme Court to extradite Armando Fernandez for his involvement in connection to Silberman's disappearance. Three months later, on January 4, 2006, the Chilean Supreme Court unanimously authorized the extradition petition.

On October 14, 2006, following established extradition requests, the Chilean embassy in Washington, DC, presented the formal extradition petition with properly certified documents to the US Department of State. The following month, I phoned the State Department to ask about the status of the extradition request. My call was transferred from office to office, until finally I reached the Office of the Legal Adviser of the US Department of State. The woman who answered my call happened to be the lawyer in charge of reviewing extradition requests from Chile.

"I haven't seen the request yet," she told me, "though the process of extraditing somebody from the United States to a foreign country takes a long time. Our office reviews it first; then we send it to the Department of Justice for further review. If the extradition judge certifies extraditability, it is then sent to the secretary of state, who is the US official responsible for determining whether to surrender, in this case Armando Fernandez, to Chile."

When I told Bob about this conversation, he said that he doubted the Bush administration would pursue extradition. "Only if the Democrats win in '08 will we have a shot at extraditing him," he said.

For the last two years of George W. Bush's presidency, the extradition request remained under review.

In 2008, President Barack Obama campaigned and won on the slogan, "This is the time. This is the moment."

In 2012, President Obama was reelected on the slogan, "Forward."

Will the United States finally surrender Armando Fernandez Larios to Chile? Will this be "the time"? Will this be "the moment"? Will the extradition move "forward" at last?

To this day, Chilean authorities are waiting for the United States to answer the extradition request for Armando Fernandez Larios.

WORKS CITED

Allende, Salvador. Last speech, Santiago, Chile, transmitted by Radio Magallanes. September 11, 1973. http://en.wikisource.org/wiki/Salvador_Allende%27s_Last_Speech.

"Inmates' Escape Attempt." Commander Oscar Haag's Military Communiqué, published in *Atacama* newspaper. September 18, 1973.

Helms, Richard. Handwritten notes from meeting with President Richard Nixon on Chile, with John Mitchell and Henry Kissinger present, September 15, 1970. National Security Archive Electronic Briefing Book No. 437, edited by Peter Kornbluh, posted September 11, 2013. Sourced from the website http://www2.gwu.edu/~nsarchiv/NSAEBB/NSAEBB437/, accessed on August 24, 2013.

Verdugo, Patricia. *Los Zarpazos del Puma [The Claws of the Puma]*. Ediciones CESOC. 1989.

All Chilean military announcements and edicts were sourced from the website
http://www.derechoschile.com/, accessed on April 9, 2013.

Deposition of Armando Fernandez Larios. Miami, Florida. August 13, 2001.

Deposition of Ariosto Lapostol. Victoria Room, Crowne Plaza Hotel, Santiago, Chile. August 27, 2001.

Deposition of Grimilda Sánchez. Victoria Room, Crowne Plaza Hotel, Santiago, Chile. August 28, 2001.

Deposition of Eugenio Rivera. Victoria Room, Crowne Plaza Hotel, Santiago, Chile. August 28, 2001.

Deposition of Iván Murúa. Victoria Room, Crowne Plaza Hotel, Santiago, Chile. August 29, 2001.

Deposition of Patricio Lapostol. Victoria Room, Crowne Plaza Hotel, Santiago, Chile. August 29, 2001.

Deposition of Enrique Vidal. Victoria Room, Crowne Plaza Hotel, Santiago, Chile. August 30, 2001.

Deposition of Victor Bravo. Victoria Room, Crowne Plaza Hotel, Santiago, Chile. August 30, 2001.

Deposition of Juan Morales. Victoria Room, Crowne Plaza Hotel, Santiago, Chile. August 28, 2002.

Deposition of Jorge Ortíz. Victoria Room, Crowne Plaza Hotel, Santiago, Chile. August 28, 2002.

Deposition of Efrain Jaña. Victoria Room, Crowne Plaza Hotel, Santiago, Chile. August 29, 2002.

Deposition of Dr. America Gonzales and Dr. Elvira Miranda. Victoria Room, Crowne Plaza Hotel, Santiago, Chile. August 29, 2002.

Testimony of Dr. Elvira Miranda. US District Court Southern District of Florida, Miami Division. September 24, 2003.

Testimony of Armando Fernandez Larios. US District Court Southern District of Florida, Miami Division. October 7, 2003.

ABOUT THE AUTHOR

Zita Cabello-Barrueto, PhD, a native of Chile and a US citizen, is a human rights activist, filmmaker, and educator. Following the coup led by General Pinochet in 1973, Zita's husband Patricio and her brother Winston were arrested without charges. While Patricio was released, Winston was killed. Cabello-Barrueto spent thirty years relentlessly searching for the truth about her brother's death. In 1998, she and her family brought a civil suit against one of her brother's murderers, a former Chilean army officer who had been living in Miami, Florida, since 1987. Five years later, in 2003, after tracking down hundreds of witnesses and with the help of a team of pro-bono US lawyers, the Cabello family set a historic precedent as the first ever jury verdict for crimes against humanity in US history.

Cabello-Barrueto hopes that *In Search of Spring* will provide important insights to the millions of Chileans affected by Pinochet's brutal regime and encourage others to speak out against human rights violations and bring an end to the impunity of perpetrators around the world. After years of teaching at UC Santa Cruz and most recently at UC Berkeley, Cabello-Barrueto is now retired and lives with her family in California.

To learn more, visit www.insearchofspring.com